PRINCIPLES OF PARALLEL AND MULTIPROCESSING

GEORGE R. DESROCHERS

QA 76.5
D45
1987

INTERTEXT PUBLICATIONS, INC.
MCGRAW-HILL BOOK COMPANY

Library of Congress Catalog Card Number 87-81304

10 9 8 7 6 5 4 3 2 1

ISBN 0-07-016579-3

Intertext Publications, Inc.
McGraw-Hill Book Company
11 West 19th Street
New York, NY 10011

To Beth, Laura, and Hannah

CONTENTS

PREFACE

The age of parallel processing is upon us. For the past twenty or so years, the field of automated computation has burgeoned so that virtually every aspect of our lives is touched in some way by new technology and applications. Through the advancement of technology and the development of new problem-solving methods, we have experienced a steady increase in computational capability and a corresponding decrease in space, power use, and cost. Also, we have seen improvements in interconnection technology, both on the chip level and between components. These factors create an atmosphere that is ripe for the creation of previously unfeasible or untried computer architectures. Some of the most exciting and promising creations fall within the realm of parallel and multiprocessor computing. Until new computational forms are developed (possibly with optics), we will realize the most outstanding gains in problem-solving capability through the use of parallelism.

We know that there are physical and architectural bounds which limit the computational power that can be achieved with single processor systems. A seemingly obvious solution, then, is to replicate the best of what we have to achieve the level of capability we desire. The way in which we replicate and the methods we use to make the replicated parts all work together, however, are not trivial tasks. The various ways to combine and operate processing elements result in the breadth of parallel and multiprocessor architectures which exist today.

There are two general trends in parallel and multiprocessing which are occurring simultaneously; I'll call them the micro trend and the macro trend. The micro trend stems from advances in integrated electronic circuit design and fabrication which allows us to pack more and more functionality onto a single chip. The trend, then, is to place a number of custom computational units on a single chip and interconnect them to form a parallel architecture. Several manufacturers have already done this, producing parallel processors aimed at solving specific problems more economically than with traditional methods. (I use economics loosely here; it could mean speed, cost, power, space, or a number of other measures.) The macro trend takes the opposite approach, which is to interconnect standard processors into parallel architectures. This trend produces systems that are more general-purpose than those of the micro trend, but they are usually of higher performance for a broad range of applications. The critical aspect of the macro trend is the maturity of efficient, high-performance interconnection systems which typically take the form of switches, buses, or shared-memory configurations.

Each of these trends is contributing to the number and type of parallel and multiprocessor system architectures from which the application designer may choose. Accordingly, the cost for a parallel processor may range from several hundred dollars for a single-chip, special-purpose implementation to over a million dollars for a high-powered, general-purpose parallel machine. There are also many choices in between, from plug-in boards for personal computers to single-user "mini" supercomputers. All these options are opening the door for many new parallel applications, as well as for the incorporation of parallel problem-solving techniques to existing standard products. Examples in existence today are pipelines in microprocessors and coprocessors in large microcomputers.

None of the hardware or architectural advances would be of much use, however, if there were insufficient means to develop, exercise, and evaluate applications. In this area, the technology dealing with parallel program development has advanced dramatically. Various machines now have environments which assist the application designer in partitioning the solution into parallel entities, compilers which can automatically detect and implement certain forms of parallel computation, and run-time packages which allow parallel applications to communicate, share information, and report results in a cohesive manner. Thus, the development of software to make the parallel architectures useful has come as far as the actual architectures themselves.

Where are we headed? We can expect to see a continuation of the two trends mentioned earlier, with both emphasizing an explosion in the number of processing elements used in a single parallel system. The maturity of fabrication techniques, such as wafer-scale integration, will greatly increase the number and complexity of processors that can be fabricated from a single piece of silicon. Also, improvements in switching networks, memory access speeds and interprocessor communication techniques will allow more dense and varied macro architectures. Coupled with the architectural advances will be corresponding improvements in development tools. Automatically detecting parallel code sections, an area under research, will be addressed (this is in addition to the vectorization techniques that are available today). Also, automated techniques for managing large numbers of processors will be improved.

With the architectural and developmental improvements will come a reexamination of many compute-bound problems and heuristic problems that are known today. A particularly exciting application area is that of Artificial Intelligence, due to the processing demands imposed by many AI solutions. Also, we can expect to see a move toward more functional architectures, systems that are configured around a single application area. Decreasing hardware development costs and improved system design capabilities will make special-purpose parallel hardware feasible for many specific problems.

Finally, the availability of parallel processing tools will free designers to think in terms of parallel solutions and know that those solutions will indeed be feasible. This change, akin to that experienced with the adoption of high-level languages as the desirable programming vehicle, is happening already and will intensify as more experience with parallel application development is gained.

This book is architecturally oriented in that it concentrates mostly on the structure of the various parallel and multiprocessor systems rather than on their individual performances or construction technologies. This orientation allows the classification of parallel and multiprocessor architectures and, subsequently, some generalization of the given classes. In this way, the reader can obtain a basic understanding from which the exploration of new or novel architectures is a natural step. I have attempted to make the book stand alone in that all of the essential areas of computer architecture are covered to some degree.

The basic organization of the book is as follows. Section I, General Principles, provides a basic grounding in computer architecture and software. The material presented therein is summary in nature and is intended to give a broad view of the issues that are important in the field. Ample references are cited to guide further study. Section II, The Implementation of Parallel Systems, furnishes a generic treatment of parallelism and the breadth of parallel and multiprocessor architectures. Also, an introduction to techniques for the analysis of parallel machine architectures is given. This section is actually the heart of the book, and those more experienced may want to concentrate on this part. Section III, Case Studies, supplies material on historically significant parallel and multiprocessor implementations as well as other, more recent, efforts. The material supplements that of Section II by providing concrete examples of many of the topics discussed there. Although not every parallel architecture class of Section II is covered by a case study, the set that was chosen attempts to give complementary information to what is typically seen in today's literature. Thus, by studying the cases presented and by surveying the published material cited in the references and bibliography, the reader should gain extensive exposure to many parallel and multiprocessor systems.

The preparation of the manuscript and the subsequent finishing touches have taken a great amount of work by various individuals besides myself. I would like, therefore, to thank my wife Beth for her support and patient translation of my scribbles and drawings into neatly formatted text and clean illustrations, Alan Rose for his constant encouragement and advice, and Bob and Shawn Wallace for their expert composition of the final illustrations. I am also grateful to my parents, Rene and Eva Desrochers, and to my employer, Naval Underwater Systems Center, for giving me the opportunities for engineering and scientific study. Lastly, I am indebted to my two daughters, Laura and Hannah, for the time not spent with them and for the constant prodding (by Laura) to "write, Daddy, write."

George R. Desrochers

Section I:
General Principles

In this section, the basic concepts that form the foundation for subsequent discussions are presented. Starting with some basic definitions and facts about traditional and conventional computer architectures, this section progresses to performance measures and the structuring of software for problem solutions. Chapter 1 introduces some topics that set the stage for the remainder of the book, including the definition of the basic architectural building blocks and a discussion on the definitions and classifications of parallel and multiprocessing computers. Chapters 2 and 3 deal with the principles of conventional computer architecture and speed, and program structure.

1. INTRODUCTION

Ever since cognitive man appeared in the struggle for survival, he has continually sought methods and means to improve his lot. Considering the total span of natural history, it took man a relatively short time to learn how to plan in order to achieve better utilization and results from his limited resources. Primordial peoples existed in groups that delegated responsibilities according to ability and position. The traits that allow us to overcome great obstacles with techniques other than raw power are characteristically human. Our ability to formulate practical laws and methods out of the mysteries of science has allowed us to make many controlled evolutions in the ways we live and use our resources. In ancient Egypt, the pharaohs organized huge labor forces to construct the pyramids. By Egyptian technological standards, this was a monumental feat. Nonetheless, effective control over scores of independent activities forced cooperation and eventual success. In modern times, the industrial revolution and subsequent dawn of the age of mechanization defined many changes in the work and social habits of a majority of the world's population. Gradually, self-reliant, close-knit communities gave way to specially trained workers existing in an interdependent society. More recently, another revolution has taken place, bringing on the so-called Computer or Information Age. All such periods in human history are marked by an initial set of significant events, which are later recognized as major technological breakthroughs, followed by a period of increasingly sophisticated exploitation of the basic technology. What began as a need for cooperation to survive led to the foundation of human society. From rudimentary shelters came the techniques and knowledge that enabled the construction of the great pyramids. The ability to harness and utilize energy resulted in the mass production of almost every consumer item. Controlling and monitoring the flow of electrons in semiconductive materials has provided a foundation for the development of electronic data processing.

In the Computer Age, we are now in the exploitation phase of this simple two-part model of technological development. This phase can also be simply described as containing two parts, which occur in roughly chronological order. The first part is usually concerned with applying the new technology to existing applications, using known techniques and methodologies. In the Computer Age, this phase is typified by the replacement of the slide rule by the electronic calculator or the use of computers for solving complex scientific problems such as the trajectory of an exploratory space craft. The second part of the technological exploitation phase is characterized by the birth of previously difficult or impossible applications that are made feasible by the new technology. Sophisticated computer graphics controllers and powerful digital signal processors are two examples of new applications using Computer Age technology. We are currently in the second part of the technology exploitation phase.

Two concepts emerge which result from the previous discussion: the capability of man to organize, plan and control resources; and the general nature of technological evolution. Taken together, these two items lead to the topic of this book: effective computer organizations that use the latest technology to attain the maximum benefit from the available resources. Throughout history, we can find examples of the types of organization embodied in many of today's parallel and multiple processor computer systems. The pharaohs used parallel efforts to quarry stone and to construct the sides of the pyramids. Assembly lines in the automotive industry use the pipeline concept to overlap the different phases of automobile production. Thus the constructions of parallel and multiprocessor architectures are often based, wittingly or not, on existing structures. There are, however, new developments in parallel and multiprocessor computers. Associative memories, in which data is accessible not by where it is stored but instead by its value, represent an advancement that is not reflected in past experience.

All of this results in a sort of philosophical opinion about computers, man, and history: that is, that parallel and multiprocessor computers are not the ultimate computational form; rather, they represent a point in the electronic evolution. Also, much of parallel and multiprocessing embodies existing principles and techniques, albeit in new mechanisms. The use of parallel and multiple processor computers will, however, have an impact on man's history. Indeed, parallel systems have already contributed greatly to weather prediction and radar processing systems, thereby giving man more information and, presumably, control over his destiny.

Computers: Evolution and Uses

Computers, in one form or another, have long been used to assist and automate computational processes. The centuries-old abacus was an early computer used for simplifying the computation of arithmetic quantities. In the late 1700's, automated mechanical computers such as the Babbage Difference Engine began to appear, supplanting humans for tedious, error-prone tasks. Looms that used punched cards to program patterns were common at the turn of the nineteenth century. Telegraph and telephone equipment spurred advances in switching theory and technology. The birth of the electronic computer is generally attributed to the development of vacuum tube technology in the mid-1900's and to the combined influence of the previous computing technologies. Today's electronic computer applications have infiltrated virtually every aspect of our lives. The uses of computers can be broadly classified into three categories: computers for computation, computers for control, and computers for automation. In each of these categories, the benefits and effects of parallel and multiprocessing have been felt.

Computers for computation are prevalent in applications that have well-defined problems or that require extensive data manipulation. Well-defined problems, whose solutions can be defined as a sequence of elementary operations, benefit from the speed, repetition, and predictability afforded by computers. Calculating the square root of a quantity can be done almost instantaneously on a computer. Performing the square root operation on all elements of a sequence is a repetitive task that is easily performed by a computer. Assurance that different instances of the same calculation will produce identical results is essential. Applications that require extensive data manipulation, such as searching and sorting, also benefit from computational assistance. In this case, logical computations are used to compare elements and control processing for applications such as expert systems, pattern recognition, and the simulation of real-world phenomena.

Computers for control are used in situations in which fast response, continuous monitoring, and decision aids are needed. The positioning of an aircraft's ailerons at supersonic speeds requires very fast response. The monitoring of conditions in a nuclear power plant must be constant. The filtering out of false alarms and low-priority occurrences aids commanders in tactical situations. All of these areas are well-suited for computer usage.

Computers for automation appear in diverse areas where jobs can be enhanced. Business applications such as spreadsheet analysis and payroll are common. In engineering, Computer Aided Design/Computer Aided Manufacture (CAD/CAM) systems automate circuit design and fabrication.

In all of the above classes, multiple computing elements are used for a variety of reasons. Computational applications can benefit from increased processing power when several jobs are performed at once. For control applications, it is advantageous to use multiple controlling elements for different aspects of a process, as well as for fault tolerance. Automation applications can benefit from increased processing power by using specialized multiprocessor architectures. Subsequent chapters will identify specific instances of parallel architectures in the context of different applications.

Process/Task States, Descriptions, and Representations

As with any unit of work performed to achieve a goal, a task (in the computer sense of the word) is an entity that has its own characteristics, can be scheduled to occur at a certain time, requires a finite time to complete, and changes the overall state of the job within which it is embedded. The overall state of a job is defined as the collection or set of values that are assigned to the set of state variables at a particular point in time. State variables are those variables whose values change with respect to some independent system variable or variables (the independent variable is typically time). Note that the association of a time with the state definition (the set of state variables) is what defines a unique state. The task state definition can be expressed as follows:

$$ST = \{a, b, c, ...\}$$

where a, b, c are the values of the state variables A, B, C at a particular time. But, as just stated, each state variable is a function of an independent variable, such as time, so that the state becomes:

$$ST = \{A(t), B(t), C(t), ...\}$$

Thus, the state is also a function of the independent variable t.

A set of tasks that together accomplish a desired goal can be loosely called a process. Before discussing this further, it is important to note that the nomenclature used in this book to describe the organization and performance of work is not based upon the conventions of any specific system or programming language. It is merely a framework to provide a basis for further discussions. Getting back to the definition of a process, a more complete definition includes the precedence of tasks and the flow of control between tasks. Graphically, a process P1, comprised of tasks T1 through T5, might

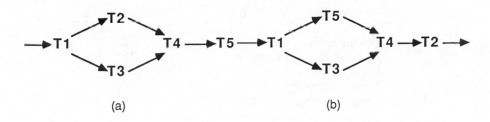

(a)   (b)

Figure 1–1. **The Tasks and Structure of Processes: (a) P1 and (b) P2**

look as shown in Figure 1–1(a). Note in the figure that the structure of the tasks T1 through T5 uniquely identifies the process P1. For example, process P2, shown in Figure 1–1(b), contains the same tasks as P1 but, unless T2 and T5 are exactly equivalent, it has a function completely different from P1.

The state of a process P, made up of a set of tasks, is just the composite state of the tasks taken together:

$$SP = \{ST1, ST2, ST3, ...\}$$

or, substituting the expressions for the individual tasks:

$$SP = \{A1(t), B1(t), C1(t), A2(t), B2(t), C2(t), ...\}$$

Note that the structure of the tasks that go into the process P does not explicitly appear in the definition for the state of P. This is true because the knowledge of the precedence or structure of the tasks is implicit in the values of the task state variables at time t.

Calculating the process state consists of sampling all of the variables in the state and then combining them in some coherent manner. Depending upon the complexity (i.e., the number of variables in the process state), the process state may be calculated using simple concatenation schemes or more complex polynomial formulas. The simple concatenation scheme forms the basis for the calculation of the maximum size of the process state. This quantity is expressed in bits and results from the summation of the number of bits contained in all of the state variables. Thus the maximum size of the calculated state will result from the concatenation of all of the bits in the state variables. As an example, the process state of a process P, executing on a hypothetical

Process State Variable	Number of Bits
Double register accumulator	32
Program counter register	16
Interrupt register	16
Stack pointer register	16
General purpose registers	64
Process information word	16
Go bit	1
Interrupts enabled bit	+ 1
Total	162

Figure 1–2.   **Process State in a Hypothetical Machine**

machine, will be calculated. Assume that the machine has a total of nine registers, one double register accumulator, four general-purpose registers, one
program counter, an interrupt register, and one stack pointer. Also assume
that there is a go/stop bit and an interrupts-enabled bit. The machine has a 16-
bit register and memory word size. Further assume that the machine is
shared among several processes, so that there is a memory word for each
process that holds information about its execution status (e.g., blocked,
waiting). The maximum process state size for a process P on this hypothetical
machine is 162 bits, as shown in Figure 1–2. [Bell82] contains a similar
derivation for the state of the processor. In fact, the processor state com-
prises a significant portion of the process state with the addition of the
process status information.

A collection of individual process states for a single process (i.e., a number of samples of the process state variables) is also referred to as a state.
These states, then, treat some of the process state variables as don't cares (i.e.,
their values need not be recorded). The relationships between these states can
be shown as edges in a state transition diagram. Figure 1–3 shows a simple
state transition diagram for a time-shared processor. The edges in the diagram are actually the values associated with a process state variable that cause
the transition to the new state. For example, a process that is RUNNING
enters the READY-TO-RUN state whenever the allotted execution time slot

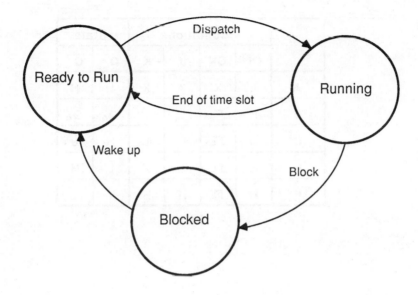

Figure 1–3. **State Transition Diagram for an Executing Process**

for the process expires. State transition diagrams are useful when describing the operation of a process under a given set of circumstances. The general form of the state transition diagram representation is used for many discrete state systems. One such system is used for representing logic level circuit designs for computer elements. Traditional next-state tables used for component behavior description are also manifestations of this same technique. Figure 1–4 shows a state transition table and diagram for a JK type flip-flop. Program compilers typically use state transition tables for parsing and lexical analysis. In this case, the diagrams are used to recognize a series of tokens in a string. The state transition diagram technique will be used where appropriate to illustrate the progression of discrete event processes.

A less-detailed method for describing the nature of tasks and processes uses descriptions for the required inputs, the transformation performed by the task or process, and the outputs produced. Figure 1–5 illustrates the general form of this representation. Although it is more difficult to perform

	Conditions				State	
	CL	CK	J	K	Q	$\overline{Q}$
A	L	X	X	X	L	H
B	H	⎍	L	L	Q_0	$\overline{Q}_0$
C	H	⎍	H	L	H	L
D	H	⎍	L	H	L	H
E	H	⎍	H	H	T	T

(a)

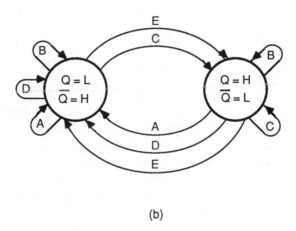

(b)

Figure 1–4. **(a) State Transition Table; (b) State Transition Diagram for a JK Flip-Flop**

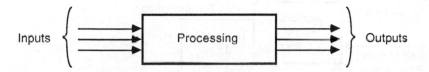

Figure 1–5. **Task Representation Model**

state transition analysis than to use the state transition table or diagram, analysis is very useful for judging the completeness and cohesiveness of a system's specification. Automatic program structure analyzers exist that work with system specification languages to help specify and design complex systems. The inputs and outputs associated with a particular task are associated with inputs and outputs of other system tasks, in such a way that a system-level data flow representation can be deduced. One structured design and analysis technique that incorporates the general philosophy of Figure 1–5 is the Integrated Computerized Manufacturing Definition Methods (IDEF). Developed at the United States Air Force's Wright Aeronautical Laboratory to support the requirements specification and analysis for the A7E aircraft program, this tool assists system designers in identifying the requirements placed on various levels of system design. This methodology identifies three perspectives from which to view the process/task structure of a large program. The first perspective, a functional view, defines what job a particular process or task must accomplish. In this view, the relationships between processes, data, controls, and resources are shown in multiple levels of detail to give the user an exact description of the goal of the program. Figure 1–6(a) shows a high-level functional diagram for an aircraft radar system. In essence, the functional representation shows what information is produced and consumed, which processes consume and produce what data, and the goal accomplished by each process. The second view provided by the IDEF methodology is called the behavioral model. Here, the dynamic behavior of the system's processing is represented in a way similar to that of the state transition diagrams discussed earlier. Events that cause transitions from one state to the next are associated with processes that embody processing states. Again, there are levels of granularity in the behavioral model representation, which facilitate a top down design approach. Figure 1–6(b) shows a behav-

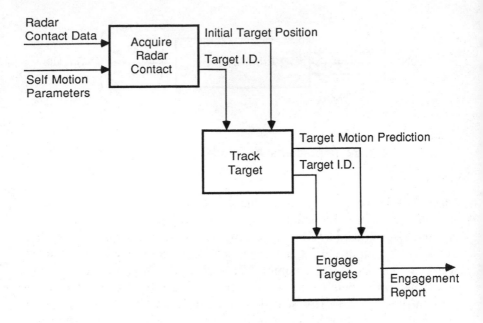

Figure 1–6 (a).   **IDEF Functional Model for a Simple Radar System**

ioral diagram for the simple radar system of Figure 1–6(a). The third modeling perspective provided by IDEF is called the informational model. In this view, the data that is produced and consumed by the processes of the function model is identified as to its size, type, range, precision, accuracy, and default values. This information is used during the construction of a system, and compliments the structural and operational information contained in the functional and behavioral models.

The various forms of process/task representation discussed above will be useful for describing the structure and behavior of process in parallel and multiprocessor environments. Combinations of these techniques form the basis for analysis to detect and identify parallelism in program and application structures.

Conventional Machine Architecture

In this section, we well review some of the basic concepts of conventional computer architecture. The review will establish a departure point for the

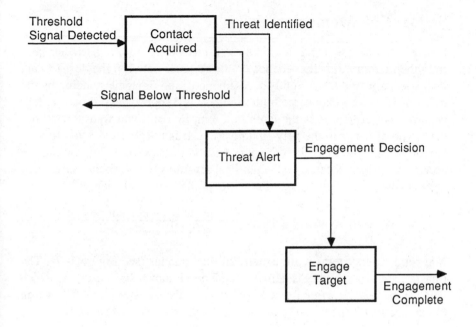

Figure1–6 (b). **IDEF Behavioral Model for a Simple Radar System**

discussion of parallel computer architectures in general. The study of computer architecture is concerned with the structure, interconnection, behavior, and design of computers. The basic building blocks for a conventional machine architecture are most commonly the memory, input/output system, arithmetic unit, and control unit. These components form the basic level of computer architecture analysis. In order to provide the necessary background for subsequent chapters, the following sections will briefly discuss the important aspects of each of the basic architectural components, listed above.

Memory

An essential element for a computing system, memory simply facilitates the storage and access of data. There are two fundamental classes of memory: sequential access and random access.

Sequential Memories

In sequential access memories, the time it takes to retrieve a particular item from the memory directly depends on the distance between the desired data item's location and the currently accessible position. Imagine standing by the railroad tracks as a long cargo train rumbles by. Suppose the railroad car that is currently before you is the tenth in a long line and you want to find out what type of car is in the fifty-first position. It is necessary for you to wait for forty-one cars to pass before your question is answered. Thus the time to access an element depends on the physical separation between the current and desired position and on the speed of travel of the train of elements.

$$a \text{ (access delay in seconds)} = \frac{l \text{ (inches from current position)}}{s \text{ (inches/sec speed)}}$$

Magnetic tape systems work exactly in this manner (see Figure 1–7). The transfer rate of a memory is defined as the maximum sustained rate at which data can be read or written. For a tape system, the transfer rate is a function of the tape travel speed and of the density of the recorded information.

$$r \text{ (transfer rate in bits/sec)} = d \text{ (bits/inch density)} \times s \text{ (inches/sec speed)}$$

Thus the time to transfer a block of n data bits is given by:

$$t \text{ (time for n bits in seconds)} = a + n/r$$

Other sequential access magnetic memories in use today are the various forms of disk storage. Disks are of two basic forms: hard disks and floppy disks. The access characteristics of both are essentially the same. Hard disks, however, offer greater storage capacity, better response time, and faster transfer rates than floppy disks. The floppy disk medium is cheaper, and it has the added advantage that it can be removed so that disks can be swapped in and out. Generally, hard disk systems are used as the main secondary storage medium in large computer systems and on high-performance personal computers. Floppy disks are more prevalent as backup devices and as the main secondary storage for low-end computer systems. New technology is also allowing the manufacture of optical disks, memories that record and retrieve information through the use of lasers. The basic mechanisms of access for optical disks are similar to those for mechanical disks and are not specifically discussed. Figure 1–8 illustrates the physical organization of data on a disk.

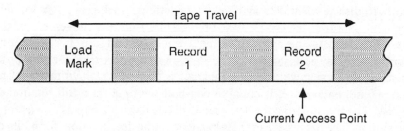

Figure 1–7.   **Magnetic Tape Sequential Access**

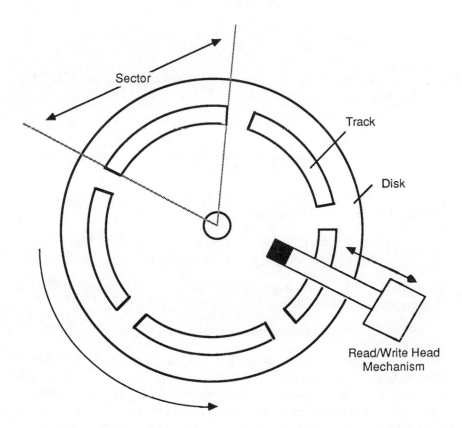

Figure 1–8.   **Physical Disk Organization**

Access to disk resident data involves three actions: track seek, disk rotation time, and data transfer. Track seek time results from the movement of the read/write head to the appropriate data track (see Figure 1–8). Latency refers to the delay associated with the rotation of the disk from the start position to the position at which the desired data is under the read/write head. The latency time, on average, is equal to one-half the time for a full rotation of the disk. The transfer time for data on a disk has the same expression as for a tape system. The expressions for seek, latency, transfer, and time for n bits of information are as follows:

s (seek time in seconds)

$$s = \frac{h \text{ (distance from current to desired track in inches)}}{n \text{ (speed of head movement in inches/sec)}}$$

One factor of a disk's density, then, is its number of tracks per inch (TPI). Latency time is given as:

l (latency in seconds)

$$l = \frac{a \text{ (arc distance from current to desired position in radians)}}{w \text{ (rotational speed of disk in radians/sec)}}$$

The data transfer rate, as for a tape, is given as:

r (transfer rate in bits/sec) = d (density in bits/radian) × w
(rotational speed in radians/sec)

Disk density, d, is the other governing factor in the determination of total disk capacity. The time to transfer n bits of data is given by:

t (time for n bits in seconds) = s + l + n/r

Some disk systems are made with one head per track, and thus the seek time is reduced to an electronic delay in selecting the proper head connection. Multiple surface disks, for which several disks are packaged with a common spindle and head movement mechanics, are also common. Disk systems are often referred to as direct access memories, because it is possible to skip over tracks of information without having to pass all data by the read/write heads. Access to data within a track, however, is still sequential.

The marking of the disk surface into sectors is accomplished in one of two ways: hard- and soft-sectoring. In hard-sectored disks, reference holes punched in the disk's surface provide physical markers from which sectors can be measured. Soft-sectored disks use a single reference hole to denote the first disk sector and use magnetic markers to denote starting points for all other sectors. For a more complete discussion of magnetic recording techniques and media, see [Stone80].

Yet another form of sequential memory, which is quite different from the usual tape and disk magnetic storage devices, is the bubble memory. Magnetic bubble memories are based on the principle that small pockets (bubbles) of magnetically polarized material can be maintained within a homogeneous area of oppositely charged material. Thus the magnetic material can be populated with a number of these bubbles of polarization. The bubbles are formed by applying a polarizing electromagnetic field to a small section of the homogeneous magnetic material. After a bubble has been formed, it can be relocated within the material by using a rotating magnetic field and an overlay of an array of fixed permalloy magnets that act as holding points for the magnetic bubbles. The two layers, magnet bubble material and permalloy overlay, form an arbitrarily long sequence of stored bubbles. Sensing electronics, which can determine the presence or absence of a bubble as the bubble stream is shifted along the path, provide the read capability for binary information stored as bubbles. Bubble memories, therefore, are commonly organized as long loops of bubble streams that can be shifted in either direction to read or write binary information. Sets of loops can be fabricated on a single integrated circuit to give parallel data-storage capabilities. The density of magnetic bubble memories is a function of the bubble size and interbubble spacing. The latter, in turn, is dependent upon the density of the controlling permalloy magnet array and hence upon the device fabrication technology. The speed of bubble memories, however, is comparatively slow with respect to hard disk and semiconductor memories. Due to its nonvolatile nature and lack of moving mechanical parts, bubble memory has found application in systems such as military field equipment, where rugged, permanent memory is required. New techniques for bubble memory construction other than that described above have been developed. The density, speed, and cost per bit have not yet, however, advanced to the point at which bubble memories can replace traditional mass storage (e.g., tape and disk) systems. See [Stone80] and [Baer80] for additional information on bubble memory construction and organization.

Random Access Memories

Random access memories are characterized by the fact that the access to any two random memory locations occurs in approximately equal time. Thus the distance from the current to the desired memory cell does not affect access time; rather, access time is a function of the speed of the electronics used to implement the device. There are two general classes of random access memory: the read only type and the read/write type. Read only memories (ROM) can only be written to (also called programmed) under certain conditions, such as the presence of a special programming voltage. The action of programming a ROM is akin to permanently making or breaking electrical connections within a device. Thus memory is attributed to the physical state of the device interconnections rather than to the storage of magnetic dipoles within a medium. Permanence of data in a ROM does not necessarily mean that the data cannot be changed. Some devices allow the erasure of the entire ROM contents by shining ultraviolet light onto the memory device. Those devices, called Programmable ROMs (PROMs), use ultraviolet-sensitive material that "mends" itself when exposed to a particular wavelength for a period of time. Another form of eraseable ROM, called Electrically Alterable ROM (EAROM) or Electrically Eraseable ROM (EEROM), allows the erasure and reprogramming of individual memory words by the use of special erasing and programming voltages. The common characteristic of all ROM-type memories, however, is their capability to permanently retain data in the absence of applied power.

In contrast to the nonvolatile ROM memories, there exist volatile, random access memories called RAMs. These come in two basic configurations, static and dynamic. Static RAMs typically use flip-flop circuits to construct elements that, when supplied with power, maintain their state indefinitely or until explicitly forced to change. As with flip-flops, however, these memories revert to an arbitrary state upon the interruption of power. Dynamic RAM (DRAM) memories, on the other hand, will not indefinitely maintain their current state with only supplied power. Their bit-cell construction, based in principle on the charging or discharging of a small capacitor per cell, allows the identifying charge to leak away over time. Also, reading a DRAM destroys the contents of the cells that are read, because the stored energy in the capacitor is used to drive sensing logic. Hence, DRAM memories must continually be rewritten to resupply the dwindling capacitance charge. This process called refresh, involves reading memory words and writing them back again over the entire memory contents. Typical DRAMs require a refresh rate on the order of several milliseconds. Advances in circuit density have permitted the placement of the necessary refresh circuitry on the memory chip itself, so that the fact that such a memory is dynamic is virtually hidden.

Another type of random access memory that was used extensively in early computer designs is core memory. Core memory is seldom used in today's computers and is not discussed here. For more discussion of memory construction and organization refer to [Stone80] and to Chapter 2.

Input/Output

Computers and computer systems would be of virtually no use if it were impossible to provide data and receive results. This is true at every level of a computer's operation, from memory access to interaction with human operators. The means of providing this access is usually delegated to the computer's input/output (I/O) subsystem. I/O can be roughly separated into two classes, serial and parallel, and can be driven by either polled or interrupt methods. In addition, access can be either I/O or memory mapped. Each of these issues is discussed below.

Serial input/output, as the name implies, transfers bits of information one at a time over a serial connection. To send words or bytes of data, then, requires the disassembly of the word into bits, the transmission of the individual bits, and the reassembly of the word at the receiving end. This process may seem like a lot of work for nothing, but we will see its advantages and disadvantages as compared to other schemes. Serial I/O is further decomposed into two forms, synchronous and asynchronous communication (see Figure 1–9). In synchronous serial transfer, a stream of data is sent at a fixed clock rate for bits within a word or byte and with a fixed interword delay. Synchronous data transmissions tend to be organized as blocks of data (on the order of hundreds of bytes per block), and resynchronization of the sender and receiver occurs only at the block boundaries. During a block transmission, either the receiver clock is kept synchronized through special data encoding that allows signal edge detection at fixed bit intervals, or it has sufficient accuracy to not drift enough during a block transmission to cause an error.

Asynchronous serial transmission, contrary to the name's connotation, still requires synchronization to allow data transfer. The two differences here are that synchronization of sender and receiver clocks occurs much more frequently than in the synchronous case (every byte or word) and that the intersynchronization time is not fixed. This form of communication gets

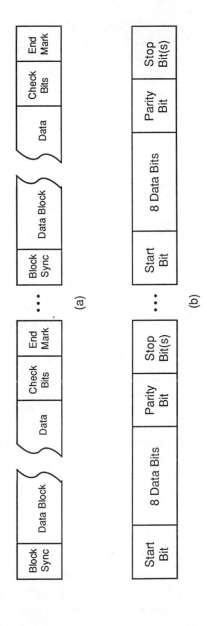

Figure 1–9. (a) Synchronous Serial Transmission; (b) Asychronous Serial Transmission

its name from the fact that byte-level synchronization occurs asynchronously. In order to provide the per-byte synchronization, special signal patterns, called start and stop bits, are used to frame the data transmission. Thus the receiver and sender clocks only have to maintain synchronization in such a way that a single byte can be recovered. In other words, simpler receiver designs are possible and a much greater drift rate for the clocks is allowed. Asynchronous transmission, however, entails a much higher overhead than does synchronous data transmission. An 8-bit datum typically requires one start bit, one parity bit, and one or two stop bits for transmission in an asynchronous fashion. This represents a 37.5%–50% overhead penalty. For a typical synchronous transmission of 256 bytes with an 8-bit end symbol, the overhead is only 12.5%, decreasing for longer blocks. Specific serial I/O devices and standards can be found in [Stone82] and in literature from integrated circuit manufacturers.

Parallel input/output implies the simultaneous transfer of more than one bit of data per clock period. Indeed, parallel I/O path widths generally range from 8 to 32 bits, most commonly in 8-bit increments, although not exclusively so. All parallel schemes are basically synchronous in nature. That is, a separate clock and control line are typically provided to control the interface circuitry. Thus a typical 8-bit parallel port will actually have approximately 10 individual lines associated with it (see Figure 1–10). Parallel I/O interfaces are usually not run for distances greater than 50 meters, for reasons of crosstalk and information skew. Crosstalk occurs when conductors in a par-

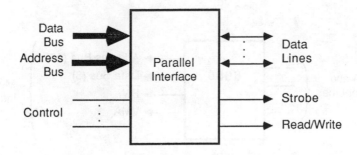

Figure 1–10. **Typical Parallel I/O Device**

allel interface are laid side by side, thus allowing the voltage fluctuations in one line to induce a signal on an adjacent line. This problem, however, can usually be prevented by using proper shielding and grounding techniques. Information skew occurs when the parallel information bits are shifted in time relative to one another and to the clock signal. This condition results from a variety of causes; among them are differences in driving electronics, contact inconsistencies, and variations in line distances. Parallel interfaces are useful, however, for high-speed, local peripheral devices such as high-speed printers, mass storage devices, and graphical displays.

Access to I/O devices from a CPU occurs in one of two ways: I/O or memory mapped. Some processors supply a separate address space for I/O devices, using read/write signals and address lines separate from those used for memory access. Figure 1–11 shows two versions of processors with separate I/O and memory address spaces. In Figure 1–11(a), control signals

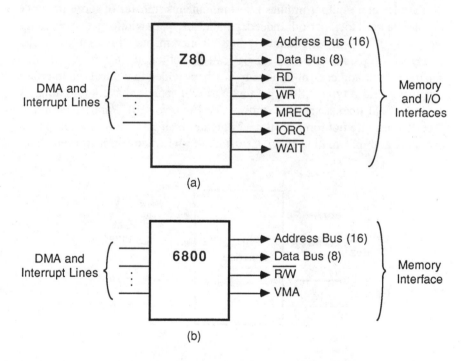

Figure 1–11. **(a) Separate Memory and I/O Interfaces; (b) Memory Mapped I/O Interfaces**

indicate whether the address on the address bus is destined for memory or for an I/O port. In this configuration, it is possible to have identical I/O and memory addresses, because they are differentiated by the MREQ and IORQ lines. This also implies that the processor has different instructions for memory and I/O access. Thus memory reads and writes will use load and store operations, whereas I/O access will use input and output instructions. For the case shown in Figure 1–11(b), there are no explicit signals to differentiate between memory and I/O access. I/O addresses therefore must be made part of the processor's memory address space, and I/O enable signals must be decoded from the memory addresses. In this situation, the same instructions are used for both memory and I/O access. Each case has advantages and disadvantages. For Figure 1–11(b), part of the memory address space must be given up to make room for I/O addresses. This in effect reduces the total amount of physical memory that can be used with the processor, depending upon the number of I/O ports that are necessary. Also, because physical memory is usually provided in chunks of several thousand bytes, the need for just one I/O address means the loss of an entire chunk of memory. The processor with separate memory and I/O spaces does not suffer this inconvenience. One advantage of the memory mapped I/O approach is the flexibility of access methods to the I/O ports, because the entire repertoire of memory access instructions, such as indirect or indexed addressing, can be used in I/O programs.

Arithmetic Logic Unit

The arithmetic logic unit, or ALU, performs all of the functions associated with data manipulation. The basic components of the ALU are the arithmetic/logic circuits (ALCs). Shown in its traditional iconic form in Figure 1–12, the ALC unit performs all arithmetic operations, as well as Boolean operations on data. In Figure 1–12, the A and B buses each supply an n bit operand to the ALC. The width n is defined by the processor word width. The operation that is performed on the operands is defined by the combination of signals presented to the control interface of the ALC. The capabilities of an ALU greatly depend upon the complexity of the ALC and the operations that it can perform. Virtually all ALC components provide fixed-point addition, subtraction, increment, and decrement, as well as the logical operations of AND, OR, EQUIVALENCE, and NOT. More advanced ALC units also perform multiplication, division, and floating-point arithmetic, as well as other logical operations such as EXCLUSIVE OR and SHIFT.

Coupled with the ALC unit in an ALU are a series of registers, busses, and latches. Figure 1–13 shows a conventional setup of ALC, registers, and interconnections in an ALU. During operation, data is gated from the accumulator (AC) and data register (DR) into the ALC unit. After operation of the ALC, the result passes through the shifter and cycles back to the accumulator. Interfaces to memory and other internal registers allow the transfer of data into and out of the ALU.

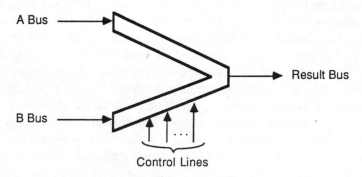

Figure 1–12. **A Typical Arithmetic/Logic Circuit Representation**

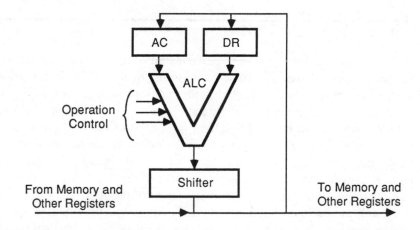

Figure 1–13. **A Typical ALU Configuration**

Although ALUs are constructed to be of the width of the processor's internal buses, bit slice ALUs are manufactured that allow the construction of arbitrarily wide ALUs. For a more complete discussion of ALU construction and operation, the reader is referred to [Hayes78] and [Baer80].

Control Unit

The control unit of a conventional processor functions to provide the controlling signals to the ALU, memory interface, and internal register hardware during an instruction execution. In general, the control unit allows useful work to be performed by coordinating the use of processor resources. Figure 1–14 shows a simplified flow diagram of the actions that must take place during an instruction's execution. From the description in Figure 1–14, it is evident that the control unit must manage the usage of the internal regis-

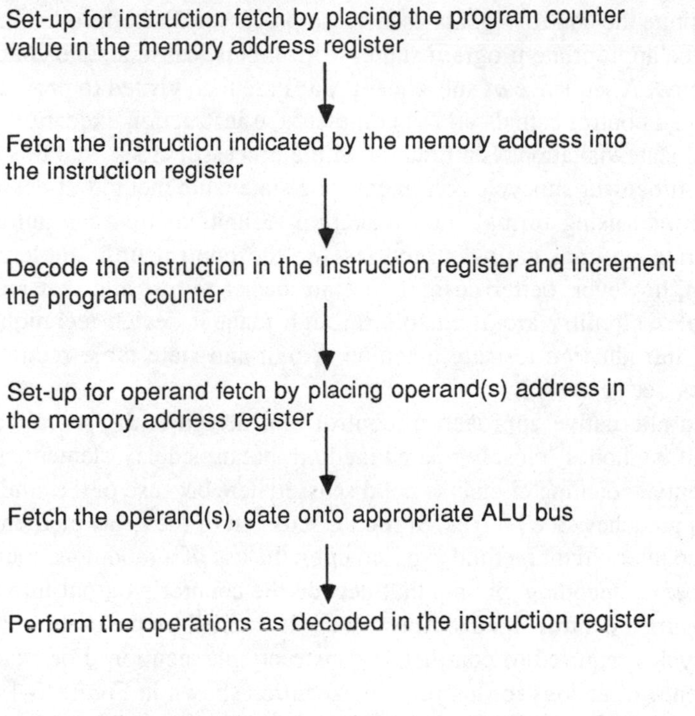

Set-up for instruction fetch by placing the program counter value in the memory address register

↓

Fetch the instruction indicated by the memory address into the instruction register

↓

Decode the instruction in the instruction register and increment the program counter

↓

Set-up for operand fetch by placing operand(s) address in the memory address register

↓

Fetch the operand(s), gate onto appropriate ALU bus

↓

Perform the operations as decoded in the instruction register

Figure 1–14. **Sequence of Operations for Instruction Execution**

ters and the paths that interconnect the registers and the ALU. Figure 1–15 shows the organization of a typical processor, with the various control interfaces illustrated by dotted lines. As shown, the control unit receives its primary data input from the instruction register and a secondary input from the program status word. From the instruction register, the operation code of the current instruction is used to derive the necessary control signals for the execution of that operation. The program status word bits become important for instruction sequences that have a dependency upon previous operations. An example of this is the execution of a COMPARE instruction, followed by a conditional branch that is dependent on the result of the compare operation. Thus the program status word acts as a memory for the control unit to assist in the setting of the control lines.

There are two basic methods for the design and implementation of the control unit logic: the state table method and the counter circuit method.

In the state table method, the control unit is implemented as a sequential finite state machine. The states in the sequential machine define outputs that constitute the control signals used in the processor. Each decoded instruction, and the appropriate program status word inputs, cause a state change in the machine. A sequence of subsequent states are then visited to provide a series of timed control signals and to complete the instruction execution. The timing of state visitations is a function of the processor clock, and this forms the basic processor subcycle increment. The state table method of design can be performed using formal state reduction techniques that can automatically generate optimal gating structures for the control unit implementation. Often, however, better designs that are easier to test and that require less complex circuitry are attainable through manual design techniques. For a good introduction to state machine design and state table reduction techniques, see [Clare73].

An alternative approach to control unit design is the so-called counter circuit method. A closely related method that uses delay elements instead of sequential counting circuits is not discussed here because of the similarities of the approaches. See [Hayes78] for a discussion of the delay element method. The counter circuit method is based upon the use of a modulo k counter and a number of decoding circuits that decode the counter's output into appropriately timed control signals. The value k is defined by the number of processor cycles required to complete an instruction execution. For example, the sequence of actions for instruction execution shown in Figure 1–14 requires six steps for the completion of an instruction. Thus a modulo 6 counter and some decoding circuitry could be used to perform the control function shown

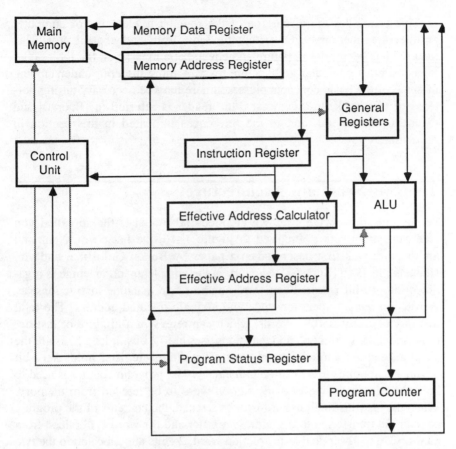

(Note: Solid lines indicate data paths; dashed lines indicate control paths)

Figure 1–15. **The Interaction of the Control Unit with
Processor Resources**

in Figure 1–15. The main advantage of this type of design is the correspondence of the controller design to the function it must perform. In other words, the design is more understandable than the state table method, from the perspective of the function of controlling CPU resources in some time-ordered fashion. This also aids in debugging and altering the functionality of the controller, because the behavior to be modified can be attributed to specific portions of the controller design.

This concludes the discussion of the four basic elements of computer architecture: memory, I/O, arithmetic logic unit, and control unit. This material has been brief in nature and covers, at a high level, the topics contained in most computer architecture texts. A more in-depth understanding of some of the basic concepts presented here may be necessary during portions of this book. In these cases, the reader is referred to [Baer80] and [Stone80] in general, and to the references indicated in this section in particular.

The von Neumann Architecture

Perhaps the most widely known architectural model is the so-called von Neumann architecture. Pictured in Figure 1–16, the basic von Neumann architecture was first described in a paper by Burks, Goldstine, and von Neumann in 1946 [Burks62]. Memory in the von Neumann machine is organized into 40-bit words. Each word contains two machine instructions; an instruction has an operation code and a single operand address. The total memory capacity is 4096 words, which can represent a mixture of instructions and data. Instruction and data addresses are 12 bits in length, as are the program counter and address register. The address register holds a 12-bit quantity that points to a location in memory. The program counter is used to hold the address of the next instruction word to be fetched from memory. When the next instruction word is to be fetched, the contents of the program counter are transferred to the address register and the word is obtained from memory. In a 40-bit double-instruction word, 24 bits are allocated to the two operand addresses, and the remaining 16 bits are allocated to the operation codes. Thus each instruction operation code is 8 bits wide, as is the instruction register. Since two complete instructions are fetched in each memory access, the instruction buffer register is used to hold the extra instruction until it is needed. This register, then, is 20 bits wide. Data paths and data registers (the data register, the accumulator, and the multiplier/quotient register) are all 40 bits wide. Arithmetic in the arithmetic logic unit (ALU) is performed using 39-bit, two's compliment arithmetic (bit 0 is reserved for the sign bit). The ALU is capable of performing addition, subtraction (using two's compliment addition), multiplication, and division. Conditional and unconditional branch instructions are provided for program control flow. Also, instructions were provided for basic data transfer operations between memory and the accumulator. Interestingly, the von Neumann architecture also allowed the modification of the operand address fields of instruction in memory. This provided the capability for the machine to alter its own instructions, which effectively allowed the same instructions to be used on different data, much like a subroutine does in today's computers. These situations, in which programs and data are stored in the same memory and in which programs can alter themselves are the characterizing features of a von Neumann architecture. The great majority of modern machines do store programs and memory together, and can also modify their own execution stream, if so desired. Thus most of today's computers are classified as von Neumann architectures. Note that the fact that an architecture permits writing to a memory location that may contain an instruction does not mean that it is always possible to do so. Many safeguards exist to ensure that this action occurs only in well-controlled situations and by deliberate program action.

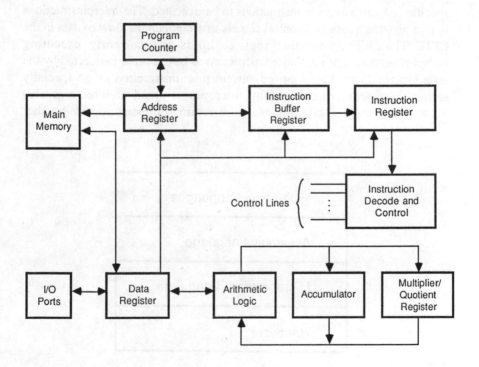

Figure 1–16. **von Neumann Machine Architecture**

An Architecture Example

An excellent way of illustrating the operation and interaction of the various architectural building blocks is to examine an existing architecture's operation under microprogram control. Before we begin this exercise, we will first define microprogramming and discuss its usefulness. In the hierarchy of programming language levels (see Figure 1–17), microprogramming lies at the foundation, closest to the CPU hardware. Note, however, that not all machines support microprogramming.

In these cases, the assembly language level is the lowest accessible. For microprogrammed systems, control instructions that can access the elements of the ALU and peripheral registers are stored in an internal control memory. Assembly language instructions brought in from memory cause a specific sequence of microinstructions to be executed. The microinstructions in turn provide a series of control signals that regulate the flow of data in the CPU. The microinstruction register holds the currently executing microinstruction. The next microinstruction to be executed is selected by the state change logic, based on the current microinstruction or on specially stored microprogram data. Many microprogrammed architectures also allow microprogram subroutines whose return addresses provide another

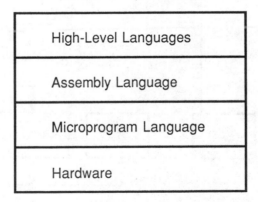

Figure 1–17. **Programming Language Levels**

source of microinstruction addresses. Thus the microprogram and its associated logic acts as the control unit for the CPU.

The advantage of microprogammed control is that the repertoire of assembly language instructions can be altered. Also, special microinstruction sequences can be created to implement new assembly language instructions.

The microprogrammed architecture that will be examined in this section is that of the Data General Eclipse Computer shown in Figure 1–18. In the Eclipse CPU, the microinstruction consists of a 56-bit word that is broken into 15 different fields. Figure 1–19 shows the microinstruction word fields. Figure 1–20 lists the significance of each field in the microinstruction.

A much more detailed description can be found in the manufacturer's literature; this discussion is intended to give a general overview of the microinstruction. In essence, the microinstruction gives the programmer full control over the internal CPU resources. The usefulness of this freedom will be demonstrated by implementing an assembly language instruction of another computer on the Eclipse CPU. The instruction to be emulated is the PDP-9 Load Accumulator (LAC) instruction. The format of the LAC instruction is shown in Figure 1–21. It operates in two basic modes (direct address mode and indirect address mode), as controlled by the indirect bit. If the indirect bit is not set, the 11-bit address contained in the instruction points to the memory location that contains the data to be loaded into the accumulator. If the indirect bit is set, the address in the instruction points to the memory location that contains the address of the data to be loaded. Thus, in the indirect case, this second address must be fetched and used to get the data from memory. The basic execution flow of the microsubroutine is as follows:

1. Read the memory word pointed to by GR3 (the Eclipse program counter).

2. Test the op code of the memory word at that location. If the instruction does not contain a LAC op code, terminate this microsubroutine. Otherwise continue.

3. Test the LAC instruction indirect bit and initiate fetch of data pointed to by the LAC address field.

4. If the indirect bit is off, jump to step 6.

5. If the indirect bit is on, use the data read in step 3 to initiate another memory access.

6. Store the data that is read from memory in step 3 or step 5 into AC0, and set up to fetch the next assembly level instruction.

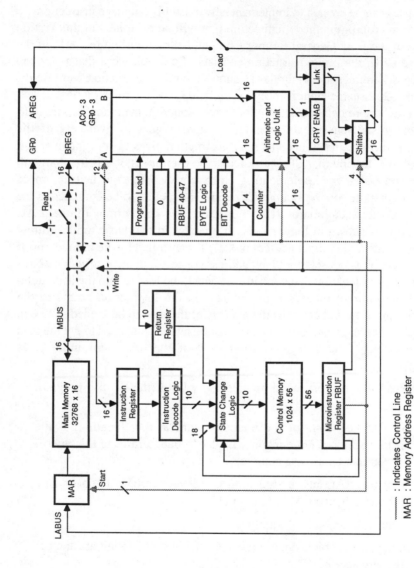

--- : Indicates Control Line
MAR : Memory Address Register

Figure 1–18.   Microprogramming Architecture of the Eclipse CPU
Arithmetic and Memory Sections Only — No I/O Shown

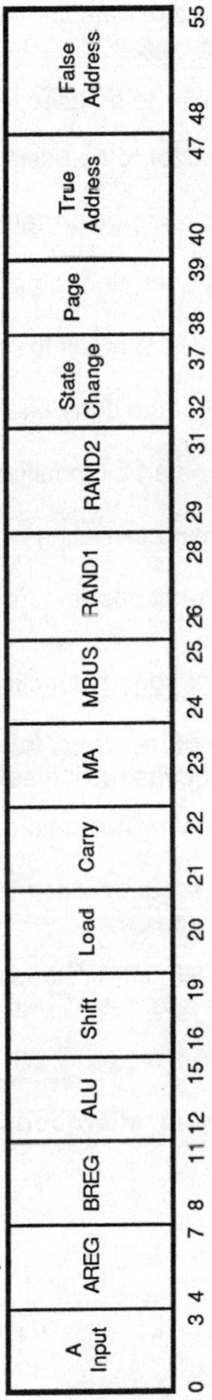

A Input	AREG	BREG	ALU	Shift	Load	Carry	MA	MBUS	RAND1	RAND2	State Change	Page	True Address	False Address
0 3 4	7 8	11 12	15 16	19	20	21	22	23	24 25 26	28 29	31 32	37 38	39 40	47 48	55

Figure 1-19. **Format of the Eclipse Microinstruction**

A Input — Defines the source of data for the A Bus for the microconstruction cycle.

AREG — Defines the register to be used as a source for the A Bus.

BREG — Identifies the register to be used as a source for the B Bus.

ALU — Selects the function to be performed on the A and B Bus data.

Shift — Defines the shift operation to be performed.

Load — If set, causes the ALU result to be loaded into the A register.

Carry — Controls the use of the carry bit.

MA — Sets the memory start bit to initiate a memory transfer.

MBUS — Controls the reading or writing actions of the memory bus.

Rand 1 — Selects special functions and helps control microsubroutine return operation.

Rand 2 — Selects additional special functions.

StateChange — Controls the use of the page, true and false address fields for the next microconstruction selection.

Page — Supplies page bits for next microconstruction address.

True Address — Holds next address; used when state change test is true; also holds constant.

False Address — Holds next address; used when state change test is false; also holds return address.

Figure 1–20.   **Definition of Eclipse Microconstruction Fields**

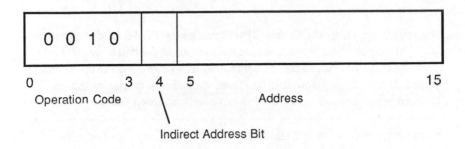

Figure 1–21. **PDP-9 LAC Instruction Format**

The microsubroutine used to perform the above functions is shown in Figure 1–22. In the routine listing, fields marked with a dash (-) indicate no action. Fields marked with an ampersand (&) indicate the next sequential microinstruction address. Instruction labels provide a convenient method of referencing microinstructions. Semicolons in column 1 indicate comment lines.

The Eclipse micro control store can hold 1024 56-bit microinstructions. The store is broken into pages 0-3, each with 256 instructions. Pages 0 and 1 are typically implemented using ROM, and they hold the microsubroutines that implement the basic Eclipse instruction set. Page 2 is called the writable control store, and it can be used to implement custom instructions, as illustrated earlier. Page 3 is reserved for future use.

The above illustration is not intended to be a tutorial on how to microprogram the Eclipse CPU. Rather, it should serve to illustrate the basic CPU components and their interaction and control. From this example, it is relatively straight-forward to envision the development of special-purpose computing units from the basic architectural building blocks. This evolution is in progress, in fact, as evidenced by the availability of special-purpose processors to handle tasks such as the control of a graphics interface or the calculation of floating-point numbers. The future of integrated electronics promises to take this evolution even further, to the point at which specialized components will perform every task necessary in a cooperative computing environment. This advancement will certainly increase the number of functions that can be performed simultaneously and make the concepts of parallel processing even more important.

```
; This microprogram for the Eclipse CPU emulates the PDP-9 load accumulator
; (LAC) instruction. This program inputs the instruction pointed to by GR3 and
; loads the effective address contents into AC0. The program is set up so that an
; indirect chain can be followed to one level. A dash (-) indicates no action.
; The next line is a reference for the Eclipse microinstruction fields.
;----------------------------------------------------------------------------------
;LBL AIN AREG BREG ALU SHIFT LOAD  CRY MA MBUS R1  R2   CHG  PG   TR   FL
;----------------------------------------------------------------------------------
; set up for memory read, address is in GR3 (PC)
 -  AR  PC   -    A   FA   -      -   S   -    -   -    NC   2    &    &
; read memory contents into AC0, increment and store GR3 (PC)
 -  AR  PC   AC0  A1  FA   L      -   -   READ -   BMEM NC   2    &    &
; form mask to strip off address bits from the instruction in AC0
; mask placed in GR1
 -  CON GR1  -    A   SW   L      -   -   -    -   -    NC   2    360  &
; AND AC0 with GR1 to strip address bits, result placed in GR1
 -  AR  AC0  GR1  ANB FA   -      -   -   -    -   -    NC   2    &    &
; form test pattern for LAC op code, place in GR2
 -  CON GR2  -    A   SW   L      -   -   -    -   -    NC   2    040  &
; XOR GR1 and GR2, if result is zero, we have a LAC, otherwise jump to END
 -  AR  GR1  GR2  AXB FA   -      -   -   -    -   -    ALUZ 2    END  &
; form mask to save address in instruction (masks op code), save in GR1
 -  CON GR1  -    A   SW   L      -   -   -    -   -    NC   2    370  &
; mask off op code and start memory, start of operand fetch
IND AR  AC0  GR1  ANCB FA  -      -   S   -    -   -    NC   2    &    &
; set up to test for indirection on bit 4, swap bytes, put back into AC0.
; swapping bytes puts bit 4 into the bit 12 position
 -  AR  AC0  -    A   SW   L      -   -   -    -   -    -    2    &    &
; test bit 12 (the indirect bit), read operand into AC0, if not
; indirect then jump to END
 -  AR  AC0  AC0  A   FA   -      -   -   READ -   BMEM ALU12 2   &    END
; indirect read so use AC0 to read again, put result in AC0
 -  AR  AC0  -    A   FA   -      -   S   -    -   -    NC   2    &    &
 -  -   -    AC0  A   -    -      -   -   READ -   BMEM NC   2    &    &
; set up to read next assembly language instruction
END AR  PC   -    A   FA   -      -   S   -    -   -    NC   2    &    &
; fetch next assembly instruction, place in IR and exit routine
 -  -   -    -    A   -    -      -   -   READ -   -    LDIR 2    &    &
```

Figure 1–22. **Microsubroutine to emulate the PDP-8 LAC instruction on the Eclipse CPU.**

Software

In the early stages of computer development, programming a computer to accomplish a specific function was a tedious task. In the 1940's, the state of the art in computers, the ENIAC, had to be programmed using a patch panel and pluggable wires. This level of programming is essentially equivalent to that of microprogramming, as discussed in the previous section. Gradually, memory technology made it possible to store programs in memory and to use standard instruction sets of possible operations. Thus one level of abstraction from the hardware level was achieved. A second level of abstraction, programs that could run on different machines having different sets of assembly language instructions, was made possible through the use of language compilers. The first compiled language, FORTRAN, appeared in the 1950's and permitted algebraic expressions to be embedded and evaluated within a controlled program flow. The move toward high-level language use has continued, with today's languages offering far superior structuring and control facilities than did the original FORTRAN. The expressiveness of high-level languages has also advanced to the point that languages exist for specialized application areas. Examples of this specialization are Cobol for business applications, Basic for small computers, and Ada (a trademark of the United States Department of Defense) for real-time, embedded systems.

The general progression in languages has been from linear, monolithic programs that were self-contained, to modular, separately compilable subprogram units. Many of these languages exist within similar development and execution environments. Development typically occurs within a time-shared computing environment or on stand-alone personal or minicomputers. The environment in these systems usually consists of a file-oriented operating system that offers services such as screen editors, compilation and link utilities, program storage, and printing commands. Execution environments are often characterized as single processor systems with varying degrees of operating system support, memory, and I/O. These conditions, at a gross level, hold true no matter what the actual application or end use may be. From a computer architecture standpoint, these systems gain their functionality through the particular technology used to implement the computer's components and through the organization of the software that runs on the hardware.

Operating systems on traditional systems provide the execution environment for application programs. Centralized operating systems are responsible for managing files, I/O, memory, and processor resources in a single processor architecture. The majority of applications and programming languages that have been developed in the past were heavily influenced by the centralized operating system mindset. This approach is entirely appropriate for two reasons: the control of time-ordered events is relatively straightforward in a centralized system, and the sequential nature of programs in these systems is easier for the programmer to conceptualize and implement. The extension to parallel systems, however, is seldom straightforward. On the development side, new tools are needed to help programmers define, detect, and exploit parallelism. Also, new languages that can adequately express the desired program constructs will need to be developed. A start on these issues, however, has been made. There are vectorizing compilers and multitasking languages such as Ada. More specialized tools such as parallel detection compilers and parallel programming languages (such as occam) do exist today, although their use is usually restricted to a specific system or application. Advancement in the area of parallel code design and development appears to depend upon the solution of two basic problems. The first is to reeducate programmers and system designers so that they can take full advantage of the power provided by parallel and multiprocessor systems. The second problem, an important factor in the solution of the first, is to provide a suite of tools that are oriented toward designing and detecting parallelism, providing formal expressions for parallel concepts, and automating the compilation, loading, and execution processes on parallel hardware. Only after these goals are accomplished will we see a widespread usage of multiprocessor and parallel systems.

Definitions of Parallel and Multiprocessing

Something can be described as being "parallel" if it is "like in essential parts." Strictly speaking, a parallel process or processor is one in which the fundamental process being performed or the processing elements used are identically replicated at least once. An entity that has the characteristic "multi," is defined as "consisting of, or having many." There are no restrictions on the nature of the constituent parts; simply having more than one is a sufficient condition. The interpretation of these meanings for computer systems generally takes on a more liberal connotation. Parallelism, as seen in the literature today, commonly means "to do more than one thing at once." From this very basic definition spring several questions as to the nature of "more than one thing." This condition could be interpreted as n users each doing their own thing, n users each doing the same thing, one user doing n things at once, or n users each doing m things. Also, the processing could be taking place on one processor, one processor with multiple CPUs, or multiple processors separated by a shared communication link, point-to-point ties, or common memory. Is the parallelism applied to all aspects of the application or only to specific parts? The granularity of parallelism could be within or across programs. The function to be performed could be partitioned into a number of independent steps, whose execution could be overlapped with the steps of other functions. All of these examples fit the liberal definition in one way or another; the formal definitions are more difficult to satisfy. This book will accept the liberal viewpoint and consider all aspects of parallel and multiprocessing computers and software. In this way, a broad range of issues will be considered, all of which are important for different reasons.

In order to place subsequent discussions within some type of framework, the general classification structure of Figure 1–23 is presented. Detailed discussions of the processor classes at the leaves of the tree will be presented in general in chapter 5 and, in reference to special computers, in section III. The intermediate nodes labeled SIMD, MISD, MIMD, loosely coupled, and tightly coupled will be discussed next.

In an influential paper presented in 1966, Flynn outlined four classes for the organization of high-speed computers [Flynn66]. These classes have become standard terminology for describing a multiprocessor or parallel architecture. The foundation of the four classes is based upon the nature of the instruction stream (the sequence of instructions performed during a process) and upon the nature of the data stream (the sequence of operands that are acted upon by the instruction stream). These two streams are classified according to their degree of multiplicity, either single or multiple. Thus there are four possible classifications: single instruction single data (SISD), single instruction multiple data (SIMD), multiple instruction single data (MISD), and multiple instruction multiple data (MIMD). Each is discussed briefly below.

SISD machines are characterized by the decoding of only one instruction in a machine instruction cycle. Included in this class of machines are those that use overlapped execution units for instructions in various stages of completion. Figure 1–24(a) shows an SISD organization. Most mini- and super-mini computers in existence today are classified as having an SISD organization. It should be noted here that, although Flynn's classifications were proposed in the context of high-speed computing systems, they have since been adopted as descriptions for virtually any class of computer.

In an SISD architecture, Flynn uses the term *confluence* to describe the process of executing an instruction in phases, as illustrated in Figure 1–25.

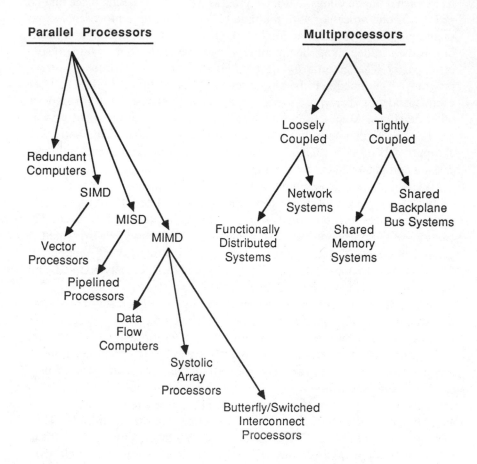

Figure 1–23. **Classification Framework for Parallel and Multiprocessors**

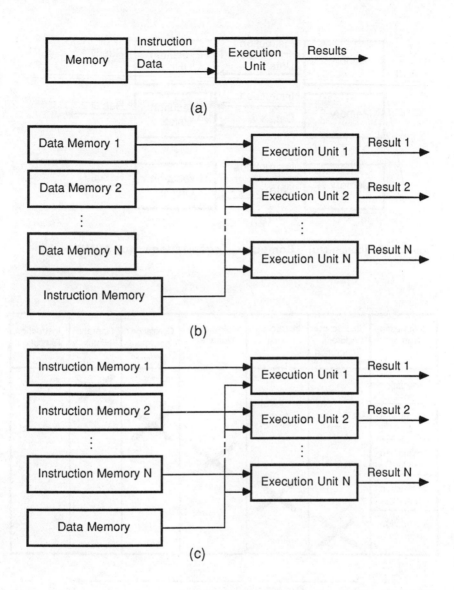

Figure 1–24. **Computer Organizations: (a) SISD, (b) SIMD, (c) MISD**

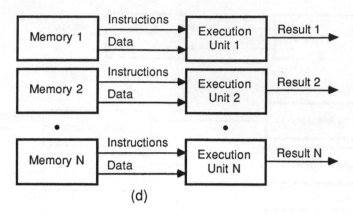

(d)

Figure 1–24 (continued). **Computer Organizations: (d) MIMD**

Instruction Number	Instruction Address Generation	Instruction Fetch	Instruction Decode	Operation Address Generation	Operand Fetch	Instruction Execution
Instruction m–2					X	
Instruction m–1				X		
Instruction m			X			
Instruction m+1		X				
Instruction m+2	X					

Direction of Instruction Flow →

Figure 1–25. **Instruction Pipelining in a SISD Computer Shown at an Instance in Time**

In the figure, several instructions, indicated by Xs, are being processed simultaneously, although they are all in different stages of completion. This concept will be discussed in greater depth in Chapter 5.

The SIMD organization, shown in Figure 1–24(b), is the classic form of an array processor. In this type of computer, the n processing elements (PEs) are identical, and they are all controlled by a master controller. The communication between PEs is typically limited to nearest-neighbor links and is also controlled by the master controller. A typical interconnection pattern, shown in Figure 1–26, illustrates nearest-neighbor interconnection in a 4 x 4 array. All of the PEs in the array operate synchronously; that is, they each execute the same instruction at the same time. Each PE, however, has its own data source and sink, which may be the output of or input to other PEs as defined by the interconnection and by the application. The interpretation of the SIMD classification has relaxed somewhat since its introduction in 1966. The original interpretation did not allow the use of confluence techniques on the individual PEs, but this restriction is generally not observed today. These types of computers will be discussed further in Chapter 5.

MISD machines, illustrated in Figure 1–24(c), are characterized by the presence of a number of PEs, each with its own instruction stream but with a common data stream. This type of organization permits the same data set to be operated on simultaneously by many different instruction streams. This could be useful for applications such as signal processing in which different solution algorithms are run simultaneously on the same data to ensure adequate coverage of the problem. A second definition of the MISD organization resembles a pipelined system in which data derived from one stage is used as input to the next stage: The single data stream is passed sequentially through and is transformed at each PE (as shown in Figure 1–27). According to Flynn's definition, the PEs operate in lockstep so that sequential data items are operated on in adjacent PEs during the same instruction cycle.

In the fourth machine category proposed by Flynn, the MIMD organization, each PE has its own, independent instruction and data stream. PEs also tend to be more general-purpose, because they must be able to process all of the instructions necessary to perform the appropriate data transformation. No restrictions are placed on the synchronization of the separate PEs in a MIMD configuration, and the communication between PEs is defined as minimal. Almost all multiprocessor systems in existence today are classified as MIMD machines. More detail on these types of systems will be presented in Chapter 5.

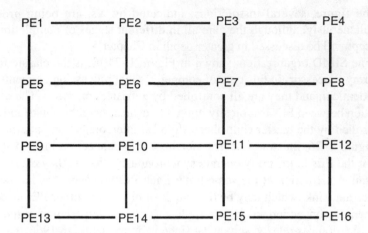

Figure 1–26. **Nearest Neighbor Interconnection in a 4 x 4 Array**

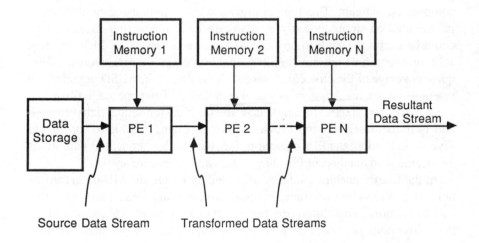

Figure 1–27. **A Second Definition for MISD Organization**

Another classification guideline that is frequently used to describe computer systems is the degree of coupling that exists between PEs. Coupling is the means by which computers exchange information: whether by shared memory, bus interconnection, or network links. In any case, coupling is represented on both the physical and the logical interconnection levels. The two extremes of coupling for both physical and logical coupling are termed loosely coupled and tightly coupled systems. These two extremes are discussed briefly below. [Enslow81] provides a good discussion of these classifications.

Loosely coupled systems are characterized by the lack of direct sharing of processor address spaces and, subsequently, no sharing of primary memory. At the physical level, this means that interprocessor communications must be message-based and that word-at-a-time interactions are not feasible. Logically, this means that the involved processes are autonomous; that is, one does not exercise direct control over another. Enslow indicates that loosely coupled systems operate at the I/O transfer level. This means that communication between processors in a system entails the use of I/O facilities and therefore forces a message-based approach to communication. In such a system, work allocated to different processes in the system is accomplished cooperatively, with each process essentially agreeing to do its share.

Tightly coupled systems, in contrast to loosely coupled ones, do permit shared memory access and promote word-by-word interaction among communicating processes. Physically, this means that the involved processors have overlapping primary address spaces, or that they are interconnected at the memory access level. Tight logical coupling implies that one process may exercise direct control over another by forcing a desired sequence of actions to occur. Of course, the system must be designed to permit this control in the first place. Tight logical coupling merely states that the imposition of this control is solely at the discretion of the asserting process; no consent is solicited or received from the controlled process.

Figure 1–28 summarizes the definitions of logical and physical, and tightly and loosely coupled systems. Note that a tight, logical coupling need not rest upon a tight physical coupling. Indeed it is entirely possible to construct a multiprocessing system in which processes are logically tightly coupled over a physically loosely coupled interconnection. The converse is also possible. In the context of this book, physically tight coupling is usually thought of as an attribute of parallel or multiprocessor *computers* whereas physically loose coupling is generally attributed to parallel or multiprocessor *systems*.

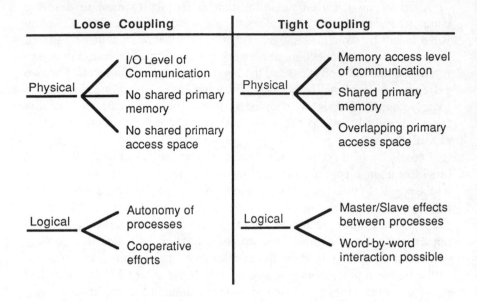

Figure 1–28. **Summary of Loose and Tight Coupling**

Several other classification schemes exist as defined in [Gajski85] and [Thurber75]. These define classes based on data- or demand-driven systems, as well as categories based on the degree of parallelism found in a computer. These categorizations will be expanded and drawn upon as necessary in subsequent chapters and are not dealt with here. For now, it is sufficient to utilize the instruction stream/data stream classes proposed by Flynn and our definitions of the extremes of physical and logical coupling.

Chronology of Parallel and Multiprocessor Systems

As a summary for this introductory chapter and as a preface to subsequent discussions, a brief chronology of parallel and multiprocessor systems is given. Figure 1–29 lists, in approximate historical order, some of the more influential and interesting computer architectures in the parallel and multiprocessor evolution. The evolution shown in Figure 1–29 does not attempt to show the lineage of the various architectures; it merely places their development in an approximate time frame. Except for families of

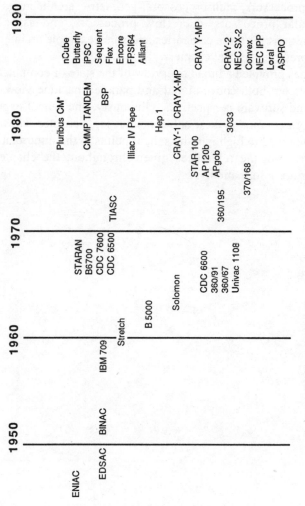

Figure 1–29. Approximate Chronology of Parallel and Multiprocessor Systems

computers from individual manufacturers, many of the computers listed use the combined influences of previous generations to formulate a more effective design. The current state of parallel and multiprocessor design does, however, allow us to lump the architectures into six basic categories: vector or array processors, multiprocessors, geometric architectures (i.e., cubes), superscalar processors, data flow processors, and associative processors. Definitions for these categories and some example architectures for each will be presented in later chapters.

This chapter has provided a broad overview of the state of computational machine science from both conventional and parallel machine views, and from hardware and software perspectives. Obviously, one cannot expect to cover every important point on these subjects in a single chapter. The author has, however, attempted to highlight the salient points in the important topic areas. For this reason, the references given throughout the chapter are suggested for further information.

2. COMPUTATIONAL SPEED AND CONVENTIONAL COMPUTER ARCHITECTURE

This chapter covers the factors, both technical and architectural, that affect the computational speed of a computer. Ignoring cost considerations for the moment, computational speed is perhaps the most important factor in the overall design for a computer system. For all time-critical applications, speed is the first item to be specified and designed for. For most microprocessor upgrades, increased speed is the biggest advantage. The desire to increase computational speed for applications is also the prime motivation for designing and building levels of parallelism in a system or computer. Increased speed through parallelism has been manifested in a number of different areas, from the use of separate I/O controllers to the calculation of floating-point operations by special-purpose coprocessors. Moreover, existing applications of parallelism to increase speed have used multiple CPU systems and hierarchies of processors. Still, there exists a set of basic factors that ultimately determine the limit of computational speed for any computer system. These factors come from two broad areas: the physical properties of the devices used to construct the component under consideration, and the architectural characteristics of the collected components within a system. This chapter will provide a survey of the important performance factors that have an impact on computational speed. The survey will consist of discussions on the physical and architectural factors that affect computational speed.

Basic Components

The transistor is the basic building block upon which the more complex elements of a digital computer are built. It stands to reason, then, that the maximum speed at which a transistor can be switched imposes a pervasive limitation on the component speed. All digital logic is based upon the binary number system and the corresponding set of Boolean algebra identities. The Boolean algebra, developed by G. Boole in the mid-1800's, allows any logic circuit to be broken down into elementary logical operations of ANDs, ORs, and NOTs. Additional laws developed by DeMorgan enable the expression of AND operations in terms of ORs and NOTs, and of OR operations in terms of ANDs and NOTs. Thus the use of only AND and NOT or OR and NOT logic circuits is sufficient to build any combinational logic design. Since AND and NOT digital logic circuits can be constructed from transistors, we can develop some criteria for the transistor switching times and subsequently for the signal propagation delay through a logic gate.

Figure 2–1 illustrates the transistor circuits for a NOT gate. The use of transistors in logic circuits is based upon the device characteristics, called the saturation and cutoff regions, that allow the transistor to act as a binary switch. Depending on the type of material used to construct a transistor, a finite amount of time elapses during the transition from the cutoff region of operation to the saturation region, and vice versa. Figure 2–2 compares the output current for a given input waveform for the transistor circuit shown. Several points can be made about this simple example. First, it is obvious that the cascaded combination of circuits of the type shown in Figure 2–2 will produce an end-to-end delay that is approximately equal to the sum of each individual circuit delay. Each circuit's delay is seen as t_on for turning on and t_off for turning off. These delays result from the time needed to accumulate sufficient charge to turn on the transistor and the time required for Ic to reach its steady-state flow value. These delays are inherent in the properties of the materials used to construct the circuit and transistor. Although some semiconductor materials exhibit faster switching time than others, the switching delay can never be completely eliminated. Building a logic gate from the basic switching element results in a gate propagation time that is measured from the input transition to the output transition. A typical transistor-transistor logic gate has a propagation time on the order of ten nanoseconds.

Another important aspect of digital circuit design is the maximum frequency at which a gate can be driven. Transistors are really analog devices that are configured to operate as bi-stable devices, either in saturation or cutoff. This is what gives a transistor the characteristic of a switch. All of this is presupposed, however, by the fact that the input signal is applied for a time that is sufficiently long for the device to switch. Thus, if an input signal is not held long enough, the desired transition will not occur and a nonfunctional circuit will result. This sufficiently long time period is defined as the sum of the setup time and hold times for a particular gate. Figure 2–3 illustrates these times. The setup time (t_s) is defined as the time interval for an input signal to reach a specified level at a gate input. The hold time is the time interval that an input signal must be held at the prespecified level before another transition can begin at the input. From these two quantities, we can calculate the maximum switching rate of a given circuit.

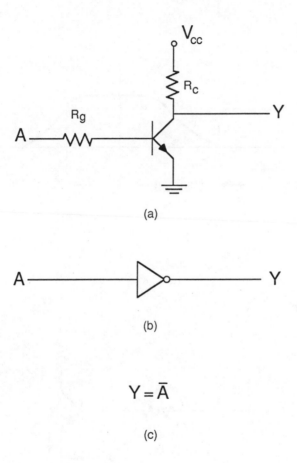

(a)

(b)

$$Y = \overline{A}$$

(c)

Figure 2–1. **(a) NOT Circuit, (b) Logic Symbol, (c) Logic Equation**

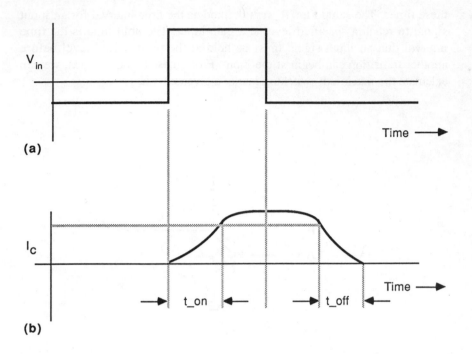

(a)

(b)

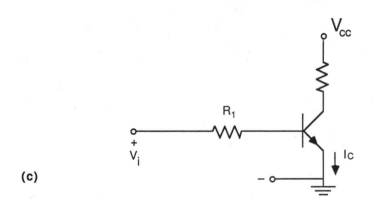

(c)

Figure 2–2. **(a) Input Voltage and (b) Output Current Waveforms
for the Circuit Shown in (c)**

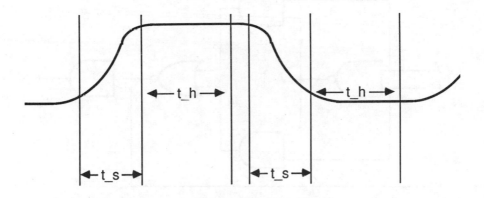

Figure 2–3.   **Illustration of Setup Time (t_s) and Hold Time (t_h)**

Using the identity:

Frequency (Hz) = 1/period (sec)

and using typical setup and hold times of t_s nanoseconds and t_h nanoseconds, we can calculate the minimum pulse period as:

Minimum pulse period = 2t_s + 2t_h seconds

and the corresponding maximum switching frequency:

Maximum frequency = 1/minimum pulse period

F_{max} = 1/(2t_s + 2t_h) Hz

Note that the illustration above has assumed that the positive-going setup and hold times are equivalent to the negative-going times, and therefore that the resultant frequency is specified as having a 50% duty cycle. This may not always be true, in which case the minimum pulse width is simply the sum of the different setup and hold times, and the maximum frequency will have a duty cycle that reflects the appropriate setup and hold times.

Now let's look at the effect of both of these measures, switching delay

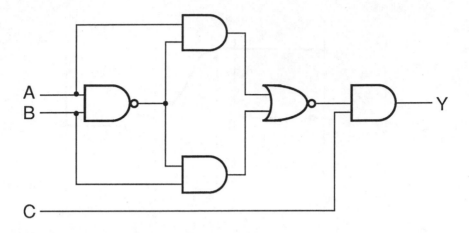

Figure 2–4. **An Arbitrary Combinational Logic Circuit**

time and maximum switching frequency, on a combinational logic circuit. Let's say we have an arbitrary combinational logic circuit with four levels of gating from input to output (see Figure 2–4). In this circuit, the propagation delay from input signal to output signal is approximately equal to the sum of the delays of each level in the circuit. The maximum switching frequency for the entire circuit, however, cannot be more than the switching frequency of the slowest component in the circuit. See [Millman72] for an in-depth treatment of electronic circuits.

Now let's consider the construction of a typical CPU and examine the definition of CPU cycle time based upon our earlier discussions. Figure 2–5 shows a simplified block diagram of the internal architecture of a typical CPU. In this architecture, each major functional block contains a number of levels of gated logic, and each has a maximum switching frequency, as described above. In addition, each functional block has associated with it a number of control lines that define the function to be performed and that provide clock pulses at the appropriate times. In a typical operation in this CPU, an operand is chosen from the register bank, is then operated on by the ALU along with another operand, and is passed through the post-ALU logic (e.g., a shifter); the result is returned to the register bank. The flow of operands through the functional boxes is sequential, and the operation of each box is synchronized, by the clock input, with the arrival of the appropriate operand(s). Because each functional box has a propagation delay associated with it, we can get a minimum round-trip propagation delay that is equal to the sum of the functional box delays. To this quantity, however, must be added the appropriate delays to limit the maximum switching frequency of all of the functional boxes. The basic CPU cycle time, then, is defined as the round-trip time from the memory bank, through the functional boxes, and back again. The basic cycle time is broken up into a number of phases, usually with one phase per functional box. Shown in Figure 2–6 are the phase definitions for the CPU of Figure 2–5. The clock phases are derived from the CPU master clock, usually by dividing the master clock into pulses that are used to clock the various functional blocks during their appropriate phases. Normally, the separation of phase pulses are designed to permit minimal delay between functional blocks, in addition to the unavoidable propagation delays within each block. Thus the clock speed for a given CPU is chosen so that it can be divided into appropriately timed phase clocks. The basic instruction cycle time, therefore, cannot always be deduced from the CPU clock rate.

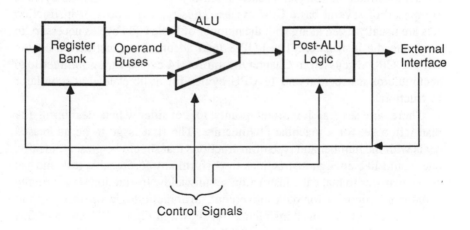

Figure 2–5. **Simplified Block Diagram of a Typical CPU**

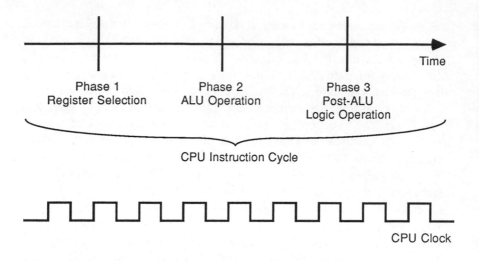

Figure 2–6. **Clock Phases During a CPU Cycle**

Processor Instruction Sets

As demonstrated in Chapter 1, each assembly language instruction cycle is composed of several basic CPU cycles. Thus typical processor instruction sets are usually listed along with the number of basic CPU cycles necessary to complete the instruction. The PDP-8 load accumulator instruction on the Eclipse CPU discussed in Chapter 1 requires 14 cycles for an indirect load accumulator instruction and 11 CPU cycles for a direct load accumulator instruction.

There are several important points to consider when designing the instruction set for a machine architecture. The first issue to be addressed deals with the number and type of instructions that should be present. Ideally, one would like enough instructions to perform any foreseeable task and yet not so many as to make the instruction set unwieldy. Instruction sets normally contain instructions for data movement, arithmetic/logic operations, and machine control. A typical instruction, as shown in Figure 2–7, contains bits to represent the operation code, the address of the operand(s), and an address mode indicator. Because the instruction repertoire for n instructions must allocate log n bits in the instruction operation code, a tradeoff between the complexity and the space required to encode the operands is encountered. A larger operand space also means that the instruction decoder must be able to

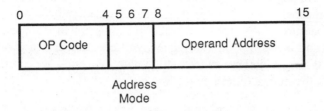

Figure 2–7. **A Typical Instruction Encoding**

handle the additional bits and that the CPU's control circuitry (or microcode) must also increase in complexity to handle the additional instruction types. Another efficiency tradeoff exists in the implementation of the machine's addressing schemes. Some machines allow certain addressing modes only with certain operation codes, so that additional decoding of the addressing mode must be performed in order to achieve the desired control. Others, however, implement what is sometimes called orthogonal instruction sets, in which any addressing mode can be used with any operation. This creates more straightforward decoding and control modules but also may permit some undesirable operand/addressing combinations.

The problem of the increasing complexity of instruction set architectures is one issue being addressed by the so-called reduced instruction set computers (RISC). The contention of RISC designers is that a smaller number of less-complex instructions will result in great gains in the number of cycles needed to execute any instruction, as well as reduce the complexity of the CPU decode and control hardware. With this philosophy, more instructions may be required to implement a given function, but each instruction is expected to be more efficient in speed and space than for a conventional instruction set. The space differential in RISC versus non-RISC architectures is arguably better or worse, depending to a great degree on the particular application used for the measurement.

The space required to store a given program can have an impact on performance. In terms of program loading and initialization, it is obvious that larger programs will require more time. Once a program has been loaded and initialized, it may not all be able to fit within a single memory segment on a segmented memory machine. Intersegment references, therefore, will require the reloading of segment addresses. Also, the effective address calculation may be more complicated than necessary because of the segment checking. On paged memory systems, a large program that spans many pages will become inefficient if it requires frequent page swaps.

One measure of the size of instruction sets is called storage efficiency. This measure is based upon the frequency of occurrence of a given instruction and its size in bits. For an instruction with frequency of occurrence f and size b bits, the storage efficiency is given as:

$$\text{Single instruction storage efficiency} = f \times b$$

For an instruction set with n instructions, the storage efficiency is given as:

$$\text{Instruction set storage efficiency} = \text{sum}(i = 1 \text{ to } n) \text{ of } f \times b$$

The measurement given above implies that different instructions may have different encoding lengths. This is in fact done in some computers in order to improve the storage efficiency (remember that a smaller storage efficiency value is better). An analysis is performed to determine the order of relative frequency for all of the instructions in the instruction set. Those instructions occurring most frequently, then, are assigned the smallest encoding pattern possible. The less-frequent instructions receive a longer encoding pattern. The only restriction on this scheme is that all operation codes are uniquely recognizable. This encoding scheme was proposed by Huffman in 1952; see [Huffman52] for a complete discussion. For example, look at the hypothetical instruction set in Figure 2–8. Given in the table are the relative frequencies for each instruction. To achieve the minimum value for storage efficiency, we must minimize each of the individual instruction efficiencies. To do this, assign the smallest encoding pattern to the most frequently used instruction. Assume that each memory reference for the instructions in Figure 2–8 requires 16 bits and that each register reference requires 4 bits. Figure 2–8 also lists the instructions, the number of bits for each instruction, and the storage efficiency for each instruction and for the encoding. If the savings in overall instruction efficiency is calculated, including the operand bits, we see a value of 16.25, as shown in Figure 2–8. For a traditional encoding, we require at least log 8 = 3 bits to encode the instruction operands. Figure 2–9 shows the storage efficiency for this instruction encoding. Thus we see an overall savings of 2.87%. If we consider only the operation code bits, however, the ratio is 2.53 for the encoded version of Figure 2–8 and 3.0 for the unencoded version of Figure 2–9, for a savings of 15% in memory required to store the operation codes. From this analysis, we can see that it actually does little good to compare the savings of

only the operation code storage without also considering the space required
for the operand addresses. Also, the increase in storage efficiency is significant only when there are a small number of instructions that are used very
frequently when compared to the other instructions in the repertoire. There
are two additional drawbacks to this scheme: increased decoder complexity
and complication of instruction fetches. For variable-length operation codes,
the instruction decoder must be able to handle codes of different lengths as
opposed to only having to worry about a single-width instruction path. Also,
variable-length instructions stored in memory may cross word boundaries or
may start and stop at places other than word boundaries. Thus instruction
fetches must handle the problems of aligning the instruction for the decoder
unit, of performing multiple memory accesses to obtain a single instruction,
and of saving portions of the fetched word for the next instruction. Also, the
branch logic must be more complex because it must now index to a particular
bit position within the target address. Needless to say, variable length
instruction formats are not often used, although we will examine one computer that used this scheme in an attempt to boost performance and to
conserve memory space (see the iAPX432 in Section III).

Instruction	Operation Code	Relative Frequency	No. of Bits	Storage Efficiency
Move R1, R2	1	35%	9	3.15
Load R, M	0 0	25%	22	5.50
Store M, R	011	20%	23	4.60
Compare R1, R2	0100	6%	12	0.72
Add R1, R2	01011	5%	13	0.65
Branch Label	010100	4%	22	0.88
And R1, R2	0101010	3%	15	0.45
Subtract R1, R2	0101011	2%	15	0.30
Total		**100%**	**131**	**16.25**

Figure 2–8. **Hypothetical Instruction Set and Relative Frequencies
Using Huffman Encoding**

Instruction	Operation Code	Relative Frequency	No. of Bits	Storage Efficiency
Move R1, R2	000	35%	11	3.85
Load R, M	001	25%	23	5.75
Store M, R	010	20%	23	4.60
Compare R1, R2	011	6%	11	0.66
Add R1, R2	100	5%	11	0.55
Branch Label	101	4%	19	0.76
And R1, R2	110	3%	11	0.33
Subtract R1, R2	111	2%	11	0.22
Total		**100%**	**120**	**16.72**

Figure 2–9. **Hypothetical Instruction Set and Relative Frequencies Using Standard Encoding**

Memory Systems

When considering the speed of execution of any processor, one cannot ignore the effect of the memory performance. In many cases, the main memory speed is not fast enough to keep up with the CPU. For this reason, systems often implement what is called a memory hierarchy (see Figure 2–10). This hierarchy applies to paged as well as nonpaged memory systems. Cache memory, however, is not always present in every implementation, whereas main and secondary storage usually are. In this section, we will look at each level in the hierarchy and characterize its performance.

Secondary Memory

Secondary memory is usually implemented as tape or disk magnetic media, with storage capability of tens of millions of bytes of data. The use of tape or removable disk media is referred to as off-line secondary storage, because some outside action must be taken to mount the tape or insert the disk to make

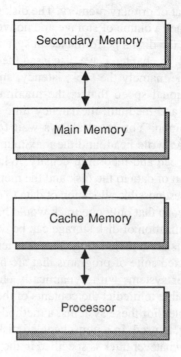

Figure 2–10. **A Typical Memory Hierarchy**

the stored data available for access. The performance of these types of memory systems are quite low when compared to processor and main memory speeds. This is acceptable, however, because their main function is to provide the largest possible storage area for the smallest possible cost. The primary function of off-line data storage, then, is to provide economical bulk storage that can be used for data and program archival and library facilities.

Hard disk subsystems with either fixed or removable media are termed on-line secondary storage repositories. On-line secondary storage is used to hold executable programs and files that are frequently used during system operation. Data bases and temporary data files are also stored here if they require frequent access by executing programs. The speed of on-line secondary storage disks is typically at least an order of magnitude faster than the off-line type of equipment. Its performance, however, is still an order of magnitude less than that of primary memory. The disk systems are necessary, however, because of their volume of storage and nonvolatility. It is therefore desirable to maximize the disk's performance in systems in which high disk throughput is essential. In chapter 1, we discussed the components that constitute disk access time, namely the seek, latency, and data transfer times. Given a certain rotational speed that is the maximum attainable for the recording technology and medium, the latency time and data transfer rate cannot be improved upon. You must always wait for the desired data to appear beneath the read/write head, and the maximum transfer rate is fixed for a given rotation speed and recording density. What can be improved is the pattern of allocation of data to the disk and the method used to access the data on the disk. The best possible allocation of data to disk tracks would be to use tracks sequentially, so that only one track would have to be traversed for a disk seek. This optimization of disk storage can be done for applications in which the disk contents are not changing. This is often the case for military systems that have a fixed suite of programs that are pulled off the disk in a consistent manner. For systems with dynamically changing disk contents, however, it is not possible to predict the contents of the disk, making storage optimization impossible. For these systems, a method of accessing the disk, called disk scheduling, is used. In a nonscheduled disk access sequence, the disk head will seek to whatever track is specified in the next access. If the data on the disk is stored in such a way that there are large track separations between consecutively accessed tracks, the disk heads thrash about for each access. This type of disk access is referred to as first in first out (FIFO) scheduling. The other two types of common scheduling are called scan and shortest seek time first (SSTF). In scan-type scheduling, the read/write heads move continually from the inner to outer cylinder and back again. Requests for data on specific tracks are serviced as the heads reach the desired track. SSTF scheduling orders the disk access requests so that the request for the track closest to the one where the read/write head currently rests will be serviced next. The relative performance of these three schemes depends heavily upon the distribution of disk accesses. For disk accesses that are localized to a set of adjacent tracks, FIFO scheduling does not suffer any serious performance loss. For low-load situations, the SSTF behaves like a FIFO system because there is never more than one request to be serviced at a time. For heavy-load situations with scattered track accesses, however, the SSTF policy will perform better than FIFO. The scan technique under these conditions performs better than FIFO but not as well as SSTF. See [Baer80] for another discussion on this topic.

Primary Memory

The second level in the memory hierarchy is called primary memory. This memory is the working memory, in which programs and data that are in the current active process set are held. This memory is typically one to several orders of magnitude faster than secondary memory but is usually less than one order of magnitude slower than the processor execution speed. Within the primary memory schema, there are several levels of organization. On the lowest level, there are dimensional classes that dictate the organization of memory components into memories of certain word widths. Above this, memory can be organized into physical banks that can be used to increase performance. On the highest level, virtual memory systems permit large logical address spaces to be implemented on limited physical memory spaces. Each of these levels is discussed briefly below. More detailed discussions on these subjects can be found in [Fortier85], [Stone80], [Baer80], and [Deitel83].

The dimensional organization level deals with the physical interconnection topology of memory components to construct primary memories of a desired word width. In use are three types of dimensional organizations: 2D, 2-1/2D, and 3D. These designations relate to the physical interconnection pattern between the memory cells and also to the interconnection of the memory array with the external interface circuitry.

In the 2D organization shown in Figure 2–11, the memory is organized into k, n, word blocks, each word containing b bits. An address to access word w in memory will be decoded to provide an enable signal for one of the k blocks, and a select for one of the n words in a block. The upper u address bits are decoded to select one of the k memory blocks, and the lower l address bits select one word in a block. The selection of the size of l depends upon the number of b bit words available in a block, and the size of u depends upon the desired depth of physical memory or on the number of bits left in the address word after subtracting the l bits required for the block address. The characteristic feature of 2D memory organization is the fact that each memory block is b bits wide.

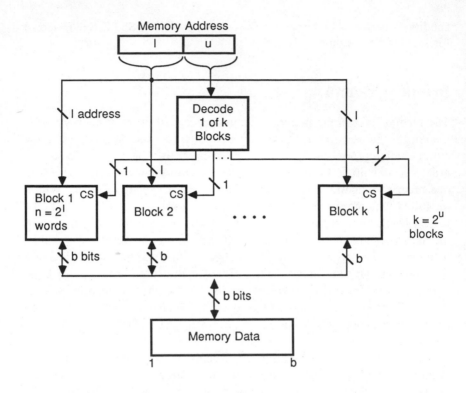

Figure 2–11.   **2D Memory Organization Using k = 2^u Chips with 2^l, b bit words per chip**

In contrast, 2 1/2D memory blocks contain m, b bit words per address and require the selection of one of m, b bit words. 2 1/2D organizations are either word-organized or bit-organized. In the word-organized 2 1/2D memory we see in Figure 2–12, the address word is broken up into upper (u), middle (m), and lower (l) divisions. Memory is organized into 2^u blocks, each block servicing 2^l addresses and having a width of 2^m, b bit words. Thus each block in a word-organized 2 1/2D memory is actually a 2D organized submemory. In the bit organized 2 1/2D memory that is shown in Figure 2–13, the memory is broken into upper (u) and lower (l) subaddresses. A memory block supplies one bit for a b bit word, so there are b memory blocks. Each of the b blocks services 2^l addresses, each address supplying 2^u bits, one of which is selected by a one of 2^u decoder. 2 1/2D bit organized memory

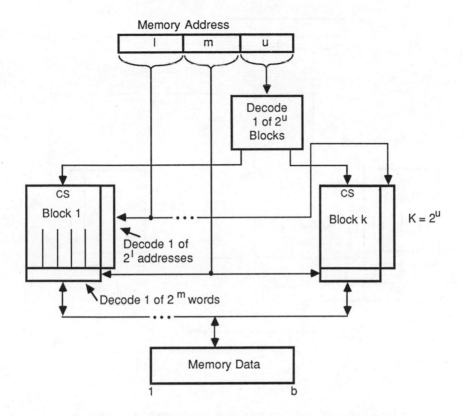

Figure 2–12. **2 1/2D Word Organization with k = 2^u Blocks, Each Block Containing 2^l Addressable Rows of b x 2^m Bits per Address**

has the advantage that single bit errors caused by the loss of a memory block are correctable. In 2D and 2-1/2D word organized memories, the loss of a memory block wipes out a contiguous section of memory words, making error correction difficult due to the multiple bit errors.

3D organizations are typically not used with today's semiconductor memory chips. This organization is of interest primarily in older, core memory technology, in which one deals with organization at the bit level. The 3D designation comes from the three basic controlling components of a 3D memory: X line, Y line, and bit line. The individual memory bit cells are arranged in a square n by n array with n X lines and n Y lines. A bit line

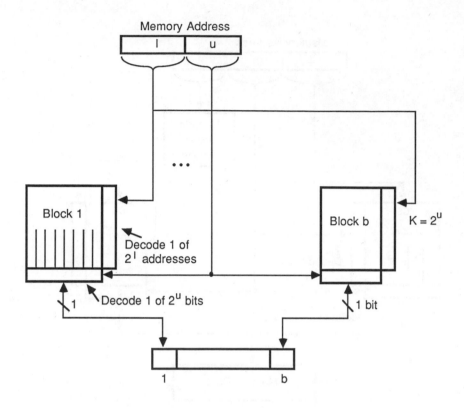

Figure 2–13. **2 1/2D Bit Organized Memory with b Blocks,
Each Block with 2^l Addresses With 2^u
Bits per Address**

connects all cells and is used to carry the information to and from the selected
cell. In operation, one X line and one Y line are energized. At their intersection point in the n by n grid, that bit cell is enabled for either reading or
writing. Thus the address field is broken in half, the upper (u) bits being used
to select the Y line and the lower (l) to select the X line. A number of such
blocks are used to each provide one bit for the memory data word. Figure
2–14 shows this organization. If a 3D memory block is more than n bits deep
but is only n bits wide, additional address bits may be used to select specific
chips within a block, say the ith chip of every block. The operation of the X
and Y lines remains unchanged. As mentioned earlier, 3D organization is
seldom applied to IC memory configurations, although it may be used to
organize memory cells within a single IC.

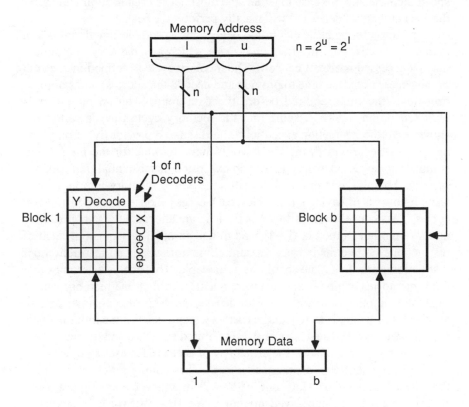

Figure 2–14. **3D Organization with b Blocks, Each Block = n x n**

In terms of performance, one would like to minimize the amount of decoding that must be done to access each memory word. For 3D organizations, the circuitry required to support the three connecting lines require additional transistors, thereby decreasing the available memory density. Less density per memory chip means that more chips are required to implement the desired memory size which, in turn, increases the amount of external decoding that must be done. For 2D organization, a large amount of decoding circuitry is needed to select the appropriate word within a single memory. In 2-1/2D organization, the decoding circuitry is shared among several banks within a single chip. The input and output circuitry is also shared in the 2-1/2D organization whereas it is not in 2D. The 2-1/2D organization, therefore, makes the most use of the decoding circuitry. Since the chip density and speed increase and decrease together, the most dense organization will suffer the least amount of delay and will usually perform the best.

In addition to the basic electronic delays one experiences with any given memory organization, the frequency with which any memory component may be accessed is also of concern. The memory cycle is defined by the sum of the access time (the time to provide and decode the address) and stabilization time (the time required before the data appears on an output or is recorded on an input). Assume that the memory cycle time is somewhat slower than the instruction execution time discussed previously. If only one memory were provided, the CPU would have to wait for the memory to complete its cycle on every instruction execution, a substantial performance penalty. To solve this problem, a technique called memory interleaving is used. It consists of having n memories, each accessed once every n instruction cycles. Thus consecutive instructions i, i + 1... are allocated to the consecutive memory modules i mod n, (i + 1) mod n, and so on. The sequential fetch of instructions will be made from sequential memories, and an instruction per instruction cycle fetch rate should be achievable. This analysis assumes that the n memories can be operated independently, so that one memory can be read while another is being set up for access, etc. This also assumes that all accesses will be made to sequential memory locations. For the more realistic case in which accesses are sequential for limited stretches and then are interrupted by program branches, the efficiency of access decreases somewhat.

The implementation of interleaved memories simply involves decoding the lower l address bits into one of $k = 2^l$ memory banks. Figure 2–15 illustrates a 4-bank interleaved memory. See [Baer80] for an analysis of interleaved memory performance.

Cache Memory

The problem of an unfavorable ratio of memory to processor speed that led us to the interleaved memory scheme also drives us to the cache memory solution. The premise here is that we can construct, at a considerably higher cost per bit than for semiconductor memory, a special-purpose memory whose cycle time is approximately that of the processor's instruction cycle time. If such an implementation is possible, then the CPU will execute at full speed without the need for interleaved memories and the CPU performance will not degrade when program branches are encountered. The basic problem here is that these memories are more expensive than semiconductor

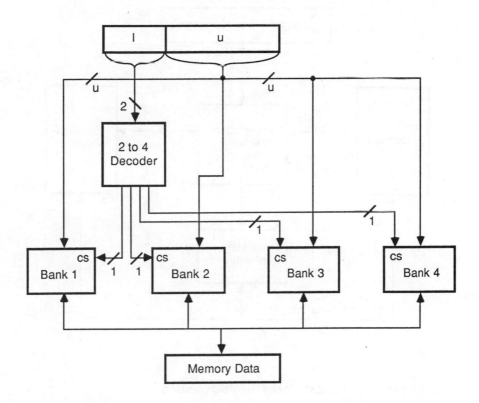

Figure 2–15. **A 4-Bank Interleaved Memory**

memories and are not feasible as a total primary memory solution. As a compromise, a relatively small amount of cache is provided, and it is managed so as to maximize its effectiveness. Since the cache operates at a speed that is close to that of the CPU, it is not feasible to manage it using software routines. Hardware support must be provided. In a typical cache implementation, as shown in Figure 2–16, the cache memory sits between the processor and primary memory and interprets memory addresses using the associative memory map. The associative map forms a correspondence between the requested address location and the contents of the cache. If the desired item resides in the cache, the associative memory will inhibit the request to main memory and supply the desired data to the processor. If the item is not in the cache, it is fetched from primary memory and also copied into the cache.

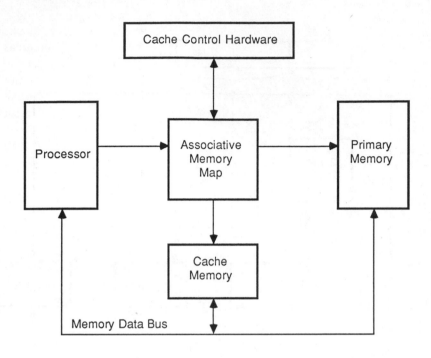

Figure 2–16. **A Typical Cache Implementation**

There are several algorithms that are used to determine which item to delete from the cache in order to make room for the new one. Perhaps the most commonly used cache replacement algorithm is the least recently used (LRU) method. This method says to replace the cache item with the oldest recorded use. This operation is based upon the assumption that program references are localized to within a certain range of addresses so that the next address will also lie within or close to that range. This thinking indicates that a cache item that has not been recently used lies outside the range of locality, and so it may be safely discarded. We may run into a problem, however, if we frequently run program loops that are larger than the available cache. In this case, every new reference will delete a cache entry that is sure to be used again on the next loop interation. For those cases, it is sometimes wise, for the sake of performance, to break large loops into a series of smaller ones that can fit in the cache. For associatively mapped caches, any word in memory can be mapped to any word in the cache. A more economical approach is to replace the associative memory map with a direct memory map. In this case, blocks of primary memory are mapped by their lower address bits into certain areas of the cache. Thus many primary memory blocks are mapped to the same cache region. In this case, there may be problems when multiple program segments that reside in different blocks are used frequently and map to the same cache area. To solve this problem, an intermediate solution, called a set associative cache, is used. This type of cache allows the associative mapping of entire memory blocks but not of individual words within blocks. The cache still contains block-mappable regions that are now allocated associatively.

Using a cache to store data items that also appear in primary memory can result in a data consistency problem if care is not taken. Generally, there are two methods of ensuring consistency: the dirty bit method and the write through method. With the dirty bit method, each cache entry has associated with it an additional bit that is set whenever that cache entry is written to. When the item is to be replaced in cache, its value is written back to primary memory if the dirty bit is set. This method is quite efficient, because it writes the value only once, when it is replaced in the cache. It does present problems if primary memory is shared among several processors and timely updates of memory resident values are important. Also, changes by another processor to primary memory data that also reside in the cache must be fed through the cache-mapping unit to ensure consistency of the cache resident data. The first problem can be solved by using the write-through method to update primary memory data. In this method, all writes to cache are immediately propagated to primary memory, thereby ensuring consistency. The second problem of update by another processor can be solved in the same way. This implies that there must be a shared processor/cache interface that will allow access from other processors. Write through, however, can result in unnecessary writes to primary memory and could slow down the cache performance if many writes occur consecutively. In that case, the cache cycle time would essentially be that of primary memory since the previous write must be allowed to complete before a new one can be issued.

I/O Systems

Another area of computer performance is that of the I/O system. In Chapter 1, we discussed conventional and memory mapped I/O in the context of computer architecture. I/O systems are also very important in performance discussions because of their typically slow access rate. The main objective of

I/O systems, then, is to relieve the processor of the task of I/O. This can be accomplished in a variety of ways, which will be discussed in this section.

There are two related functions that define the purpose of an input/output subsystem. The first of these is that of peripheral control, and the second is of data movement to and from the external processor environment. Peripheral control involves the management and timing of external devices that require some form of control. This control may involve tasks such as the lighting of indicators, the response to interrupts, or the positioning of electromechanical mechanisms. Data movement implies the need for memory access and control and for block data transfer capabilities. Although these two functions cannot be totally separated, block data transfer is more easily relegated to special-purpose I/O devices. Peripheral control tasks, however, are not as easily subsumed by the devices themselves, because their actions must be coordinated with the operational state of the processor.

For either type of I/O, there are three factors that must be considered: timing, speed, and translation. The timing of I/O interactions ensures that internal and external events take place with the proper synchronization. This control must preserve the internal timing of the processor while allowing data exchange with peripheral devices. Speed factors are important because the transfer rates of the processor and the external devices may be (and usually are) different. Some mechanisms must exist to allow orderly data transfer among the different speed devices. Translation is often required to convert data from an external representation to one that the processor can understand, and vice versa.

Before concentrating on the special-purpose devices and structures used to implement I/O systems, we will first review conventional processor I/O. Conventional I/O systems use the processor to handle each I/O request and transaction. The CPU must have special-purpose software routines that accomplish the task of transferring data to and from memory and that provide special I/O setup commands. Usually, the data to be transferred to or from the external world passes directly through the CPU, making a temporary stop in the accumulator or other register. A conventional I/O program might look as shown in Figure 2–17. The program is written in a pseudo-assembly-language format. The major disadvantage of this type of I/O structure is that the processor execution slows down to the rate of the transfer device. There are three solutions for this performance problem: polling, interrupt driven, and direct memory access (DMA). Each solution is discussed briefly below in order of increasing performance.

In a polled I/O environment, the processor is programmed to periodically check the status of the I/O device. This method is more efficient than the conventional method because useful work can be done between polls to the I/O device. The disadvantages are that fancy program constructs may be required to ensure the periodic check, the I/O device may not be serviced within an acceptable time limit, and the processor must contain some special-purpose internal interrupt scheme to periodically run the polling software. The conventional and polled I/O constructs actually represent two implementation options that differ only in the amount of time between queries to the I/O device status indicator and, therefore, will both be considered as variations on conventional I/O.

In an interrupt-driven I/O system, the time spent waiting for the I/O device to become ready (Figure 2–17) can be used instead to perform useful work. Interrupt systems are usually constructed so that, upon receipt of an interrupt, the processor is provided a memory address that is the start of the interrupt service routine. The code that resides at this memory address, for the example of Figure 2–17, would consist of the third and fourth lines of code, only that necessary to actually move the data. The actual interrupt signal is derived by the ready status indication of the I/O device. Thus the processor does not have to perform a busy-wait sequence until the device is ready. There exist two types of control of the interrupt routine address generation, called vectoring: The first type simply forces processor execution in an interrupt situation to a specific memory location that is reserved within the processor's address space. A number of memory words (1 to 4) are provided at this address to hold the code to be executed for each interrupt. Because of the limited number of locations, the code at this location usually contains program jumps to the actual interrupt service routines. Figure 2–18 illustrates this interrupt/memory structure. The second type of

```
Loop :   Input A, I/O_Status      ;  Read the I/O port's status indicator

         Jump_zero A, loop        ;  Loop until the I/O port is ready

         Input A, I/O_data        ;  Read the datum from the I/O port

         Store M, A               ;  Store in memory

         Jump_zero done, loop     ;  Continue until done
```

Figure 2–17.   **A Conventional I/O Program**

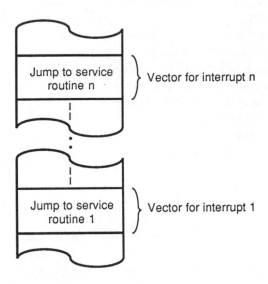

Figure 2–18.   **Fixed Interrupt Structure**

interrupt vector generation forces the processor to read all or a portion of the address of the interrupt service routine from the data bus. In this case, special interrupt control devices must be capable of providing the routine address at the proper time. The processor then uses this address to form the actual jump address for the service routine. A variation on this scheme allows the special I/O device to supply an operation code to the processor, which is then decoded and executed. This operation code could be a call to the interrupt service routine or another instruction, such as an add or output instruction. This scheme allows considerable flexibility of interrupt processing by allowing several service routines to be mapped to the same interrupt, and vice versa, or for providing a special external processor control, such as an immediate halt. This structure is shown in Figure 2–19.One factor that is common to all of the I/O implementations presented so far is that the processor must somehow be involved in every I/O transfer. An alternative to this, direct memory access (DMA), is discussed next.

Because each datum is explicitly handled by the CPU in the previous modes of I/O, the processor must be directly involved with every transfer between the outside world and primary memory. In addition, the interrupt modes, although more efficient in terms of time spent executing I/O code,

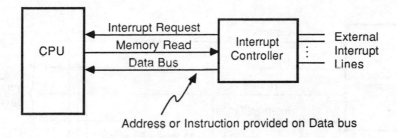

Figure 2–19. **Forced Processor Read Interrupt Structure**

require the processor state to be saved and restored on every I/O transfer. This whole process can be made much more efficient if the amount of processor involvement can be kept to a minimum. This can be accomplished through the use of direct memory access (DMA) techniques. A DMA mechanism consists of three basic components: an electrical interface to the processor data bus and read/write and memory control lines; an internal memory address register and an increment circuit; and interrupt and memory transfer logic. A typical DMA device is shown in Figure 2–20. There exist many versions of this basic device which incorporate control for several I/O devices. Some processors contain built-in DMA devices.

The basic operation of a DMA device is as follows: The processor programs the DMA device with the amount of data to be transferred, the starting memory address for the transferred data, the direction of the transfer (e.g., to or from memory) and the address of the I/O device. The DMA device then handles the device control and memory access for the transfer, in essentially the same manner as shown in Figure 2–17 for the CPU. Upon completion of the programmed transfer, the device indicates the completion to the processor (either by setting a flag or by interrupt). The processor has to be concerned only with initially setting up the DMA device and with handling the completion interrupt. The only other consideration is that the processor reserve a memory buffer to hold the transfer and then avoid use of the buffer until the I/O completes. Performance of the CPU is greatly increased when DMA is present, because almost the entire I/O process has been off-loaded to the DMA controller. This solution also makes economic sense, because the DMA controller architecture can be much simpler than that of the processor, therefore not wasting CPU power on menial I/O tasks.

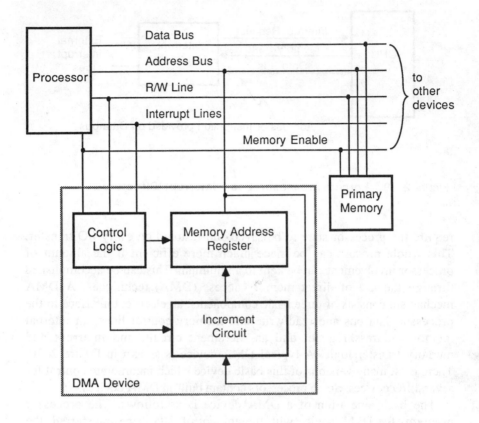

Figure 2–20. **Typical DMA Device**

Because the DMA device connects to the same interfaces as does the CPU, the use of the various busses and control lines must somehow be shared. Two methods of sharing are commonly implemented, burst and cycle stealing. In burst mode, the CPU is blocked from using the memory address and data busses until the specified number of words have been transferred. The blocking is accomplished through the use of a special CPU input signal that prevents the processor from using the memory bus until the signal is deactivated. This type of DMA transfer is useful if the I/O device is capable of transferring large blocks of data at speeds close to that of the primary memory speed. A disk subsystem in a paged memory environment is a good example of when this type of transfer is appropriate. Also, if the processor is waiting for the data block to perform some action based on its content (e.g., in a message-based system), the block DMA mode is valuable.

In the cycle steal transfer mode, only one or two words of data are transferred at a time between memory and the I/O device. The DMA device still asserts the memory block signal, but only for a cycle or two. Since this blocking is interleaved with the normal program execution, the "stolen" cycle may or may not have caused the CPU to wait for access to memory. Thus cycle stealing may or may not impact CPU performance during a DMA transfer. This mode proves useful when there is a consistent, periodic burst of one or two data words that are to be stored in memory. A good example of this mode would be the updating of a clock value in memory every n milliseconds. Interrupting the processor each time would waste CPU power, whereas the DMA solution impact is negligible. A good discussion of several DMA controllers and some implementation details can be found in [Stone82].

This concludes our discussion of the basic factors that influence computational speed. The analysis of the performance of computer systems will be discussed in Chapter 6.

3. SOFTWARE ON CONVENTIONAL SYSTEMS

This chapter will provide an overview of software on conventional computer systems. We will discuss levels of programming, programming languages, the software development process, and operating systems. These issues will be discussed within the context of centralized uniprocessor computers, and will be extended to parallel and multiprocessor environments, as appropriate, in Section II.

What is software? Loosely defined, it is anything that is part of an operating computer that is not hardware. Operating is a key word here because, if a computer were to be halted or the power removed, the software would do absolutely nothing to help define the characteristics of the computer in question. Thus software is not really a physical entity that one can touch or weigh. Rather, it is the embodiment of ideas, methodologies, and structures that gives meaning to a dynamic computer environment. Software, then, bridges the gap between general-purpose hardware and special-purpose applications. It is the basic material used to mold resources to fit different situations and uses. In the early days of computers, as Figure 3–1 describes, machines were built more or less with a single-minded purpose, and the software necessary to use these machines was minimal. Gradually, due to falling hardware costs and generalization of resources, software became almost as important to the successful implementation of an application as hardware. Today software-related activities form the bulk of the effort necessary to achieve a desired computer system. The importance of software in general therefore cannot be ignored in any serious discussion of computational systems. This chapter will explore the major topics that are common to all software environments: the languages with which we instruct computer hardware to perform specific tasks; the process by which we arrive at a functioning software system; and the tailored environment that hosts software applications by providing the appropriate management of computational resources.

Early Computers: Hardware-oriented for specific applications.
_____   Basic software provided with hardware to assist
                              hardware usage (bundled software).

Second Phase: Software unbundled from hardware, software
_____   becomes critical for specific applications,
                              generalization of hardware.

Today: Software a major factor in virtually all
_____   applications, general-purpose hardware.

Future: Two Trends: 1. Sophisticated software development
_____   environments to increase productivity and
                              re-useability and decrease costs.
                              2. Special-purpose, functional hardware
                              through advanced design and fabrication
                              technology.

Figure 3–1. **Evolution of Software/Hardware Relationship**

Levels of Software

Most computer environments support several levels of software that can be
used for writing programs. The levels span an area from hardware-dependent to hardware-invariant languages and from relatively simple to complicated. Figure 3–2 shows an approximate ordering for the various levels of
programming that may be found in a computer.

At the lowest level of programming lies the microcode programming
interface. As discussed in Chapter 1, this facility is not always present in a
computer design. For those implementations in which it is present, however,
microcode programming provides a powerful interface that allows direct
run-time control of many of the basic architectural components. Whereas
typical computers have word widths of 16, 32, or even 64 bits, microcode
words are arbitrary in length from computer to computer, depending upon
the machine complexity and the amount of control that is extended to the
microcode programmer.

As the microprogram example of Chapter 1 illustrates, a number of parallel actions must be specified within each microcode instruction (see Figure
1–22). Thus the programmer at this level must be cognizant of the hardware
state over time.

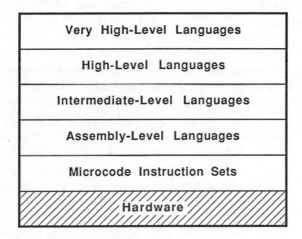

Figure 3–2. **Levels of Programming**

Because microcode instructions so closely reflect the architecture of the computer to which they belong, each instance of a microcode instruction set is different. This is not necessarily an undesirable situation, however, because the accessibility of the underlying hardware directly affects the versatility of any microprogramming facility.

The practice of microprogramming, then, is one in which there are very few restrictions on the form and content of a program and also few or no guidelines that define what constitutes a correct program. As is true in any of the programming levels in this section, there are no guarantees against constructing incorrect programs. It is however, somewhat easier to err at microcode level, because of the factors discussed above.

The next level up in the software hierarchy is that of assembly languages. The assembly language instruction sets form the "native language" of the given processor. A native language is a language for which instructions can be decoded by the processing hardware; that is, there is direct support in the architecture's control unit for initiating and carrying out all of the actions necessary to perform the intended function. On hardware-based control units, the native language instruction set is fixed. On some microcoded machines, the set of instructions that are recognizable by the basic CPU hardware (e.g., when the CPU is not embellished via microcoded routines) form the processor's natural language. In these cases, the microcode facility is used only to enhance the CPU's functionality, and the default (hardware implemented) assembly language instructions are not alterable. Other microcoded machines implement the default assembly instruction set, partially or entirely via microcode, thereby allowing modifications to be made to the default instruction set as well as enabling the addition of new instructions. This level of programming, namely the native language mode, is incorporated into virtually every CPU design, although the level (i.e., closeness to the hardware) of this language may vary substantially.

It is appropriate now to discuss the concept of the semantic level of a language. The semantics of a programming language are defined as the meanings that are given to language statements and constructs, according to their syntactic definition and the dynamic operation of instructions. For example, the PL/M-86 construct:

For i = 1 to n do

—

—

        end;

results in the condition $i = n + 1$ upon completion of the loop, a fact that is part of the language semantics. Syntax, in contrast, defines only the allowable sequences of characters from the alphabet for the particular language in question. The syntax of a language is precisely defined using formal notations (e.g., Backus-Naur form (BNF)), whereas the semantics of a language are often indicated by descriptive prose and can be somewhat dependent upon a language implementation. A semantic level, then, is defined as the amount of abstraction from the hardware level that is necessary to describe the language semantics. Put another way, the descriptions used to define the meaning of language constructs and instructions implicitly define that language's semantic level. Thus the order of discussion of languages in this chapter proceeds roughly in the order of semantic levels. In Figure 3–2, microcode language instructions are defined in terms of their effects on the basic architectural components, such as ALU, registers, and interconnections. They are therefore seen as having a low semantic level. As we progress through the various levels, we will qualitatively discuss the semantic levels of different classes of programming languages. No attempt is made here to quantify this characteristic.

The next level up in the language hierarchy is that of intermediate-level languages. An intermediate-level language is defined as one that possesses characteristics of both high-level and assembly-level languages. The instruction set that gives a language this form is one in which the instructions can be loosely grouped into two categories, ones that can "see" and operate on certain hardware elements, and ones that operate on an abstract machine. These languages are sometimes called high-level machine-dependent languages because they possess many of the features of high-level languages but are implemented for a specific machine. All of the PL-like languages (e.g., PL/M-86, PL/65) are of this intermediate language class. The two characterizing features of these languages are that expressions are written in normal high-level language notation, thereby allowing better structuring and ease of programming; and that there exist direct correspondences between some language features and the underlying machine architecture (e.g., the existence of specific addressing modes), thereby limiting the portability of the language. Figure 3–3 shows an incomplete genealogy for the language hierarchy. The edges in the figure show the influences of earlier languages on later ones.

High-level languages are the next category to be discussed. This level of language is perhaps the most widely used and familiar of all of the levels in Figure 3–2. For this reason, many programming language texts deal almost exclusively with the topic of high-level languages.

High-level programming languages typically are designed and implemented around a virtual machine concept. The virtual machine is essentially an abstracted version of a conventional computer architecture. The result of this abstraction is that high-level languages do not incorporate hardware-dependent features, at least not in the general case. This makes the use of these languages more portable across machine architectures and also encourages language uniformity, a benefit in terms of programmer training, productivity, and code maintenance. The incorporation of hardware-dependent features is made to occur explicitly, thereby making the identification of nonstandard code easier and its incorporation deliberate.

Within the scope of high-level languages, there are several subclasses that are defined according to various criteria. One of these is the strongly typed class, in which languages require that all variables, subprograms and resources be explicitly defined, and that these definitions be enforced by the language compilers and execution environments (e.g., Pascal, Ada). Another is characterized by the modular nature of program structures and the ability to reuse subroutines in different programs (e.g., Ada, FORTRAN). Yet another defines interpretive facilities for program development and execution (e.g., Lisp, Basic). It should be clear that these subclasses are not mutually exclusive, a fact that results from the common ancestry of some languages as shown in Figure 3–3.

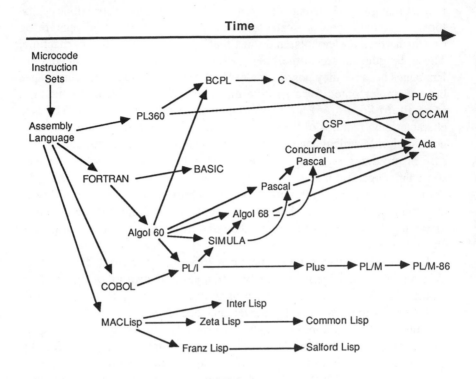

Figure 3-3. **Approximate Genealogy of Programming Languages**

Very high-level languages (VHLLs) constitute the most advanced point in the current evolution of programming languages. Until this discussion, we have concentrated on languages that are primarily used to specify how a certain job is to be performed. Exactly what job is being specified is not explicitly stated; it must be described within the program documentation or deduced from the general structure and flow of the program. VHLLs, on the other hand, attempt to take the reverse approach, to specify what is to be done instead of how it is to be performed. This step places a significant new burden on the design and operation of software development utilities, because there is now an added degree of freedom between the program specification and its final form that must be resolved by the utilities. Some examples of very high-level languages include functional languages, in which the order of computation is not and need not be specified; data flow languages that rely upon concurrent actions, as represented by Petri-net structures; some artificial intelligence outgrowths such as the Planner language that is used to develop action sequences based upon a given set of conditions, and other special purpose languages that embody these general philosophies. Wulf [Wulf80] offers a short discussion of this topic. Additional information on some specific VHLLs can be found in [Backus82] for functional languages, and [Barr81], [Barr82], and [Cohen82] for AI applications.

The Software Development Process

Like any discipline that involves the transformation of ideas to implemen-
tations of some form, the development of software requires a formal process in order to be effective. The basic phases of system design, development, and life cycle are shown in Figure 3-4. Although these phases are generalized for a nonspecific system, they apply to the process of software development as well. There are several formal methodologies in existence that embody all or some of the phases shown in Figure 3-4, and that are in general agreement with the basic methodology presented here. We will not attempt to develop a formal methodology based on Figure 3-4; rather, we present a logical progression of events that lead to sensible system-design practices. Briefly, let's examine each phase in relation to software systems.

Concept formulation entails the definition of what it is we wish to accomplish with a particular software system. If we are in a consumer/producer relationship, there is usually an iterative process between the two parties to help perform this task. The consumer specifies, in general terms, what is required, and the producer, using knowledge about current technology and design, helps to bound and define the customer's needs.

Once a general concept of the product desired has been formed, specific requirements about the performance, size, cost, and other factors are determined. For example, the customer and producer may have determined that the basic product concept is a multiuser, real-time software execution environment. The requirement specification phase, then, will establish the definitions of real-time, define the maximum number of users, set performance requirements for the system based upon the number of users, and possibly fix the maximum allowable cost for the program. In addition, restrictions such as the use of special equipment or methods are translated into requirements for the final product.

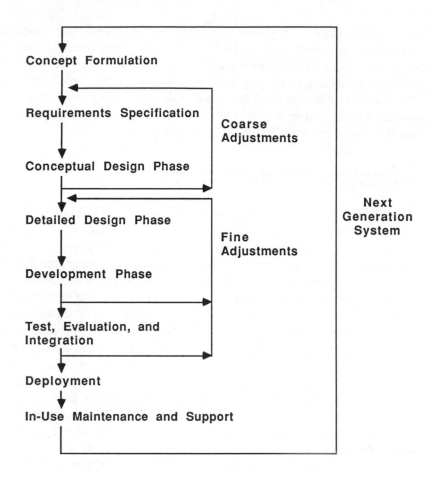

Figure 3–4. **The Basic Phases of a System's Life**

Next, in the conceptual design phase, a high-level design is created that accounts for as many of the requirements as possible. This phase accomplishes two things: it establishes a baseline of existing and needed components from which to work, and it identifies areas in which additional effort is necessary to meet the harder requirements. Note that the conceptual design phase may identify overly stringent, unnecessary requirements, or it may suggest additional guidelines. These results are fed back into the requirements specification effort until a stable situation is reached or some outside event causes the termination of this iterative process (e.g., the expiration of a deadline). This iterative process serves to make coarse adjustments to the overall goals and direction of the project.

Once the project has been firmly established, the detailed design of the specific system components is initiated. Limited resources (CPU time, memory space, etc.) are budgeted to portions of the overall design and further broken down to the lower-level components.

As designs mature, specific components are developed. Individual components are then tested, evaluated for adherence to allocated resource restrictions, and integrated with other system components. During this time, lessons learned from development and testing may cause alterations to the detailed component designs. The inability to meet a resource budget, for example, may cause the realottment of resources and another design/development/test iteration.

Finally, the system is complete and is ready for shipment and installation at the customer site. During the normal usage and maintenance of the system, new ideas for additions and improvements form the basis for system revisions or new system designs.

For several interesting and pertinent essays on the subject of software development for large systems, the reader is encouraged to consult [Brooks74].

Software Environments

Few computational systems are built in such a way that an application program must provide all of its own execution control and support. Although some examples of this do exist for special applications, most software systems execute with the aid of support services. The intention of these support services is to make the basic hardware usable for a variety of users. These services, therefore, provide a layer of access to the hardware that attempts to bridge the gap between the semantic level of the software and the actual hardware (semantic level is defined in the previous section).

The organization of a system that contains end user applications, support service programs, and the hardware is frequently shown in a picture called an onion skin diagram (Figure 3–5). In the picture, the innermost layer represents the basic computer hardware (i.e., the level typically seen by an assembly language program). At this level, the "raw" computer is available with no additional support for special purpose capabilities. This means that, in addition to those operations that are directly aimed at performing the intended task, a user at this level must also provide all of the mechanisms

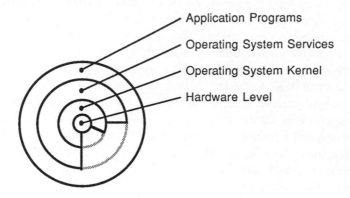

Figure 3–5.   **"Onion Skin" of System Layers**

necessary to control the process loading, initialization, operation, and termination, as well as to manage the hardware before, during, and after execution. This level of system support (or lack thereof) is generally appropriate only for small applications, or for those that require the absolute maximum performance and cannot afford any overhead associated with general purpose utilities. The next two layers of the onion form the support services that make the hardware more usable for a variety of different application programs. Since the development of software packages to help effectively utilize batch processing systems, these services have been known as operating systems. An operating system's name implies its function: It makes the basic hardware operational by providing a system of functions that perform tasks that were previously done explicitly or not at all. After the original operating system concept for batch processing systems, these programs evolved to control systems for large mainframe processors, to time-sharing operating systems for multiuser mainframes and minicomputers and finally to relatively small, disk-based operating systems for today's personal computers. Also, a number of other special-purpose operating systems exist for specialized computer applications such as real-time systems and process-control environments.

The operating system represented by the innermost layer of the onion is called the operating system kernel. Usually the OS kernel consists of a set of basic utilities and a protected data area. The basic utilities are those functions that perform generic processor services, such as programming of the processor devices (e.g., timers, interrupt controllers, etc.) and the loading of other programs in an organized manner. The protected data area typically contains the basic operating system parameters, such as the hardware addresses for devices, memory block size, and processor state information. This data area is protected, because the data contained therein must be maintained so that it cannot be accessed incorrectly by a nonprivileged program (operating system utilities typically run in a privileged or protected mode versus a normal user or nonprotected mode).

Another issue of importance in the OS kernel is performance. For this reason, the basic utilities and the shared, protected data area are optimized for the particular machine on which the kernel is to be executed. This fact results in the lack of portability of kernel software from one machine to another. By providing a standard interface and set of basic functions to the operating system's services layer, however, that portion of the operating system can be ported to other machines. A good example of this is the widespread use of the Unix operating system on many different machines.

The operating system services layer of the onion rests upon the functions provided by the operating system kernel. This operating system level implements services such as paged memory management, file and directory systems, timing services, timesharing of the processor, and schedulers for the processor resources. Operating system services also provide command processors, resource management, facilities for event flags and process communication, specialized I/O services such as printer and console controls, and other specialized utilities. The two layers, operating system services and kernel, comprise the total operating system that will be further discussed later in this chapter.

The skin of the onion in Figure 3–5 is the application program layer. Any type of user program may reside here, even those that extend the functionality of the operating system services. In the diagram, the application layer has the capability to penetrate down to the operating system kernel and to the hardware level. These interfaces are necessary for some applications that either require low-level kernel functions or cannot afford the overhead incurred by the various software levels. We will now discuss operating systems on conventional computers.

The purpose of a traditional operating system is to manage the processor, the memory hierarchy, the file system, and the peripheral devices. So far, we have been discussing the kernel approach to operating system construction. The idea of a kernel is that the essential operating system functions are implemented as semi-independent software processes that are bundled together around a basic kernel data set. Another operating system organization type is referred to as the monitor approach. In this organization, all control and interprocess communication passes through the monitor. The monitor is sometimes referred to as monolithic because it embodies both the kernel and operating system services mentioned earlier. We will not continue our discussion of operating system structures beyond this point; rather, we will approach the functional aspect of such a system. The reader is referred to [Deitel83] and [Madnick74] for further discussions of operating systems structure.

Processor Management

We will now discuss the four dimensions that contribute to operating system resource management: The processor, memory, files, and I/O devices. These four dimensions are sometimes represented in an onion diagram to form the physical hierarchy shown in Figure 3–6.

Processor management is concerned with the allocation of the processing resource (time) to the set of processes requiring service. There are three basic components to processor scheduling: deciding which of the waiting jobs is to be assigned to an available processor, called job scheduling; deciding the order of execution of the constituent tasks or processes of a job, and the time that should be allotted for each, called task or process scheduling; and the synchronization of processes or tasks that run concurrently and require some

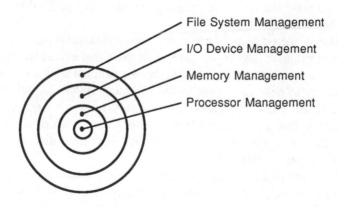

Figure 3–6. **Physical Hierarchy of Operating System Resource Management**

degree of controlled interaction. The following discussion will examine each of these three components.

Job scheduling is concerned with assigning a waiting job to an available processor. A waiting job could be a batch process run in off-peak time on a large mainframe processor; an interactive request, such as a program compilation; or a response to an external event in a real-time control system. Specifically, the job scheduler performs the following tasks:

1. Imposing an ordering on the waiting jobs according to some algorithm, thus controlling the transition of jobs from the waiting to ready state

2. Upon the transition of a job from waiting to the ready state, allocating (or requesting) the required resources (e.g., memory, display, etc.) on behalf of the new job

3. Upon job completion, reclaiming the resources allocated in item 2

4. Maintaining the states of the jobs in the system (regardless of their current state) and making this information available

5. Creating and setting up the component processes or tasks that are required to complete the desired functions and controlling the termination of the processes upon task completion

The ordering of jobs that are waiting to be run is given by the chosen method of arbitrating among waiting jobs. Some job-scheduling algorithms require very little computation and need only some sort of queue structure to hold the waiting jobs. First in first out (FIFO) scheduling is an instance of this type of scheduling algorithm. A second class of scheduling algorithms require the readjustment of the queue contents every time a new job arrives. These scheduling algorithms are referred to as static scheduling algorithms, because a given set of waiting jobs will yield the same ordering regardless of the passage of time. Fixed priority and shortest time first (STF) algorithms are examples of static scheduling algorithms. A third class, dynamic scheduling algorithms, require constant reexamination of the job queue based upon the occurrence of external events, such as the passage of time. Value function or dynamic deadline schedulers are of this class. A number of scheduling algorithms are analyzed in [Madnick74] and the reader is referred there for a more complete discussion.

Resource allocation by the job scheduler requires that the scheduler act as an agent for the waiting job. After the required resources have been acquired, the job proceeds from the waiting to the ready-to-run state. Each job will typically have associated with it a block of information listing its resource requirements for completion of the task at hand, as well as the job's priority and an estimate of running time. For example, a compilation job may require a block of n memory words to hold the compiler's state transition tables, some scratch disk space for intermediate compilation results, and possibly a printer reservation for compilation result output. Other resource types may include special processing capabilities, such as floating-point or graphics processing. Some of these resources may be requested by the processes that make up the job, rather than by the job scheduler using job control block information.

The reclamation of resources after the termination of a job is performed in conjunction with other resource controllers, such as the memory and I/O device managers. In some cases, jobs may enter the ready state, partially complete, and then return to the waiting state. This may be common for jobs requiring large amounts of processing time. In these cases, the reclamation of resources must be such that the semicomplete job may resume where it left off. In some instances, certain resources may not be reclaimed until after the job completes, provided a deadlock situation does not arise (e.g., the printing of job's progress requires use of the printer until complete). Other resources may be temporarily surrendered and then reallocated with no ill effects (e.g., scratch memory locations).

Maintenance of a job's state is one function that is essential to the successful operation of the scheduler, resource allocation and reclamation software. For example, jobs that cycle between the waiting and ready states during their execution will decrease their time to complete each time they complete a cycle. Thus the estimated time required to complete the job, held in the job's control block, must be decreased by the amount of time already invested in the job's execution. Keeping track of this investment and correcting the estimated time to complete are the responsibilities of the status maintenance function of the job scheduler.

Finally, when a job is making the transition from the waiting to the ready state, the job scheduler must associate the appropriate control information with each component process of the job. This information is then handed off to the process scheduler. The determination of how to break up a job into processes, or whether to break it up at all, depends upon several factors. One of these is the presence or absence of a multiprogramming environment. If multiprogramming is not present, then a job that has been allocated to a processor will run to completion. If multiprogramming is present, several jobs may share the CPU. In the former case, it makes little sense to break up a job into pieces that cause additional overhead to interface. In the latter case, however, it may be attractive to form several, semi-independent processes that can exploit CPU bandwidth that would otherwise be wasted waiting for I/O to complete or for an externally controlled event. Another factor in creating processes from a job is the degree of independence of the created processes. Also, the determination of the processes that constitute a job must be done by a human or by some intelligent partitioning software, so this information is passed to the job scheduler.

After the job scheduler has performed its function and a set of processes (which constitute a job) is presented, the process scheduler is responsible for managing the dynamic mapping of the process requirements to the processor resources. The functions of the process scheduler correspond fairly closely with those of the job scheduler. They are:

1. Coordinating the switching of the processor's resources from one process to another (in a multiprogrammed environment)

2. Maintaining the state of each process during periods in which the process is ready or blocked (suspended)

3. Performing the arbitration of which process gets to run and when

The action of coordinating the process switching is a critical factor in achieving optimal performance from a processor given a certain set of tasks. One factor that is used to control this switching, called the quantum time (or simply quantum), is the maximum time a process can run each time it has a turn on the processor. The quantum value may be uniform across all processes in the system, although it is more common to determine the individual quantum times based on the priority of a process, the estimated time to complete, or deadline information. Once a process is allocated to a processor, it runs until its quantum has expired or until some other condition causes it to stop or become suspended. A process will become suspended, or blocked, when it has to wait for resource allocation or services that are orders of magnitude slower than the CPU speed. Process switching, then, must recognize the situation in which a process switch will occur, store the blocked process's state, place the blocked process into the blocked process queue, restore the state for the new process, and start the new process running.

Maintaining the state of all processes in the system is another important aspect of process scheduling. As mentioned in the previous paragraph, processes whose quantum times have expired are circulated back to the process scheduling queue for rescheduling. Because these processes are in a state of incompletion, the pertinent state information must be available when they are again ready to execute. Thus the state information that is saved during a process switch must be associated with the proper entry in the scheduling queue. In the case in which a process is blocked, the process state at the time of the blockage must also be saved. In addition, unblocking events such as the availability of an I/O device or a memory page will cause the state of the blocked process to change to a ready condition. An entry must then be made for the process in the process scheduling queue. Thus the process state must be updated even though the process is not currently executing.

Performing the arbitration of which process gets to run for a quantum time and when it can do so are the jobs of the process scheduler. Essentially, this function operates exactly like the job scheduler discussed earlier. There are criteria that cause the use of certain types of scheduling algorithms to become appropriate. The major difference between the functions of scheduling jobs and scheduling processes, then, lies in the degree of resource allocation that occurs at the respective scheduling levels. At the job scheduling level, the totality of a job's resources (with those exceptions discussed earlier) are allocated and reclaimed upon the transition from waiting to ready, and vice versa. In the process scheduler, however, most of the process's resources are maintained while the process is idle. The motivation here is that some resources are plentiful enough to allow multiple allocations and that the overhead necessary to claim and reallocate resources would be counterproductive.

With so much switching in and out of processes and their associated process states, one might think that it would be easy to mistakenly interleave process execution and cause unwanted and unpredictable results. Take the following example of two simple identical processes operating on the data item X:

Process 1	Process 2
read X	read X
$X = X + 10$	$X = X + 10$
write X	write X

Assume that X has a given value (say C) before either of the processes executes. Depending upon the interleaved order of execution of the instructions for processes A and B, the value of X after both processes have completed could be either C + 10 or C + 20. This situation is unacceptable and is called the update synchronization problem. There are many different examples of problems that can arise as a result of this type of inconsistency. In order to avoid this situation, synchronization methods are required. Any synchronization method is based upon the premise that if a sequence of transactions can be made to execute serially, then consistency can be maintained. (A transaction is defined as a sequence of actions that, when executed without any other interleaved actions, transforms the system from one consistent state to another). [Soh87] contains many excellent discussions and examples of various synchronization methods for distributed systems. [Madnick74] also discusses some basic synchronization mechanisms for centralized systems.

Another function that comes under the broad heading of synchronization is the passing of messages between processes, called interprocess communication. Interprocess message communication frequently uses the synchronization facilities to help manage the transfer of information from process to process. This facility is usually provided as a basic service in a centralized, multiprogrammed operating system.

Summarizing processor management, it is evident that the main objective is to make the most efficient use of the main processor resource, time. Through the use of intelligent control, scheduling, synchronization, and communication methods, the complex job of managing the processor can be accomplished.

Memory Management

Memory management is concerned with the allocation, control, and usage of the different levels in the memory hierarchy discussed in Chapter 2. Although the name "memory management" is used, the scope of this service actually includes all of the memory hierarchy levels and can be interpreted as "storage management." Both terms will be used interchangeably here. The management of storage encompasses the following functions:

1. The logical structuring of memory into allocatable entities and the maintenance of the status of the entities (logical memory organization)

2. The method of mapping user requests from logical representations to physical ones, and vice versa (virtual storage)

3. The implementation of policies that determine when and where memory resource actions will occur (virtual storage management)

In Chapter 2, we discussed the physical organization of memory components within the memory hierarchy. For the purposes of the discussions in this chapter, such organizations are transparent to the memory management software. Instead, a level of the memory hierarchy is viewed as a monolithic, physical entity upon which logical organizations can be placed. This brings us to the first topic in our discussion of memory management, the logical structuring of the physical memory. Perhaps the most basic organization is that of partitioning. Simply stated, partitioning cuts up a linear array of memory into smaller memory regions. Partitions can be made in one of several ways. They can be constructed and allocated either statically or dynamically, and they may be of constant or variable size. In static partitioning, a number of memory blocks of specific sizes are created prior to the processing of the jobs in the job queue. These partitions may then be allocated to the various processes, using some sort of fitting algorithm (e.g., first fit or best fit). In dynamic partitioning, memory partitions are created only when needed by a process, and for variable-sized dynamic partitioning, reclaimed partitions are combined and reallocated as needed. Variable-sized partitions, then, are usually associated with dynamic allocation and fixed-sized partitions with static allocation.

The process of allocating and reclaiming memory partitions leads to the creation of many small, noncontiguous memory sections, called fragments. This problem can be alleviated by a process called compaction, which moves memory partitions to contiguous locations (see Figure 3–7). The technique of memory partitioning is usually not used alone to manage memory systems. Rather, it has evolved into more sophisticated schemes that are termed virtual storage techniques.

Mapping from logical representations to physical ones is the job of a virtual memory system. The term *virtual memory* implies memory that is not really there, or that is being substituted for by other resources. In partitioned memory, some mapping takes place from the logical address space to the physical locations in memory. Thus job 2 (of Figure 3–7) addresses its first allocated memory location as location zero (or whatever the starting address is) both before and after compaction, even though different physical memory locations are involved.

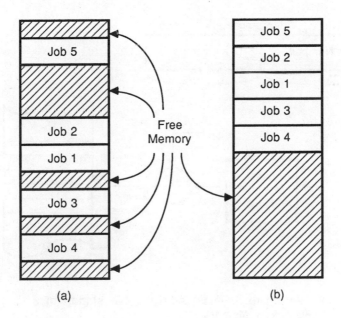

Figure 3–7. **(a) Fragmented Memory; (b) After Compaction**

Virtual memory typically refers to the appearance of a larger memory space than is really there. The memory space being considered here is in main memory, that area in which program execution and data manipulation take place. The whole idea of virtual storage, then, is to give the user the illusion of a much larger main memory address space than is actually allocated to the user or than actually exists. This is accomplished through the intelligent management of the different levels in the memory hierarchy discussed in Chapter 2. Another feature that is part of a virtual memory system is that of contiguous logical memory on noncontiguous physical storage. This is accomplished by the use of memory mapping, the act of translating logical to physical addresses, and vice versa.

A basic underlying service that must exist in order to implement a virtual memory system is that of memory blocking. Memory blocking is a combination of the partitioning described earlier and a block address mapping system, which translates a virtual address into a block location (or physical block number) and a displacement within the block. Figure 3–8 shows the

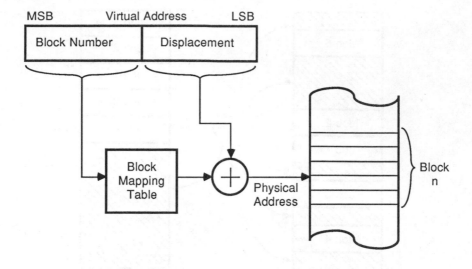

Figure 3–8. **Virtual to Physical Address Translation of Blocked Memory**

mapping process from virtual to physical addressing for a typical blocked, virtual memory system. The block mapping table holds an entry containing the block address in memory for each physical memory block and, for variable-size blocked memory systems, the size of the memory block. The block number is used to index the correct entry in the block mapping table. In using blocked, virtual memory, it is desirable to be able to place a virtual memory block at any of the memory's physical block locations. This implies that all of the physical blocks must be the same size in order to facilitate this interchanging of block locations. This type of memory system is typically called paged memory, and each block is referred to as a memory page. An additional characteristic of paging systems is the fact that not all of the virtual pages reside in primary memory at any one time. In fact, it is usually the case that all of a process's virtual pages are not in primary memory at once. Secondary storage, usually disk, is used to hold the remainder of the pages.

Mapping from virtual to real (physical) addresses in a paged memory system proceeds much in the way shown in Figure 3–8. Since all of the pages may not be in primary memory at any given time, however, there must also be a field in the block (or page) mapping table to indicate the physical page location (in primary or secondary memory). The implementation of the page mapping table is sometimes done using associative memory to speed up the address translation process. The method of block (or page) mapping described earlier is also called direct mapping. In addition to the basic virtual memory organizations described above, there are variations that involve programs with noncontiguous storage requirements (segmentation) and overlaying of large program sections. See [Madnick74] for discussions of these.

The process of keeping track of which pages are in primary memory and when to move pages between primary and secondary storage, called page swapping, is part of virtual memory management. The emphasis here is on the strategies and policies used in replacing pages in main memory with ones from secondary storage and writing main memory pages to secondary storage.

Basically, a virtual memory system operates as follows:

1. An executing program produces a virtual address to memory.

2. The virtual to physical mapping of the address occurs as shown in Figure 3–8.

3. The location (in primary or secondary memory) of the desired page is checked.

4. If the page is in primary memory, the access proceeds.

5. If the page is not in primary memory, it is swapped into primary storage.

Steps 3, 4, and 5 define the bulk of the work in a virtual memory management system. The situation in which the desired page does not reside in primary memory is called a page fault. The memory management system must intervene when a page fault occurs.

What functions must be performed by the memory manager? For one, the desired page must be brought in from secondary storage so that it can be used. If free memory space is available, it can be placed there, and the job is done. This implies, however, that the memory manager must keep track of free memory space, which is the case. If free space is not available, the memory manager's job becomes more difficult. A decision must now be made as to which of the pages currently in primary memory will be overwritten with the new one. Also, if the page being replaced is no longer consistent with the copy that resides in secondary storage, it must be written there before replacement.

Several strategies exist for deciding which pages should be replaced when a new page is needed. Some of these are the first in first out (FIFO) strategy, random page replacement, the least recently used (LRU) criterion, the least frequently used (LFU) strategy, and the not recently used (NRU) method. The names of the strategies listed above are indicative of the operation of each replacement algorithm. See [Deitel83] for a discussion of these algorithms.

Another dimension of the page replacement problem involves the timing of page swapping actions. So far, we have loosely described what is called demand paging. That is, no action is taken until it is forced by a page fault, and then only a minimal corrective action is taken (i.e. only one page brought in at a time). Other, more effective strategies exist. These methods are all based upon the principle of locality of reference. This principle is a kind of law of inertia for programs that states that the next memory reference that a program makes will, with high probability, be to the next sequential memory location. For example, if we assume that one of ten program instructions is a branch, then 90% of the instructions pass control to the next sequential instruction. More complex justifications for this principle can be constructed, but the intuition remains the same; most instructions do not alter a program's sequential flow of control. The intelligent paging strategies, then, take advantage of this fact. Another characteristic that supports these strategies is that data references tend to be clustered around a set of main data sets used by a program.

The use of locality of reference leads us to the conclusion that it may be possible to predict, with a good chance of success, which pages will be required by a process during execution. Intelligent paging schemes, then, attempt to exploit this fact by preloading memory with the pages that are likely to be used during a processes execution. Some systems attempt to load a sufficient number of process pages, called the working set, when the process is initiated and then use one of the other paging strategies when a page fault occurs. Others use the occasion of a page fault to load a number of pages that are expected to be required, a process called anticipatory paging.

As the preceding discussion illustrates, the topic of memory management in operating systems is very important from the standpoints of both resource utilization and system performance.

Device Management

The third layer of the operating system onion is that of device management. Included in this layer are the responsibility for controlling peripheral devices as they operate, for allocating the device resources to processes, for providing the necessary interfaces that allow processes to effectively use the devices, and for providing buffering for data areas to and from the devices.

The control of peripheral devices, entails two specific tasks. One is maintaining the current operational status of all of the devices in the system. This can be accomplished through the use of software that either interrogates or passively ascertains the device status, and through appropriate data structures to maintain the status of all devices. The other control task is concerned with the provision of the appropriate device control signals or parameters in real time. Device control signals may be in the form of a state change on a physical I/O line, or in the form of device control information that is programmed into the device to define certain operational characteristics. There exist generic peripheral device categories, such as disk, printer, monitor, etc., which require certain standard types of control procedures, customized to the specific device make or model. These standard control programs are typically provided with an operating system and tailored to the specific environment by the system installers. Nonstandard devices require special control programs that are not part of the basic operating system capability.

Channel programs are one method of providing device control. These programs are run by a channel controller and consist of a sequence of channel control words that are really just specialized instructions for channel control. These programs are not part of the operating system, but their control (i.e., when to invoke the channel program, which processes can access them, etc.), is an operating system function.

Peripheral devices can be broadly categorized as dedicated, shared, or virtual. Dedicated devices are those that are usable by only one process at a time. Devices that record stream output, printers, or tape drives, for example, would be allocated as dedicated devices.

Shared devices are those that can support interleaved access by a number of different processes. Generally, any random access device such as a disk can be allocated in this way. The critical factor here is that all data accesses are accompanied by data addresses that direct the read or write to the appropriate location. The sharing of sequential devices is difficult because all data items are referred by their relative position to the other data items. Since interleaved access requires the determination of the data item's location, much searching back and forth for the appropriate address is required, making sharing impractical.

One way to alleviate the problem associated with having to dedicate devices for the duration of a process is to provide what is known as a virtual device interface. This type of interface actually tricks the process into thinking that it is communicating with the real device, when it is actually using a front (some software interface) and a portion of primary and/or secondary storage. The use of the actual, physical device is then removed one level to the operating system. Thus the device is dedicated to an operating system process that meters its use.

The common factors that permeate all of device management are the capabilities of buffering and device status reporting. Buffering of transactions allows the involved process to execute an I/O transfer at CPU speed rather than at the slower device speed. This is necessary to optimize the CPU performance. The maintenance and reporting of the status of an I/O transfer is also important to control the blocking and resumption of processes or to provide status indicators that can be periodically checked by a process.

File Management

Within the combined context of device and memory management, there is an entity that has become so important that it requires its own separate management function. Unlike processes, memory, or devices, however, this entity is not a physical resource. Rather, it is a logical ordering of the physical resources. This is the system's information storage and retrieval function, called the file system. Since many specific file system organizations exist (virtually one for every operating system), a generalized organization will be discussed here.

There are three basic components to any file system:

1. The *files*: Sets of related items that are logically associated and stored within the memory hierarchy

2. The *directory*: A data structure that contains organizational information about the files

3. The *file access system*: A program that allocates and controls access to files and that enforces the structure imposed by the directory

A file is nothing more than a collection of data items that have some significance when associated as a unit, much like a normal paper file that holds a set of related papers. Files can be of the sequential or direct access type, the definitions corresponding to those for storage devices. Special markers in the file signify the beginning and end of the information in the file. This facilitates the location of the file and gives a reference point for information in sequential files. Files may reside anywhere in the storage hierarchy, although they are commonly associated with secondary storage organization. The actual organization of the data in a file follows basic guidelines. At the lowest level, bits of information are grouped into bytes (one byte equals the concatenation of eight bits). Bytes form the basic unit of data that is represented on the storage medium. Strings of bytes are formed into records, fixed-length sequences that form the basic organizational unit. A number of records, in turn, make up a file. Although the bits in a byte and the bytes in a record must all be physically contiguous on the medium, records that are logically contiguous within a file need not be physically contiguous. Records themselves are sometimes organized into groups, referred to as logical records. In either case, the record (or logical record) forms the basic unit of information that is transferred for each file access. In addition to the actual data that is contained in a record, each has a header and trailer that contain identifying information and a special delimiter pattern, respectively. The combination of noncontiguous record storage and the identifying information facilitate the imposition of the next level of organization, the directory.

A rudimentary directory is just what it says, a list of files in some order. The actual information contained in a directory entry varies greatly from system to system. The information, though, is of two types, user-visible and system-specific. The user-visible information is pertinent to the end user of the file system and contains items such as the name of the file, its size and creation date, the access protection that it has, and its type. System-specific information helps to map the user-visible items to internal file system parameters such as the location of the file in memory, the format of its data, and perhaps a map of the file's storage organization. Thus the directory provides an organization that enables files to be stored, accessed, and protected. A basic directory can itself become a component of a larger directory structure that may be organized in a number of ways (e.g., hierarchical, networked, associative). A hierarchical structure of directories within directories is by far the most popular and straightforward to implement.

A combination of the file and directory organizations provides the static view of the overall file system, what you would get if you drew all of the items and associations on a large sheet of paper. A file system, however, is not static; it constantly changes according to the wishes of the system users and processes. Therefore a mechanism must be in place to ensure that file access is controlled and that the integrity of the file system's structure is maintained. File management provides users with the interfaces necessary to access the file system, handles the allocation and deallocation of storage resources for use by files, and interprets the physical organization of the file system.

User interface functions that are provided by the file system manager include commands to create, destroy, copy, and update files. In addition to these high-level commands that treat a file as a single entity, lower-level commands, such as get and put, allow record or byte level access to files. This is necessary for the construction of file editors and other special purpose programs.

The management of file storage space on secondary storage is a major responsibility of the file manager. Usually, a table that maps sections of storage is kept, to indicate free and occupied memory. The allocation of this memory is performed according to some metric deemed important to the system. For example, if performance were a major issue, then it would be wise to allocate records in such a way that a disk-scheduling algorithm would perform optimally. Similar tradeoffs can be made for other parameters, such as storage efficiency and transfer rate. Also, the reclamation of storage space must be handled when a file is deleted from the system. This normally requires only the setting of a flag in the mapping table.

Another responsibility of the file manager is to make sense of the directory and record-identification information so that the physically dispersed files can be retrieved. There are generally two methods of achieving this. One is called chaining or linked-list organization. In this method, each record (or logical record) contains information on the location of the next logically sequential record in the file. This information can be placed in the record header or trailer, depending on the system. Access to a file, then, is performed by sequentially chaining down the records until an end-of-file marker is reached. This organization yields a sequential-type file.

The other file retrieval method, called indexed access, uses a table to hold the locations of the records in the file. In this method, each record or logical record has a table entry stating the starting address of the record. Large files may require several of these tables, which may themselves be chained or indexed. File access in this organization can be direct, however, because the address of each record can be found by looking in the table.

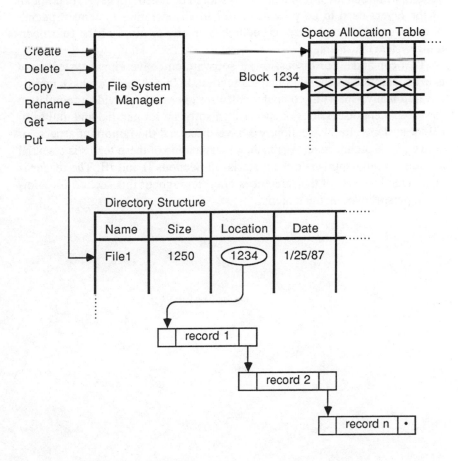

Figure 3–9. **File System with Sequential File Structure**

Making additions or deletions to the contents of a file requires the manipulation of the location information that is in the records or in the index table.
A picture showing a generalized file system, with some of the associated data
structures, is shown in Figure 3–9. A topic that is closely related to that of file
systems is that of information storage and retrieval, or data base systems.
These systems are not discussed here, however, as they are beyond the scope
of this book. The reader is referred to [Ullman82], [Date81], and [Date83].

Looking back to our onion model of Figure 3–6, we have discussed each
layer. Application processes that execute in this environment have inter-

actions with each layer in the onion. It should be noted, however, that not all
of the layers need to be present in full in all operating systems. Special-
purpose systems emphasize or deemphasize one or more of the four operating system managers.

This concludes our discussion of software on conventional systems and
also concludes the general principles section. In this chapter, we have rapidly
covered many aspects of computer software in order to provide a foundation
for subsequent discussions of specialized software for parallel and multiprocessor systems. In this section, we have discussed the important aspects of
conventional architecture. Again, an understanding of these topics is essential
in order to fully appreciate the material in Sections II and III. The reader is
encouraged to consult the references cited throughout this section for additional perspectives on the material.

Section II:
The Implementation of
Parallel Systems

This section will cover a wide range of parallel and multiprocessor systems, from array processors to pipelines and from associative to multiprocessors. Also, this section will address some of the basic issues that permeate parallel designs of any type. This section is meant to build upon the material in Section I by showing extensions, alterations, and departures from conventional machine architectures.

Chapter 4 covers several topics that are germane to many parallel and multiprocessor architectures. These include methods of detecting, representing, and implementing parallelism, and definitions of terms used in these areas.

Chapter 5 presents an architectural review of a number of generic parallel and multiprocessors. These architectures are chosen to cover the greatest possible breadth of systems and to attempt to place the often-confusing gamut of these systems into perspective. Special issues that relate to the particular architectures are also presented where appropriate.

Chapter 6, the last in Section II, attempts to round out the architectural presentations of Chapter 5 by discussing various methods of evaluating and measuring the performance of computer systems. The chapter illustrates the basic tools and methods necessary to allow the modeling, evaluation, and measurement of computer system performance.

4. PARALLELISM

We will now turn our attention to the topic of parallelism in applications for computers. This chapter is broken up into four topics: methods for representing parallelism; a loose classification of the types of parallel execution; detecting parallelism in applications; and implementing parallelism.

Let's begin by first reviewing the basic definition of parallelism: the ability to do more than one activity at once. Doing n different activities at once; doing one activity in n simultaneous parts; doing n activities staggered in time; using k resources for n jobs; and k resources for one job — all of the above represent instances of parallelism. The common thread that runs through these examples is the utilization of multiple resources in an instance of time to increase the amount of work performed per unit of time.

Representing Parallelism

Before delving into the categorization, detection, and implementation of parallelism in computer systems, it is useful to discuss methods for representing the parallelism that is found in various applications. To this end, we will discuss the use of graphs as applied to problems and solutions for computers. First, a review of the terms and definitions used in graph theory are given. Next, some graph algorithms and applications are discussed, which will lead us into the discussion of the classification of various forms of parallelism.

A graph is simply a model that represents the structure of computations and data for a given problem. The graph representation has its origin in mathematics, where it is used to represent the elements of a set and the relationships among the elements. All of us are probably familiar with graphs of one form or another, since they are frequently specialized for use in many different applications. A flow chart, for example, is a specialized graph, with set elements consisting of logical program blocks, and the flow of control and data manifested in the relationships.

As stated earlier, a graph consists of a set of elements and their relationships. The set's elements are referred to individually by the following interchangeable names: node, vertex, object, and point. Node and vertex are the most commonly used, with node appearing more frequently in discussions of a computer science or architectural nature, and vertex appearing in algorithm analysis and graph theory discussions. We will use the term "node" here, with the occasional substitution of the others. The relationship of the elements of a set, or the nodes of a graph, is known as the edge, link, connection, branch, or arc. The term "edge" is commonly used and will be used here.

Figure 4–1(a) shows a simple graph called an undirected graph. The undirected nature of the graph is signified by the absence of direction arrows on the edges. Undirected edges between nodes, represented by the parenthetical pair denoting the nodes connected by the edge, indicate that the nodes are adjacent. A directed graph, shown in Figure 4–1(b), contains directed edges between nodes. Here the edges are denoted by the angle brackets, and the order of the nodes in the edge identifier indicates the direction of the edge. Sometimes, the wording "node a is *adjacent to* node b" is used to indicate that a directed edge exists from node a to node b. Alternatively, node b can be said to be *adjacent from* node a to describe the same situation.

A path between n_1 and n_2 consists of the set of edges, arranged in sequence, that one must transverse to get from n_1 to n_2 in the graph. An undirected path, consisting of a sequence of undirected edges, exists between any two nodes in an undirected graph. The same is not true for a directed graph, however, because the directed path is made up of directed edges, which are ordered pairs. A cycle in a graph is a path in which the first and last nodes in the edge list are the same. In Figure 4–1 (b), the path $<n_1, n_3><n_3, n_2><n_2, n_1>$ is a cycle. A simple path is one that passes through any node only once.

An undirected graph is said to be fully connected if there exists an edge between every pair of nodes. Figure 4–1(a) is a fully connected graph. For a directed graph, if for any two distinct nodes, n_i and n_j, there exists the edges $<n_i, n_j>$ and $<n_j, n_i>$, then the graph is said to be strongly connected. Figure 4–1(b) is not strongly connected. Strong connection is also called symmetry. Fully connected, undirected graphs and strongly connected, directed graphs are essentially the same, because undirected edges imply bidirectional links between nodes.

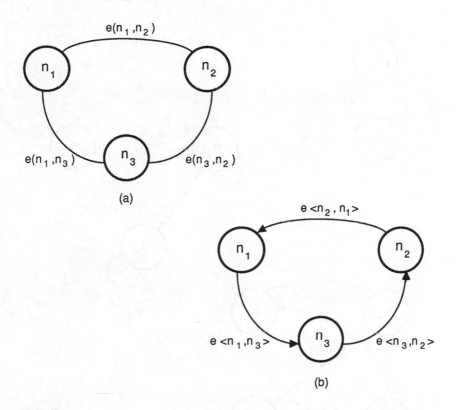

Figure 4–1. **(a) Simple Undirected Graph; (b) Simple Directed Graph**

Further classifications exist for directed graphs. A reflexive node n_i exists when an edge $<n_i, n_i>$ exists. A reflexive graph is totally made up of reflexive nodes. A complete graph is one in which, for every pair of distinct nodes n_i and n_j, there exists at least one directed path from n_i to n_j or from n_j to n_i. Figure 4–2 shows several graph classifications.

One important use of graph representation is for the analysis of the connectivity of a number of nodes. For this purpose, a data structure, called the adjacency matrix, is used. The purpose of this structure is to produce a representation of the relationships between nodes that can be easily manipulated by automatic means. The adjacency matrix may be structured in a number of ways: with the rows and columns representing edges and the entries representing nodes, with rows and columns as nodes and entries as edges, or as variations on the above. It is perhaps easier to understand the

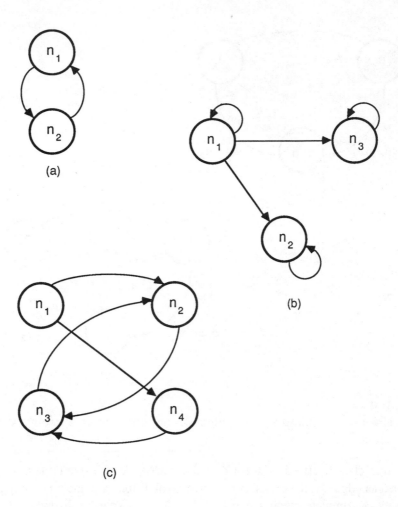

Figure 4–2.   **(a) Strongly Connected Graph; (b) Reflexive Graph;
(c) Complete Graph**

structure that uses nodes for row and column indices and entries to indicate
the absence or presence of an edge between nodes. The adjacency matrix is
read by reading across the row for n_i and finding that node n_i is adjacent to n_j,
where the matrix entry contains a one in the column for n_j. The adjacent from
relations are read by scanning down columns instead of across rows. Notice
that no weight (e.g., distance, cost, capacity, etc.) is attached to the

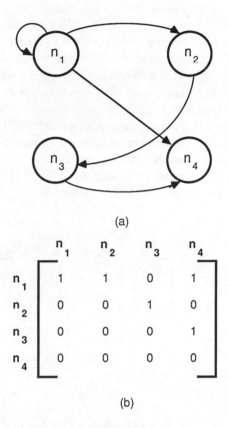

(a)

$$
\begin{array}{c c c c c}
 & n_1 & n_2 & n_3 & n_4 \\
n_1 & 1 & 1 & 0 & 1 \\
n_2 & 0 & 0 & 1 & 0 \\
n_3 & 0 & 0 & 0 & 1 \\
n_4 & 0 & 0 & 0 & 0
\end{array}
$$

(b)

Figure 4–3.   **(a) Directed Graph and (b) Its Corresponding Adjacency Matrix**

entries in the adjacency matrix; they simply represent connectivity. Figure 4–3 shows an example graph and the corresponding adjacency matrix. The adjacency matrix is obviously always square. An adjacency matrix for an undirected graph is always symmetrical, as is that for a strongly connected directed graph, hence the equivalence of the two. The adjacency matrix represents all paths that involve the traversal of single edges only. That is, the paths that involve the traversal of more than one edge are not explicitly represented, although the information is embedded in the matrix. This information can be made explicit, however, by taking powers of the original adjacency matrix. Thus the square of the adjacency matrix will result in all directed paths consisting of two edges being marked by appropriately placed nonzero elements in the matrix. In general, the nth power of the adjacency matrix identifies all directed paths involving the traversal of n directed links. Figure 4-4 shows the adjacency matrices for the various path lengths of the graph in figure 4-3. For the square of the original matrix A, we see that there exists a path of length 2 from n_1 to each of the other nodes, including itself and from n_2 to n_4. For the cube of matrix A and higher powers, there are paths of length $(3 + k)$, $k = 1...m$, from node 1 to any other node, including itself. The matrix at this point is idempotent, a result of the reflexive node n_1. For any power R of A, the number of nonzero entries in row n_i represents the number of paths of length k that originate at n_i. For the matrix A, this number is called the outdegree, or fan-out, of n_i. Similarly, counting nonzero column entries gives the indegree, or fan-in, for a node n_j.

$$
A^2 = \begin{array}{c} \\ n_1 \\ n_2 \\ n_3 \\ n_4 \end{array}
\begin{array}{cccc}
n_1 & n_2 & n_3 & n_4 \\
1 & 1 & 1 & 1 \\
0 & 0 & 0 & 1 \\
0 & 0 & 0 & 0 \\
0 & 0 & 0 & 0
\end{array}
$$

(a)

$$
A^{(3+k)} = \begin{array}{c} \\ n_1 \\ n_2 \\ n_3 \\ n_4 \end{array}
\begin{array}{cccc}
n_1 & n_2 & n_3 & n_4 \\
1 & 1 & 1 & 2 \\
0 & 0 & 0 & 0 \\
0 & 0 & 0 & 0 \\
0 & 0 & 0 & 0
\end{array}
$$

(b)

Figure 4–4.   **Adjacency Matrices for Figure 4–3: (a) Path Length of 2 and (b) Path Length of 3 + k**

Any node in a graph is considered to be reachable if there exists at least one adjacent-from edge connected to it. This edge will be part of a path that is identified in the adjacency matrix. A node is also defined as being reachable from itself. Thus we define the reachability matrix as follows:

$$R = I + A + A^2 + ... A^n$$

where I is the identity matrix. The sum is carried out until either A^n is zero or until it is idempotent. The nonzero elements in row n_i, then, indicate that there is a path from n_i to the n_j whose columns correspond to these elements. For our example of Figure 4–3, the reachability matrix is given in Figure 4–5. Zero entries indicate that there is no path from node n_i to n_j.

The element product, R dot R (transpose), forms a symmetric matrix whose nonzero elements indicate that n_i is reachable from n_j, and vice versa. Here, *dot* refers to the dot product of the matrices (the product operation forms the product A dot B = C by forming the individual products $c_{ij} = a_{ij} \times b_{ij}$, where a_{ij}, b_{ij}, and c_{ij} are individual elements of A, B, and C, respectively). From this product, referred to as the matrix Q, columns with entries in the same rows form sets of commonly reachable nodes that can be combined into single nodes. This is a reduction technique that can continue until a basis for the matrix Q is found. Figure 4–6 shows the matrix Q for the graph of Figure 4–3. In the figure, there are no reductions possible.

The adjacency matrix discussed earlier is also referred to as the value matrix, when the element values represent some numerical value for the corresponding edges. These entries could represent the cost incurred when

$$R = I + A + A^2 + A^3 = \begin{array}{c} \\ n_1 \\ n_2 \\ n_3 \\ n_4 \end{array} \begin{array}{cccc} n_1 & n_2 & n_3 & n_4 \\ \left[\begin{array}{cccc} 3 & 3 & 2 & 4 \\ 0 & 1 & 1 & 1 \\ 0 & 0 & 1 & 1 \\ 0 & 0 & 0 & 1 \end{array}\right] \end{array}$$

Figure 4–5. **Reachability Matrix for Figure 4–3(a)**

$$Q = R * R^T = \begin{bmatrix} 3 & 3 & 2 & 4 \\ 0 & 1 & 1 & 1 \\ 0 & 0 & 1 & 1 \\ 0 & 0 & 0 & 1 \end{bmatrix} * \begin{bmatrix} 3 & 0 & 0 & 0 \\ 3 & 1 & 0 & 0 \\ 2 & 1 & 1 & 0 \\ 4 & 1 & 1 & 1 \end{bmatrix} = \begin{bmatrix} 9 & 0 & 0 & 0 \\ 0 & 1 & 0 & 0 \\ 0 & 0 & 1 & 0 \\ 0 & 0 & 0 & 1 \end{bmatrix}$$

Figure 4–6. The Element Product Indicating Mutual Reachability

using a link, a probability of taking the specified link when transitioning between nodes, or any number of other interpretations.

One of the most important uses of the value matrix is to attempt to find a path of a specified length between any two nodes that has the minimum or maximum value (length refers to the number of edges traversed). A path value is calculated by summing all of the individual edge values that lie along the path. This task can be performed by tracing all paths emanating from the source node for a specified length (i.e., a specified number of edges), and then picking the most suitable path that ends up at the desired destination node. This calculation can be automated, however, by the process that is now described. The main objective is to perform an operation on all paths of length n to obtain the values for paths of length n + 1. Let us adopt the notation V(n) for the value matrix, where n is the path length whose cost is represented in the matrix. Thus V(1) is the original value matrix. The matrix V(n + 1) is calculated from the elements of V(n) as follows:

$$v_{ij}(n + 1) = op\ (sum(v_{ik}(n) + v_{kj}(n)): k = 1, ..., m)$$

where m is the dimension of V (the number of nodes) and op is the desired operation (e.g., max, min, avg, etc.). The elements on the right side of the equation are from the V(n) matrix and v_{ij} is an element of the V(n + 1) matrix. From the resultant matrix V(n + 1), the entry corresponding to the source node's row and destination node's column represents the value of traversing a path of length n + 1 from source to destination. Modifications of the above algorithm can be made to find the minimum distance between any two nodes and the path that yields this value, the average value of a specified path length, and a number of other useful procedures.

Various graph algorithms have been documented in the literature, and we will consider a few of them here as a prelude to discussions of parallel classifications. We will discuss several useful algorithms and analyze them in terms of their application to parallel processing. First, the discussions will focus on problems involving unweighted graphs, those graphs in which the adjacency matrix is equal to the value matrix. Next, weighted graph problems, with significant value matrices, will be discussed.

One problem that arises frequently in many computer science problems is that of searching a graph from a given starting node. Several search strategies exist, including depth first, breadth first, minimax search, and others. We will discuss here the case of breadth first search. The general breadth first algorithm is given below. This problem assumes an undirected graph. Repeat the following steps until no new nodes are encountered:

1. From the originating node, follow each edge to the connected node and remember only the nodes not previously encountered

2. For each node found in step 1, repeat step 1 using the new node as the originating node

This algorithm searches all paths on a given level before moving on to the nodes on the next level. Figure 4–7 shows a sample graph and the corresponding breadth first search. The order of visitation of the nodes is given in parenthesis beside each node and n_1 is the assumed starting point.

How much time does it take to perform this search? First, let's define the average degree of an undirected graph to be given as:

$$d_{ave} = 2e/C$$

where e is the number of edges in the graph and C is the number of nodes in the graph. Here, because of the bidirectional nature of undirected edges, one edge contributes twice to the degree of a node; hence, the quantity 2e. If we further define the two operations involved in searching a graph as node expansion and node selection, then we can characterize the complexity of the breadth first search algorithm. This complexity will translate to an upper bound of the amount of time required for a search, given the time needed for each operation.

For the breadth first search, therefore, we require n node selection operations, one for each node in the graph. For each node, there is an average of 2e/n edges, where e is the total number of edges in the graph. We have a total, therefore, of n(2e/n) operations to expand all of the nodes in the graph. The

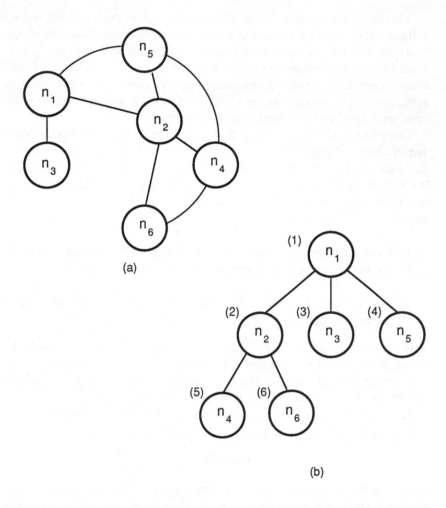

Figure 4–7. **(a) Example Graph and (b) Its Breadth First Search Representation**

upper bound on the number of operations, then, is given by:

$$\text{Bound} = 2e + n$$

In fact, this expression gives the upper bound of complexity for any algorithm (e.g., depth first search) that sequentially searches a graph.

Now let's examine a parallel implementation of this algorithm. For a parallel system with p processors, let's assume that we have the two operations given above. Let's further assume that node expansion, the process of following edges to nodes and adding new nodes to the search list, also takes care of combining the partial lists of the p processors and redistributing the new partial lists. Operations on the processes that run concurrently are counted as one operation when finding the upper bound on search time.

At each level in the search tree, all of the nodes are expanded before combining the partial lists. The expansion of each node requires the traversal of each edge that is incident upon that node. On a processor with p processing elements, p of the edges can be followed at once, and a partial list can be kept at each processor. The bound, then, for performing a breadth first search on p processors is given by:

$$Bound = sum((deg(i)/p + 1): i = 1, ..., n) + l(roundup(log\ p))$$

where deg(i) is the number of edges incident upon node i and l is the number of levels in the search tree (Logarithms are base 2 and roundup rounds the argument to next whole number.) [Quinn84] states that, for $p \geq 2$ and an average vertex degree of $\geq$ roundup (log p)+5, parallel breadth first search is superior to the sequential version. Figure 4–8 illustrates the algorithm for the graph of Figure 4–7. The numbers in parenthesis indicate the order of visitation for p = 2.

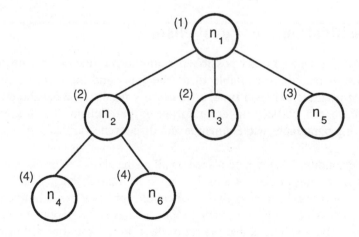

Figure 4–8. **Visitation for Breadth First Search on Two Processors**

The breadth first search algorithm is useful, for example, in finding the connected components of an undirected graph. Other algorithms that solve this problem utilize the adjacency matrix to find collections of nodes that are mutually reachable. These sets are then collapsed into a "supernode" that is used as a new node in the calculations. A supernode is a set of nodes that are commonly reachable, as defined earlier. [Quinn84] provides a good survey of a number of algorithms to solve this and other parallel graph problems.

There are also several useful parallel algorithms that make use of weighted, directed graphs. One such algorithm finds the shortest path between all pairs of nodes in the graph. Performing this task requires the computation of several matrix multiplications, where multiplication is defined as it was above in the calculation of the value matrix V with minimum as the operator. If we have a parallel processor with the appropriate interprocessor connections and with n^3 processing elements, then we can solve the shortest path problem in order $(\log n)^2$ time for an n node graph. For this algorithm, the adjacency matrix A contains the weights of the edges and the resultant matrix A^n contains entries that correspond to the minimum path length between any pair of nodes in the graph. Again, consult [Quinn84] for a survey of directed graph algorithms.

Now that we have given a brief introduction into the representation of parallelism and have discussed some of the algorithms that can be useful with the representation, we will move on to discuss the basic classes of parallelism.

Classifications of Parallelism

Because there are so many possible permutations of the number of jobs, the number of resources available to do the jobs, and the different ways of organizing these two over time, a framework needs to be developed within which we can classify different forms of parallelism. To this end, the following paragraphs will enumerate and discuss the various forms of parallelism.

One condition that will be placed on all of the classes to be discussed here is that the n jobs, or parts of jobs, be somehow interrelated. This relationship may be very weak, such as two independent jobs that are submitted to the same processing resource, or very strong, such as two complimentary pieces of a job. The gist here is that the set of the n jobs taken together must have some real significance. Restricting this condition further, it will also be assumed that the set of n jobs to be performed somehow applies to a common goal or set of goals. With this condition, the processing is focused, and the imposition of parallel or multiprocessor organizations on the application makes sense.

We now present three general classes of parallelism. These classes do not specify the control methods, as do Flynn's classifications. Instead they provide an organizational viewpoint. The purpose of this classification, then, is to provide a loose mapping from the kinds of parallelism that are found in various applications to high-level machine organizations. These classes are intended to compliment those presented by Flynn by providing the more general models over which his control methods can be laid. The three classes are named vector, pipeline, and n-dimensional.

Vector Parallelism

In mathematics, a vector is defined as an ordered set of elements, each element having significance in one dimension of the problem space. Vector parallelism, then, is also characterized by the presence of elements that have both individual significance and set significance. Furthermore, the elements of a set are all operated on simultaneously. No conditions on the duration or complexity of the operations on the individual elements are imposed. The only stipulation is that the operations, once initiated, proceed independently until all are complete. At these completion points, interactions between the elements may occur. Figure 4-9 shows a graph that represents the general form of vector parallelism.

Vector parallelism is usually found in applications in which the same operation must be performed on all elements of a set or sets of data elements. Cases do occur, however, in which only a subset of the data is to be operated on during any one cycle. Figure 4-10 shows the graph of such a case, in which all of the nodes in the graph of Figure 4-9 do not participate in every operation. Note the visitation of node n_1 during each cycle. It is here that the results of each operation are combined into the proper resultant form.

Another structure that uses vector parallelism on a large scale is the co-begin/co-end construct. Shown in Figure 4-11, this type of application requires synchronization at the beginning and end of each processing cycle. Although the operations performed during each cycle may consist of entire processes, the characteristics are still those of vector-type parallelism.

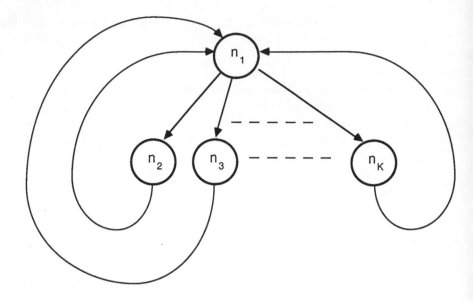

Figure 4–9. **A Graph Showing Vector Parallelism**

Pipeline Parallelism

The second class of parallelism is called pipelined parallelism, because the operations on items are performed in steps. Each step occurs at a discrete period in time, and the operations performed in each step may be different. Items that undergo pipeline operations are acted upon in sequence, and each new item is skewed by one or more step in time. Pipeline parallelism has the appearance of Figure 4–12, with a new item able to be accepted at n_1 at each step in time. The parallelism occurs when there are items at more than one node during the same time period. This type of parallelism is found in any application in which the same sequence of operations is performed on a number of data items. Data items that are in various stages of completion (i.e., in various stages of the pipeline) do not interact; the operations are independent. The other restriction on this type of parallelism is that each stage in the pipeline consumes the same amount of time to complete the designated operations. All items are then shifted to the next station, much like units on an assembly line conveyor belt. Pipeline parallelism in an application, then, requires that all of the operations of short duration not suffer while waiting for the longer ones to complete.

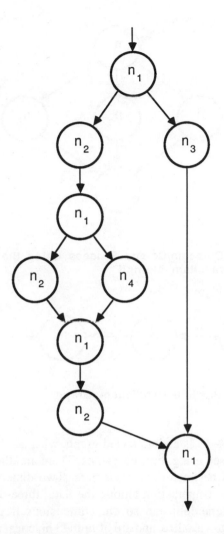

Figure 4–10. **An Example of an Application Using the Vector
Parallelism Model**

n-Dimensional Parallelism

N-Dimensional parallelism is characterized by the interaction among the data
in a model of computation. For instance, one-dimensional parallelism has
interactions between all adjacent data along some path (see Figure 4–13).

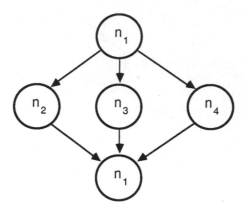

Figure 4–11. **A Co-begin/Co-end Process Using the Vector Parallelism Method**

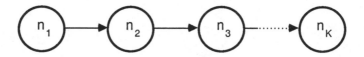

Figure 4–12. **A Pipeline Parallelism Graph**

Note that Figure 4–13 is an undirected graph, whereas the previous classes have been expressed using directed graphs. There are, then, two-way (or n-way) interactions between data items here. Two-dimensional parallelism permits two axes of interaction among the data; three-dimensional allows three axes of interaction; and so on. Dimensions larger than three are possible but hard to visualize, and are of limited practical importance. Figure 4-14 shows a three-dimensional graph of a parallel application that has interactions along the edges of a cube.

No restrictions are placed on the operations that take place at each node, the duration or complexity of the operations, or on the frequency of interaction between the data on connected nodes. Also, the geometry of the graph is not fixed to any particular interconnection pattern.

In practice, this type of parallelism is found in many applications in which a continuous physical phenomenon is to be modeled. One example is the simulation of weather conditions across a geographic region. The nodes of a two-dimensional graph would represent the conditions in a geographic area, and the edges would convey information that would influence the calculation of the next weather state. Thus the whole system would evolve over time to produce likely weather patterns.

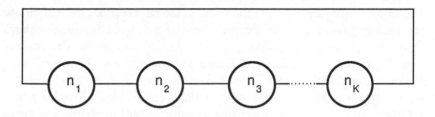

Figure 4–13. **One-Dimensional Parallelism**

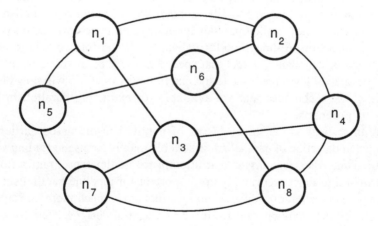

Figure 4–14. **A Three-Dimensional Parallel Graph with Cube Edge Interactions**

Detecting Parallelism

Assuming that we have some form of parallel hardware and a method for programming applications on that hardware, the question of how to detect parallelism must be answered. There are two forms of parallelism in any application: explicit and implicit. Explicit parallelism refers to programmer cognizance of parallelism in the application program and to the express identification of such parallelism in the code. In the next section, we will discuss programming languages that provide a vehicle for expressing explicit parallelism. In this section, however, we will concentrate on the detection of implicit parallelism. Implicit parallelism is defined here as that concurrency that can be wrought from the code of standard programming languages such as FORTRAN or Pascal. Many of the techniques discussed here have been built into parallelizing compilers that accept standard programs and create code for parallel computers. The success of these compilers in attaining maximum parallelism is limited, however, by factors such as the language used, the programming style used in creating a specific application, and, of course, by the target machine architecture. One point that becomes clear when investigating these techniques is that, in order to achieve the greatest benefit from any given parallel or multiprocessing computer, the programmer must be made aware of the machine architecture in order to fully exploit the potential performance benefits. In other words, implicit parallelism will only get you so far; explicit parallelism is required to achieve the maximum performance gain. Although no formal analysis is performed here to justify the previous statement, the fact that special-purpose parallel languages have been developed gives credence to the claim. In any case, we will now discuss some of the techniques that are available for extracting parallelism from existing programs.

With respect to the three classes of parallelism discussed earlier, the automated detection of parallelism is suitable mainly for use in finding vector parallelism. Also, techniques that attempt to predict a program's flow of control and to react accordingly are important for pipeline parallelism. The automated detection of n-dimensional parallelism is much more difficult and usually requires explicit help from the application designer. The following discussions, then, will focus on vectorization techniques.

Let's begin with the analysis of some standard programming constructs in search of parallelism. We will discuss four basic statement types: assignment statements, array operations, conditional branch (IF) statements, and loops.

An assignment statement is of the form:

$$Variable = expression$$

where the variable may be of scalar or array type, and the expression is any valid program expression. When a program contains a sequence of assignment statements with no intervening statements, it is possible to transform the sequence into a parallel set of expressions. A process called statement substitution is used to do this, and it works as follows:

For a sequence of assignment statements in which the result of a previous assignment is used in a latter assignment expression, substitute the expression from the previous assignment for the variable use in the latter statement.

An example should make this clear. The sequence of assignment statements

$$(1) \: X = A + B \times C \qquad (2) \: Y = X/D \qquad (3) \: Z = Y + 1$$

can be replaced by three parallel statements, by repeated substitution of the expressions for the variable names on the right-hand sides of each expression. Thus, we have the parallel statements:

$$X = A + B \times C ; \quad Y = (A + B \times C)/D ; \quad Z = (A + B \times C)/D + 1$$

This process can be automated by forming dependency graphs of the assignment statements and then by using a node-collapsing operation (such as creating "supernodes," as described earlier in this chapter). A dependency graph is simply a directed graph in which the nodes represent individual assignment statements and the edges represent usage of the variable on the left-hand side of the statement. The dependency graph for our previous example is shown in Figure 4–15. A dependency exists between statements if the left-hand side of an assignment statement is used in another statement. More formally, if X is the output of statement i and X is an input to statement j, then statement j is data dependent on statement i. If X is an input to statement j and the result of statement i is not an input to statement j, then there is no data dependency between statement i and statement j (indicated by the absence of an edge in the dependency graph). If there is a time ordering such that statement j must be computed after statement i, then we say that statement j is data-output-dependent on statement i.

In a dependency graph, a strongly connected region denotes the situation in which there is a cyclic data dependency among the statements. In this case, sequential execution is necessary and no parallelization is possible. Statements that are not contained within a strongly connected region, how-

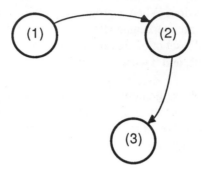

Figure 4–15. **Dependency Graph for the Assignment Statement Example**

ever, may all be executed in parallel, given a sufficient number of processors. In figure 4-15, we see that no statement is contained in a strongly connected region and so they may all be executed in parallel. Let's add another statement,

$$(4)\ D = Y + C$$

so that the dependency graph now appears as shown in Figure 4–16(a). Using the criteria for creating a supernode based on equivalent columns in the reachability matrix shown in Figure 4–16 (b), we can see that nodes (3) and (4) are strongly connected and can be fused into a single node. Because of the strong connection, statements (3) and (4) must be executed sequentially in the given order. Their sequential execution, however, may proceed in parallel with the other two statements.

The dependence of statements that contain array references is not nearly as straightforward as that for the simple assignment statements discussed above. In the trivial case in which we are performing array-to-array assignments, as shown in Figure 4–17, each assignment is essentially a simple assignment and the loop can be "unrolled" to create a sequence of assignment statements, as discussed previously. More complex situations often occur, however, when there is circular dependency among array statements, as shown in Figure 4–18. Here, what is called a layered dependency between the statements exists. This terminology arises because statement (1) is dependent on statement (2) only when considered in the context of the outermost loop. When considered with respect to the innermost loop only, the variable j

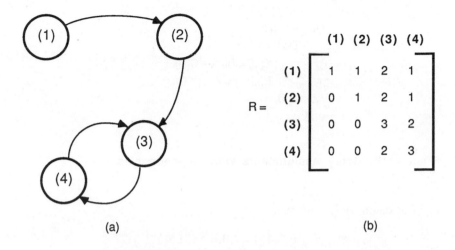

Figure 4–16. **(a) New Data Dependency Graph and (b) Its
Reachability Matrix**

appears as a constant, and hence B[i, j + 1] and B[i, j] are clearly different
pieces of data. The dependence of statement (2) on (1), however, is independent of the loop structure because the form A[i, j] is used in both statements.
It is possible, therefore, to vectorize the operations over the span of the
innermost loop. The operations that depend upon the outer loop variable,
however, cannot be vectorized due to the circular dependency that remains.

```
Do j = 1 to k
    Do i = 1 to n
        A[i,j] = B[i,j] + C[i,j];
        D[i,j] = A[i,j] * 10
    end;
end;
```

Figure 4–17. **Simple Array Assignments**

```
        Do j = 1 to k
            Do i = 1 to n
    (1)         A[i,j] = B[i,j] + C[i,j];
    (2)         B[i,j+1] = A[i,j] * C[i,j]
            end;
        end;
```

Figure 4–18. **Array Assignments with Dependencies**

Suppose statement (2) had read:

$$B[i+1,j] = A[i,j] * C[i, j]$$

instead of the original form in Figure 4–18. It would appear that this sequence could not be vectorized because of the circular dependency that arises from the use of the innermost loop variable. It is a trivial matter, however, to merely swap loop control statements without altering the intent of the sequence and thereby make vectorization possible, as before.

A conditional branch statement (IF statement) consists of two parts: the condition expression that contains arithmetic and logical operations, and the body, which contains n statements of any form. [Kuck77] describes a method for putting blocks of IF statements into canonical form that can then be implemented with some degree of parallelism. A block of IF statements is a sequence of statements in which the ratio of IF statements to all other statements is sufficiently high. Sufficiency can be established on a number of conditions, one of which may be the number of available processors and subsequently the potential gain in constructing the canonical IF form. The canonical form is given as:

1. A set of assignment statements whose elements may be executed simultaneously.

2. A set of simultaneously executable Boolean functions.

3. A binary decision tree that represents the control structure implemented in the IF block. There are n paths through the tree.

4. n blocks of elementary assignment statements, each block corresponding to a path through the decision tree.

The items in the canonical form are executed in sequential order 1-2-3-4. Step 1 calculates the results for all of the IF statement bodies, using whatever means available to attain the maximum speedup. Step 2 computes the conditions for each IF statement in the block. Step 3 computes the binary decision tree for the combinations of conditions found in step 2. Finally, based upon the path that is followed in step 3, the results that were calculated in step 1 are stored into the proper variables. There are no computations on the right-hand side of the assignment statements in step 4.

A block of statements that is nearly a pure IF block can be transformed into a pure IF block by simply moving the offending statement outside the block or by factoring the statement into every path of the binary decision tree (i.e., into every block in step 4).

We discussed loops to some extent when we presented the methods for vectorizing array operations. It turns out, however, that the combination of loops and arrays also form the crux of the problem of loop vectorization. Again, this is because we are dealing with a set of variables whose elements (the variable names themselves) change with every loop iteration. A problem that we have not yet discussed is that of self-referential cyclic dependency. This occurs, with arrays of dimension greater than 1, when the right-hand side of an assignment contains the same variable as is being used in the left-hand side of the statement. Figure 4–19 illustrates this problem for a simple loop.

Because, in the example, there is a cyclic dependency as a result of both subscripts, the methods described previously will not work here. One method for achieving a speedup in this situation is called the wave-front method. In

```
Do i = 1 to n
    Do j = 1 to k
        A[i,j] = B[i,j] * A[i-1,j] + A[i,j-1]
    end;
end;
```

Figure 4–19. **Cyclic Dependency on a Single Statement**

the wave-front method, we essentially propagate a wave of calculations through the array at an angle that is prescribed by the array subscripts. In our example, an angle of 45 degrees is appropriate because we are using the elements of the reverse diagonal in the calculation. Thus we would compute

$$A[1,1] = B[1,1] * A[0,1] + A[1,0]$$

during the first wave, A[2,1] and A[1,2] in the second wave, using the values of A[1,2] and A[2,1], and so on. Figure 4–20 illustrates the third wave calculation of the loop on the array A. The example shown reduces the number of steps in the loop from an order of n squared to an order n. Different arrangements of array subscripts and loop variables will yield different wave shapes and angles of attack. Also, cyclic dependencies involving several statements and loop variables may be treated in a similar fashion.

Other statement combinations on which it is difficult to perform vectorization have been addressed in the literature. An example is the presence of an IF statement within a program loop. In this case, one is faced not only with

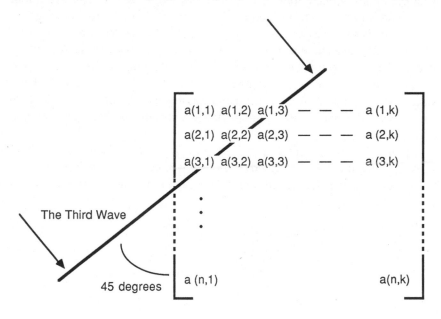

Figure 4–20. **Illustration of the Wave-Front Method**

the problem of dependency but also with changing dependency graphs according to the program flow through the IF statement. These are advanced topics that have more limited applicability than those techniques discussed earlier and are beyond the scope of this text. The interested reader is urged to consult the references listed in [Kuck77] and [Allen85] for detailed discussions.

Implementing Parallelism

Now that we have discussed the representation of parallelism, some algorithms that can take advantage of those representations, and the detection of implicit parallelism in applications, we will turn our attention to the topic of explicit parallelism. As stated earlier, explicit parallelism is purposefully imposed upon the structure of an application in order to exploit certain control or data structures that are recognized by the application designer. Thus the implementation of explicit parallelism is a conscious task; someone must decide where, when, and how the parallelism is to be applied. To this end, we will discuss here a few of the techniques and tools that are available to aid in this task.

First, we will discuss the concept of a programming environment in which the user can specify and develop both the nature of the task to be performed and the parallel architecture that is desired. After that, we will examine some parallel programming constructs that allow the implementation of the where, when, and how aspects of a parallel solution.

An environment that is suitable for parallel program specification and development must contain support tools that will allow the detailed specification and coding of the individual tasks to be performed, the definition of the structure of the tasks relative to the hardware that is to be used for execution, and the communication protocols and mechanisms for transferring data between tasks and in synchronizing task execution. Let's look at an example of a parallel programming environment, the Poker environment [Snyder84].

In the descriptions of algorithms, there are five characteristics that are commonly exhibited [Snyder84]. These are:

1. A graph consisting of nodes (processors) and edges (communication within the algorithm)

2. A computation set that specifies the parameters associated with the processing at each node

3. A mapping of computations to processors that defines how the application is to be performed

4. A specific action of the synchronization that must occur between the computations on the processing elements

5. A description of the data formats for input, processing, output, and the rates at which these must occur

These five attributes can be used to effectively specify a program that contains both implicit and explicit parallelism. [Snyder84] describes a novel programming environment, called Poker, in which the user specifies computations and then maps them to the appropriate parallel graph using a graphical tool to arrange the graph's nodes and edges. One example application that is given in the reference is an implementation of an algorithm to find the maximum of n(log n) entries using n processing elements. The solution for this problem is arranged as a complete binary tree so that each node compares the values of its two children nodes with its own local maximum and supplies the greatest of the three to its parent node. This algorithm assumes that each node initially has at most roundup(log n) of the values and computes a local maximum for each node. The algorithm structure, shown in Figure 4–21, will find the maximum value in the order of log n steps. To actually make the algorithm workable, roundup(log n) elements are assigned to each node, if n is not divisible by 2. In other words, up to n × roundup(log n) elements can be sorted in order log n time on n processing elements. In the case of Figure 4–21, we can sort 21 elements by using three steps. In step 1, all nodes perform a three-element compare to obtain the local maximum. In step 2, each node in level two performs another three-element compare using its local maximum and the maximums propagated upward from the leaf nodes. Finally, the root performs a similar operation and outputs the maximum result.

In the preceding informal discussion and figure, we have specified all five characteristics as listed above. The graph was specified in Figure 4–21. The computational set and its mapping consists of two elements: the task for the leaf nodes and the task for the interior nodes. We have described the synchronization in both the description in the text and in the illustration. Although the specific type of the data items to be maximized is not explicitly

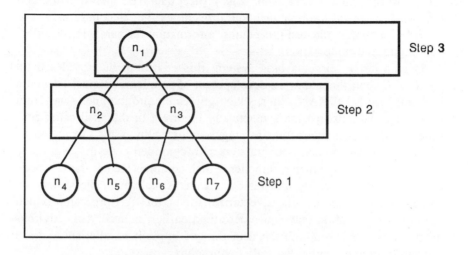

Figure 4–21. **Binary Tree Algorithm to Find Maximum of
7 log 7 Elements**

stated, it is implied that the data items must be compatible to enable the comparisons and that the communication paths must handle these types. In the
Poker environment, a graphical display allows the user to build the graph
from a collection of blank nodes and edges. Next, the communications along
the edges, called ports, are named and defined. At this point, we can specify
the tasks and finally provide the mapping of tasks to nodes in the graph. The
tasks are coded using a data-driven language called XX. *Data-driven* simply
means that read operations must complete before subsequent sequential code
can execute. Thus the synchronization of processing and communication can
be done automatically by a code optimizer due to the data-driven nature of
the programs and the structure and task map of the graph.

In general, the environment described above provides a tool that lets the
application designer see the structure of the desired explicit parallelism.
Another environment for programming parallel systems has been developed
at Rice University [Allen85]. The main emphasis of this environment is to
allow large parallel programs to be developed without having to compile the
entire body of code every time a change or addition is made. This feature
becomes important when there are interprocedural synchronization and

communication parameters that are important for each compilation. The key feature of this environment, then, is its project data base facility that maintains such pertinent information about procedures. The data base saves and provides program code, test procedures, information for parallel processing, and program documentation.

In addition to the data base system, this environment provides three specialized tools that aid in the development of parallel programs. These are an intelligent FORTRAN editor, which guides the programmer away from program constructs that are syntactically incorrect or that will cause runtime problems; an interactive debugger, which allows the correction of interpreted source code in conjunction with compiled code that is already debugged; and an optimizing compiler, which compiles the program sections into a form that is easily integrated with the remainder of the system. In conjunction with these tools, a vectorizer for FORTRAN programs, which uses the vectorization techniques described earlier, is used. This environment, then, addresses both the detection of implicit parallelism and the implementation of explicitly parallel programs.

One of the most influential papers in the past decade on the topic of parallel languages was presented by Hoare [Hoare78]. Entitled "Communicating Sequential Processes," this paper proposed several new programming constructs that could be used in multiprocessing environments. The ideas presented therein have formed the basis for further work, including at least one commercial language for a parallel processor. The details of the Communicating Sequential Processes (CSP) paper are summarized below.

The main premise of the CSP paper is that the actions of input and output form the backbone of concurrent processing. To support this, CSP uses simple and consistent input and output commands that identify the source and destination processes, the source expression, and the target variable. The reduced Backus-Naur form (BNF) syntax for the set of input and output commands is given in Figure 4–22 (for a complete description of CSP and its syntax, consult [Hoare85]). Communication using these I/O facilities is completely synchronous in CSP. Thus a forced rendezvous of sender and receiver will occur when the specified data transfer actually takes place. A process will block if the other involved process is not ready to communicate. The set of I/O commands is part of a larger set that includes commands for assignment, parallel evaluation, normal arithmetic operations, and program control (e.g., repetitive commands).

<input command> : : = <source>? <target variable>

<output command> : : = <destination>! <expression>

<source> : : = <process name>

<destination> : : = <process name>

Figure 4–22. **Partial BNF for CSP I/O Commands**

The major benefit of CSP is realized in its ability to specify concurrent processes that communicate via the I/O commands. The symbol || is used to denote parallel processes, as shown in the BNF for parallel commands in Figure 4–23. The curly brackets, as in [Hoare78], denote zero or more occurrences of the enclosed construct. All processes specified in the parallel command start at the same time and run to completion. The command completes when all of its constituent processes complete. A series of commands, then, is executed serially, with the exception of those processes specified in a parallel command. Also note that processes may be subscripted, thereby allowing the creation of n unique but identical parallel processes in a single command. The individual processes are then referenced, using the appropriate subscript.

Another important CSP construct is called a guard. A guard may appear before any command list and itself contains a series of Boolean expressions and/or declarations, all of which must be satisfied before the command list may be executed. In addition, a guard may contain an input command, a useful way of synchronizing operations. Figure 4-24 gives the BNF for the guarded command. An alternative command will execute only if its con

<parallel command> : : = [<process> {||<process>}]

<process> : : = <process label> <command list>

<process label> : : = <empty> | <identifier> : : | <Identifier> (<label
                      subscript> {, <label subscript>}) : :

Figure 4–23. **Partial BNF for CSP Parallel Commands**

<alternative command> : : = [<guarded command> { [ ] <guarded command> }]

<guarded command> : : = <guard> --> <command list> | (<range> {,<range> })
                                      <guard> --> <command list>

<guard> : : = <guard list> | <guard list> ; <input command> | <input command>

<guard list> : : =   <Boolean expression> | <declaration>
                         {;<Boolean expression> | <declaration>}

Figure 4–24. **BNF for CSP Alternative and Guarded Commands**

stituent guarded commands are satisfied. Repetition is accomplished by preceding an alternative command with a star (*). This denotes 0 or more repetitions.

The combination of these and the other CSP facilities provides us with a powerful tool for expressing parallel applications. As an example of this expressive power, the CSP code for the k interior nodes of the maximum finding algorithm of Figure 4–21 is shown in Figure 4–25.

In the figure, k processes (each called node and referenced by the subscript i) are created, one for each interior (i.e., nonleaf) node. All k of these processes run in parallel, but they may become blocked because of an input or output command. We assume that the nodes are numbered as shown in Figure 4–21. Within each node process are three additional concurrent processes: max, rounddown, and an unnamed process that consists of four

```
[ node (i : 1 .. k) : :   [ max : : maximum
                          || rounddown : : ROUNDDOWN
                          || max! (e1, e2, e3); rounddown!(i/2); max? local max;
                                max! (localmax, node(i*2)?, node (i*2+1)?);
                                node(rounddown?)! max? ]
                          || node (0) : USER ]
```

Figure 4–25. **CSP Code for the Interior Nodes of Figure 4–21**

sequential commands. The process max is defined by "maximum," a set of commands that are not elaborated here. It accepts three elements using an appropriate input statement and returns the maximum value using an appropriate output statement. Max is, then, a kind of subroutine that can be executed concurrently with the other processes in the parallel statement. The process rounddown is defined by the commands specified by "rounddown." and it rounds down the input number and returns the result. Access to rounddown is similar to that described for max. To use either max or rounddown, an output command is issued to the process with the appropriate data. At a later time, an input command is issued to collect the result. Since these are concurrent processes, other commands can run while the routine is acting on its input. This is illustrated in the third process, in which the maximum process is "called" with the three initially allocated values, e1, e2, and e3. We are not concerned with how these values are input to the process. The next statement invokes rounddown to obtain the index for the process of the parent node. This calculation can proceed concurrently with max because the two processes are parallel. Next, the local maximum value is retrieved from max, and max is invoked again with this value and the maximums from the two children nodes. Finally, the maximum for the node is passed to its parent, whose index is input from rounddown. The proper synchronization is maintained, because of the blocking that occurs in the I/O commands. The additional process node 0, which is in parallel with the other k nodes, represents the user that accepts the final result.

One commercial language that has been built upon the concepts presented by CSP is the occam language (Occam is a trademark of INMOS Limited). Occam incorporates the principles of CSP, as well as some expansions that make the basic CSP constructs a complete language. Some of the additions include support for different data types, conditional statements, buffering for I/O commands, and facilities for real-time programming and for interfaces for hardware devices. For a complete description of the occam language and a discussion on its usage, see [Pountain86]. The occam language is the native language for the INMOS Transputer, a parallel machine.

Another language that has been extended for use in a parallel environment is FORTRAN 77. As part of the Pisces project at the University of Virginia, researchers have added various constructs that facilitate the definition, implementation, and synchronization of parallel tasks, as well as expressions to implement special purpose intertask communication facilities [Pratt 85]. The BNF notation for some of these extensions is given in Figure 4–26.

The program unit expressions define new FORTRAN program module types in the same sense that subroutines and functions are FORTRAN program modules. The tasktype keyword identifies the attached program code section as a concurrently executable entity. A tasktype may be communicated with via a signal or a message. If message communication is used, the task must have a handler program unit that specifies the name of the handler routine. The handler declaration identifies the FORTRAN subprogram code that performs the necessary processing for incoming messages. A signal is simply a message that carries no data and that does not require processing by a message handler. The signal declaration, then, defines which incoming message types are to be treated as signals. Send does just what it says: It sends a message to a task. An accept statement is used to control which incoming messages get routed to the handler, which get counted as signals, and which are ignored.

Program Units

    <task type> : : = tasktype <name> <arguments>

    <handler> : : = handler <name> <arguments>

        <arguments> : : = (<formal argument list>) | <empty>

Declarations

    <taskid> : : = taskid <variable list>

    <signal> : : = signal <message type list>

    <handler declaration> : : = handler <message type list>

Statements

    <initiate task> : : = on <cluster spec> initiate <name of task type> <arguments>

    <send> : : = to <task specification> send <message type> <arguments>

    <accept> : : = accept <count> {<message type> <message count>}

        <arguments> : : = (<arguments list>) | <empty>

        <count> : : = <integer> of | <empty>

        <message count> : : = (<integer>) | <empty>

    <parallel do> : : = pardo <normal Fortran Do statements>

    <parallel begin> : : = parbegin <statement sequence> parend

Figure 4–26. **BNF for Pisces FORTRAN Extensions**

Several of the extensions deal with specifying and controlling explicit parallelism. The tasktype program unit explicitly specifies tasks that can run in parallel. The initiate statement controls when and where such a task will be run. Parallel begin specifies that the statements that are contained between parbegin and parend can all run concurrently. The parallel do statement indicates that the loop iterations can be vectorized; that is, they can be run concurrently.

Figure 4–27 gives the extended FORTRAN code for the example of Figure 4–21. The tasktype "interior node" contains the code for each nonleaf node in the graph. We define some local task variables and a two element array to hold the maximum values found by the children nodes. The IF statement and its associated do loop create two children tasks for each interior node task, up to the prescribed node number (given as k in the CSP solution). The children tasks are also of type "interior node" and will run concurrently with the parent. Next, the local maximum is computed, using the max subroutine (not defined here). Again, we do not worry about obtaining the values of e1, e2, and e3. The task then waits for two messages, one from each child, that contain the maximums computed by the children nodes of this task (these could be leaf node tasks that are not shown here). The task forwards to its parent the maximum of the local maximum and the two child values received by the accept statement. The task then terminates.

The handler is defined to accept the child identifier (a 1 or 0 to denote left or right child) and the value calculated by that child. The values are stored in the child array in the common block that is shared with the task. The handler could contain other FORTRAN code if necessary. It is not needed in this case because the only action being performed is data input. Note that the accept statement defines the handler to be used to receive the messages. The function ODD returns a 1 if its argument is odd, a 0 otherwise. The child array is assumed to have indices 0 and 1. Also, it is assumed here that there is a user or master task that kicks off the first interior node task with the value for node number and accepts the final result.

From the example, we can see that this style of parallel programming is more cumbersome than the CSP notation. It is important, however, because of the large investment in FORTRAN code that already exists today. Some of the keywords used in the program of Figure 4–27 are specific to the Pisces parallel execution environment and are not elaborated upon here. [Pratt85] gives a description of the Pisces environment and a more complete definition and example of the FORTRAN language extensions.

```
Task type interiornode (nodenumber)
        real maximum, e1, e2, e3, child (2)
        handler childmax
        common child
end declarations

* Task body
        If  (nodenumber/2 ≥ 1) then
                Do I = 0 to 1
                        On same initiate interiornode
                                (rounddown (nodenumber/2) - I)
                enddo
        endif
        maximum = max (e1, e2, e3)
        accept 2 of
                childmax
        end accept

        to parent send childmax(odd(nodenumber),
                                        max(maximum, child(0), child(1)))

        end
        *end of task body
            Handler childmax(childid, child(childid))
                    real child (2)
                    integer childid
                    common child
            end declarations
            return
            end
```

Figure 4–27. **Extended FORTRAN Code for the Interior Nodes
of Figure 4–21**

Additional explicit parallelism exists in many programming languages, which employ the fork and join or cobegin and coend operations. In these cases, an independent instruction stream can be initiated on another processor and executed until a join or coend statement is encountered. These facilities are usually associated with a multiprocessor system. In fact, the semantics of these operations can be implemented using the CSP and extended FORTRAN languages discussed earlier. See [Baer80] for a discussion of this subject.

5. PARALLEL ARCHITECTURES

Several forms of computer architectures are referred to as parallel or multiprocessors. This chapter is organized as a kind of glossary of these architectures so that the reader can quickly find the discussion on a desired organization. Each section will describe the basic architecture and its variations, will discuss the salient points of that organization, and will identify any special requirements that are related to the use of the architecture.

All of the architectures included in this chapter have one goal, to increase computational power by using replicated processing elements that are connected to and can communicate over some type of network. This goal results from the bounds on performance in traditional von Neumann architectures. First, we are reaching the physical limitations of the current semiconductor design and fabrication processes. We have seen a one hundred times reduction in the size of integrated circuits since their early fabrication. The process will eventually reach the point at which a single processor cannot be made dense enough to ensure the miniscule time delays that mean high speed.

In traditional architectures, we are faced with what is called the von Neumann bottleneck. This results from the use of a single memory interface through which all data and control information (i.e., programs) must pass. Parallel architectures address this problem in a variety of ways, from simply replicating the conventional architecture to utilizing completely new machine organizations.

This variety of factors has spurred the research and development of at least a dozen different forms of new computer architectures, which are surveyed here.

The three essential issues that must be considered for a parallel architecture are: the granularity of the processing elements; the topology of the interconnections between processing elements; and the distribution of control across the processing elements. Granularity refers to the power of each processing element in the architecture ranging from many single-bit processors to a few powerful general purpose ones. Topology refers to the pattern and density of the connections that exist between the processing elements. Control distribution is concerned with allocating tasks to processing elements and synchronizing their interactions. Figure 5–1 illustrates the parallel computer architecture space with these three variables as the axes. As we discuss the various architectures, we will place them in relative perspective by illustrating their approximate position within the space. The criteria used to position the architectures are somewhat subjective and qualitative, because the various architectures are often so different in their structure and operations that a one-to-one comparison of their features is virtually impossible. We see this situation even in less-complex architectures when we consider the very subjective process of benchmarking processors. An attempt is made, therefore, to qualitatively justify the placement of each of the architectures within the organizational space.

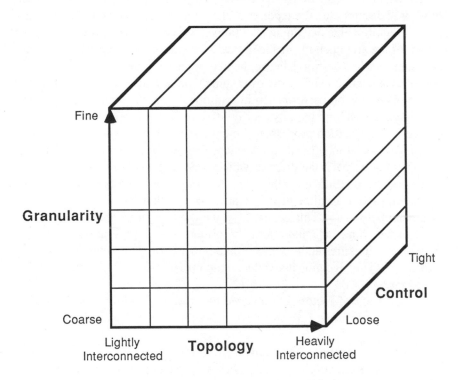

Figure 5–1. **Organizational Space of Parallel Systems**

Multiprocessors

The term *multiprocessor* has many connotations that encompass virtually all architectures with more than one processor. Some surveys of multiprocessor systems cover everything from array processors to data-flow machines. The reader should be aware that this name may imply more than will be included in the multiprocessor definition given here. A multiprocessor architecture, in our context, consists of a number of processors connected through some kind of communication system to a common shared memory, a shared I/O system, and possibly (although not necessarily) to each other. Figure 5-2 shows a typical multiprocessor architecture. The memory and I/O interconnection networks may be separate, as pictured in Figure 5–2, or they may be one and the same. Multiprocessors are also characterized by the existence of a common or global operating system that controls the jobs performed on each processor. Synchronization between jobs is also provided by the common OS. Usually the processors themselves are considered autonomous;

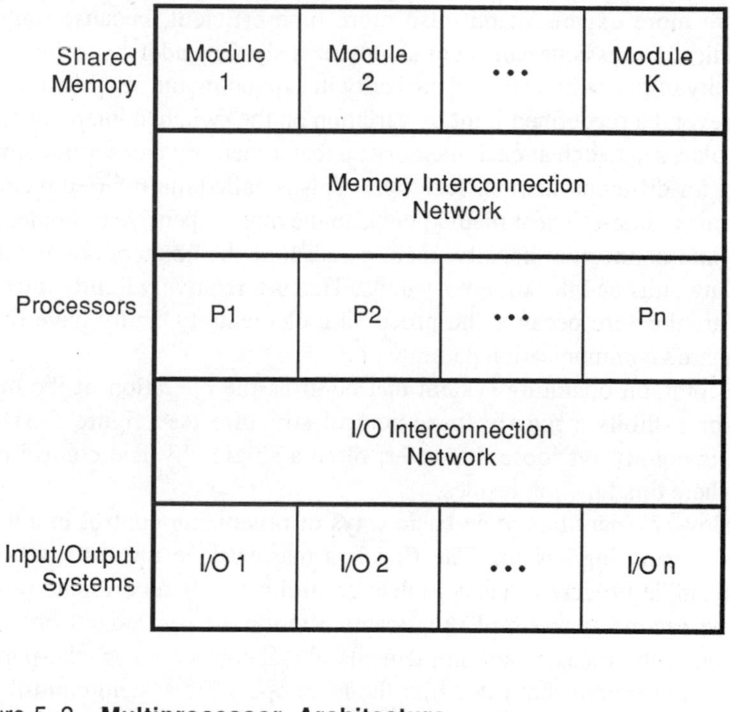

Shared Memory	Module 1	Module 2	• • •	Module K
	Memory Interconnection Network			
Processors	P1	P2	• • •	Pn
	I/O Interconnection Network			
Input/Output Systems	I/O 1	I/O 2	• • •	I/O n

Figure 5–2. **Multiprocessor Architecture**

that is, each processor is free to execute under local control as long as no outside interaction (e.g., I/O access or synchronization with another processor) is required. Finally, most true multiprocessors are composed of a number of like, general-purpose, medium- to coarse-grained processors. The region occupied by multiprocessor architectures in the organizational space is shown in Figure 5–3.

The granularity of a multiprocessor systems can vary from microprocessor-sized components to full-scale CPUs, as found in some large minicomputers and mainframes. Interconnection techniques for multiprocessors generally come in two flavors: shared busses and switches. Shared busses are time-multiplexed so that only one communication session (i.e., memory to processor transaction) can occur at a time. Switched networks allow multiple sessions concurrently, but not with the same memory unit or processor. Generally, shared busses are less expensive but also less time-efficient, because only one memory can be accessed during any bus cycle. Busses are also more readily expanded to accept another processor or memory since only one connection, to the bus, needs to be made. Switches, on the other hand, are more expensive but also more time-efficient, because multiple communication sessions can occur simultaneously. The added cost lies in the complexity of the switch and the difficulty in expanding the number of access points beyond a predefined limit. A variation on the switched interconnection system places a switch at each memory so that a memory can service several requests for different memory locations. This is called multiported memory. It is the most time-efficient method but also the most expensive to implement.

The interconnection density, then, consists of the connections for the n processing units and the k memory units. This is a relatively lightly interconnected architecture because the processing elements typically have only a single shared communication path.

The common operating system that controls the operation of the multiprocessor exhibits a mostly loose-control structure (see figure 5-3). The control is not always loose, however; often a single physical control point exists where this function resides.

[Enslow77] identifies three basic ways of organizing control in a multiprocessor operating system. The first is a master/slave implementation in which a single processor has complete control over all subordinate processors. The second type simply replicates a modified centralized operating system on each processor and implements global control via special-purpose application programs that run under the local operating system control. The third takes the view that all processors are autonomous but that they coop-

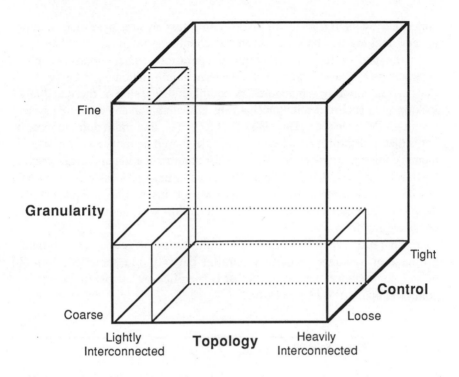

Figure 5–3. **Multiprocessor Region in the Organizational Space**

erate to control the multiprocessor operation. In the last case, the global control is integrated into each local operating system so that the operating system control and associated tables are globally allocated and controlled. This contrasts with the second case, in which control and OS data are local for each processor. Control in a multiprocessor, then, is not performed on an instruction cycle basis and is therefore defined as mostly loose.

Synchronization in a multiprocessor is usually accomplished through the use of memory-based locking techniques. The basic principle is that only one access to any memory location can occur in any one memory cycle. Hence, a test and set operation (read/modify/write memory cycle) on a predesignated memory location can be used to control access to a memory area, thereby enforcing a level of synchronization. The lock in this case has two possible values, on and off, so that a process wishing to access a memory region that is controlled by such a lock can do so with a test and set operation. A more general locking mechanism, called the counting semaphore, is also based upon the use of indivisible memory operations. The operations, characterized as P and V, respectively, decrement and increment memory locations called counting semaphores. A complete discussion of these and other locking and synchronization mechanisms is available in any operating system text (e.g., [Madnick74], [Deitel83], [Soh87]). The important point to remember is that multiprocessors, because they are shared memory systems, use the memory for synchronization as well as for communication and data storage.

In relationship to Flynn's classifications, a multiprocessor is an MIMD machine. Each processor executes its own job instruction stream independently of the other machines, unless interaction with another processor or I/O is required.

In operation, each processor in a multiprocessor gets either a separate program or separate, explicitly parallel parts of the same program. In occam, for instance, each process that is specified by the parallel command could end up on its own processor.

Vector Processors

Vector processors, as their name implies, are adept at performing computations on vector data. Vector parallelism is characterized by the performance of the same operation on all elements of a vector at once. Vector processors, then, do exactly this. In order to perform this function, however, vector processors, or vector processing units, as they are called, are usually attached to and run in conjunction with a scalar processor. The scalar processor is usually a conventional, SISD computer that handles the execution of scalar instructions in the instruction stream. Typically, a vector processor works in conjunction with an attached mainframe or supermini-computer that functions to control the job stream and operation of the vector processor.

The architecture of a vector processor is shown in Figure 5–4. Access to data in memory is accomplished using n bit transfers, where n is the word width of the processor. Memory is usually constructed in banks so that interleaved bank access can be used to increase memory throughput. The vector unit typically handles n element vectors, where each element is n bits wide. Thus each vector register contains n^2 bits. The registers can be grouped together into a number of register files in such a way that k vectors can be obtained from k of the register files simultaneously. Each register file appears as a two-dimensional array of n bit elements. The vector unit contains an array of processing elements, each of which can operate on k, n bit quantities. Thus, on each cycle of the vector unit, k vectors can be operated on to produce a single n element vector result. Each of the processing units can perform a variety of arithmetic and logical functions. In some vector machines, these functions are allocated to special-purpose PEs in such a way that vector operations of different types can proceed simultaneously. In this case, the array of processing elements is two-dimensional. The result of a vector operation is channeled back to the register file or, in the case of special-function PEs, to another PE. This practice, called pipelining, will be discussed in a later section. On a vector machine with n PEs, vectors with up to n elements can be processed efficiently. Larger vectors are broken into parts that can fit into the n element space, and the parts are processed serially through the vector unit. For operations on vectors with less than n elements, some of the PEs are turned off and produce no result for that cycle.

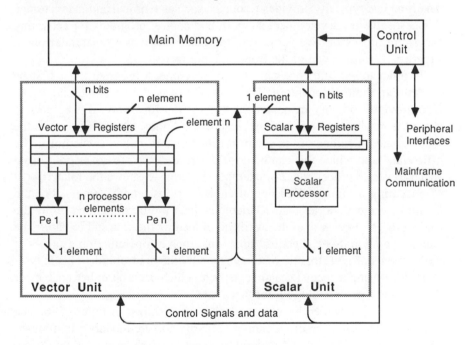

Figure 5–4. **Vector Processor Architecture**

The scalar unit can operate on single-element (n bit) quantities that are obtained from memory or from the vector unit. The unit contains a set of n bit registers, k of which can be accessed simultaneously and fed to the scalar processor. The scalar processor can typically execute all of the functions that a PE of the vector unit can, with the addition of program flow control instructions (e.g., conditional branches, Boolean operations) and other special-purpose instructions. The results from a scalar operation can be deposited back into a scalar register or fed into an element of a vector register. Scalar results can also be deposited in memory.

The control unit may or may not exist as shown in Figure 5–4. Its function may be embedded in the vector and scalar units, along with the necessary peripheral and mainframe interfaces. The control unit must perform two main functions, communication with the outside world and the setup and execution of programs. Outside world communication consists mostly of interactions with the attached mainframe computer, also called the front end. The front end typically provides resources such as terminal and mass storage devices, software development support, and control programs for activating the vector processor. The peripheral interface, shown as a separate arrow in Figure 5–4, is often part of the front-end interface.

In order to execute code on a vector machine, a program must first be loaded into the main memory. The control unit performs this function and also provides memory management support to allow several programs to share the machine's computational resources. Another important task is the loading and unloading of the vector register files from and to memory. The efficiency with which this can be done determines the crossover point from scalar to vector processing. For example, Figure 5–5 shows the relative cost of executing an unspecified operation on various length vectors. For the example, vectors shorter than 10 elements long are best operated on by the scalar processor because of the overhead of loading the data and initiating the vector operation. Special control functions, such as operating on a subset of the elements of a vector, are also managed by the control unit. This is typically done using a special scalar register in which each bit either enables or disables the corresponding PE for that cycle.

The region occupied by vector processors is shown in Figure 5–6. The processing elements are of medium granularity and are moderate in number. The PEs are not considered general-purpose (coarse) because they do not perform all processor functions, and are not of a fine granularity because they operate on multibit elements. The topology of a vector processor is defined here as fairly heavily interconnected, because communication is performed at a low level and without the need for contention to access a

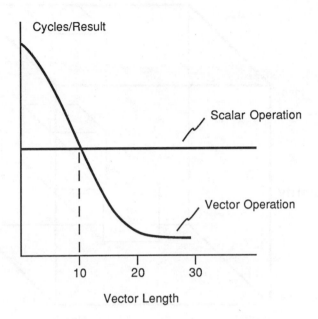

Figure 5–5. **Comparison of Scalar and Vector Processing for a Given Vector Length**

communication path. Also, the scalar unit can readily interact with the vector unit via direct hardware interfaces. The operation of a vector machine is tightly controlled. This must be so in order to provide synchronized data exchanges between memory, the PEs, and the scalar processor.

According to Flynn's categories, a vector processor is an SIMD machine. This is so because all PEs in the vector unit perform the same operation on the individual elements of the vectors. Software for vector machines is developed using vectorizing compilers, which use many of the techniques for discovering implicit parallelism discussed in Chapter 4. The parallelism, then, is obtained not on a process basis, as with the CSP language, but rather on an instruction or loop basis. Most vector machines, in addition to the vectorizing compiler, provide language instructions that specifically call out vector data and operations. These instructions may be explicitly used by the programmer or may be inferred by the data type of the operands.

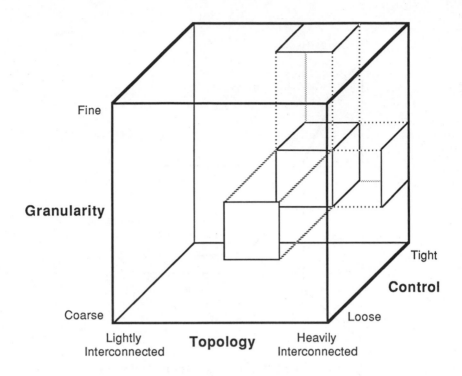

Figure 5–6. **Vector Processor Region in the Organizational Space**

Pipeline Processors

Pipelining is a technique that has been successfully applied to a number of different computer architectures, notably vector and floating-point processors. In a pipelined processor, the execution unit consists of a number of stages, each of which performs a specific function within a specified time period. The summary effect of all of the pipeline stages on a data element constitutes an operation. Pipelines are generally of two types: single-function and multifunction units. Single-function pipelines are capable of performing only one operation on a stream of data. Multifunction pipelines contain reconfigurable links between the pipeline stages, so that different combinations of the stages can perform different operations. Figure 5–7 illustrates these two alternatives.

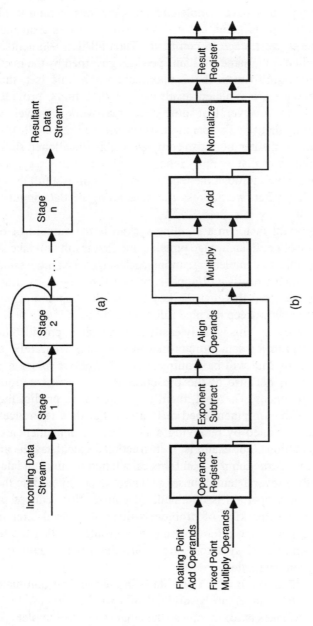

Figure 5–7. (a) Fixed Function and (b) Multifunction Pipelines

All pipelines have the characteristic that the data in the pipe is shifted from stage i to stage i + 1 at the same time for all n stages. At the shift time, all stages in the pipe must have completed their operations on their local data. The intershift time, or pipeline cycle time, cannot be less than the time required for the slowest stage to complete. Thus all data elements move through the pipeline at the same constant speed, as governed by the maximum of the stage processing times. If the maximum stage time is t, then the pipeline can produce a completed result every t time units, provided the pipeline is full. Note, however, that some stages may work iteratively on the pipeline data during that stage's operation, as shown in Figure 5–7(a). This is of no consequence if the iterations can complete within the allotted shift time. Multiplication pipelines that work by repeated addition in this way. Another case, in which each pass through the repeated stage requires a full cycle, will be discussed later, when we address the scheduling of data input to the pipeline.

Another important factor in a pipeline system is the amount of time it takes to fill the pipeline. In an n stage pipeline, the first result will take $sum(t_i: i = 1, ..., n)$ time units to complete, assuming each stage has a processing time of t_i. Each subsequent result will appear every t time units, as described earlier. We can see from this that the key to attaining maximum pipeline performance is to always keep the pipe full of data by supplying a new set of operands on every cycle. This is fairly easily accomplished, provided that we have a linear program or data structure so that we can accurately predict which instruction or data will be required next. A problem arises in many programs, however, because of the presence of branch instructions and irregular data references. The goal, then, is to attempt to predict the next access in light of the aforementioned difficulties. For data references, this problem can be alleviated by removing data reference dependencies from consecutive instructions. For example, if instruction n calculates the address of the operand for instruction n + 1 and this calculation occurs at a late stage in the pipeline, then several "null" entries will have to be shifted into the pipe until the appropriate operand is obtained. Of course, this reduces perfor- mance. Solutions to this kind of problem will be discussed later in this section. Nonlinear program references create a problem called the branch prediction problem, whose symptoms are as just described. Again, this will be discussed later in the section.

If we have a situation in which one stage in the pipeline dominates the processing time, that stage can be divided into smaller stages. In Figure 5–8(a), the stage S_2 takes twice as long as the other stages to complete. Thus a result can be produced only every 2t time units. If we break S_2 into two

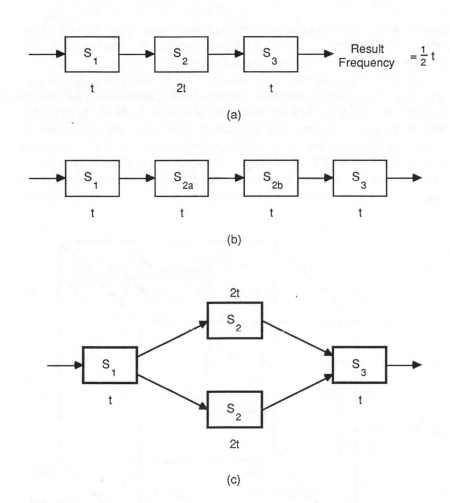

Figure 5–8. **(a) Pipeline with a Dominating Stage and
(b), (c) Improved Performance Pipelines**

stages, each with a processing time of t, then we can produce a result every t
time units, a significant improvement. Also note that it takes no longer to fill
the pipeline of Figure 5–8(b) than it does for Figure 5–8(a). It may be
difficult, however, to find a suitable division within stage S_2 that will yield
such nicely timed substages. Another method used to overcome this problem
is to perform the cumbersome stage in parallel parts, as shown in Figure

5–8(c). Again, we will achieve better throughput and retain the same fillup time. In the parallel case, the S_2 units are alternated for input and output so that a data item is produced from stage 2 every t time units.

Any operation—arithmetic instruction fetch and decoding, or user specified—that exhibits a sequence of uniquely identifiable and separate steps can be pipelined. This may not always be advisable, however, because one step may largely dominate the processing time while the others are insignificant. In the organizational space, pipeline processors are situated as shown in figure 5-9. The granularity of each processing element, in this case of each stage, is moderate to fine. The range is determined by the overall capability of the pipeline (e.g., multifunction pipes may have more complex

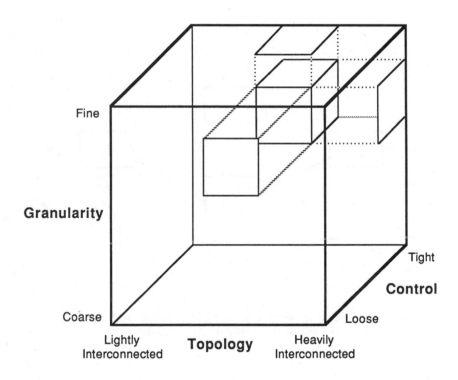

Figure 5–9. **Pipeline Processor Region in the Organizational Space**

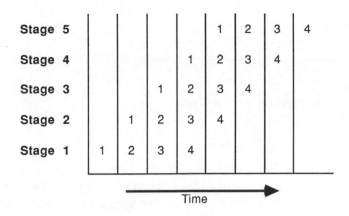

Figure 5–10. **Pipeline Data over Time**

stages). Control in a pipeline is tight because of the synchronization requirement between stages and the mechanisms used to keep the pipe full and manage its operation. The topology of a pipeline is moderately interconnected, because the routing of data may change, though only in a restricted sense, and because data transfers are always synchronous.

Figure 1-25 shows instruction pipelining in an SISD computer. Figure 5–10 provides another view, which shows the data in a pipeline at various pipeline cycle times. Multifunction pipelines can be classified as statically or dynamically allocated. Statically controlled pipelines retain the same functional interconnections for the duration of any given task. Dynamically controlled pipes, on the other hand, can change to perform different operations during a task's execution. Because of the complexity of control in a dynamically controlled pipe, they are seldom used in practice.

For pipelines of the type shown in Figure 5–7(a), a problem occurs during the feeding of elements into the pipeline. For example, the order of visitation of the stages in such a pipeline may be S_1, S_2, S_3, S_2, S_3, S_4 for the pipeline in figure 5-11. It is possible to create a situation in which two data elements are shifted into the same stage at the same time. This can be avoided by following the technique described below.

At the start of an operation in the pipeline, we can create what is called a reservation table that shows which stages will be utilized in which cycle. For Figure 5–11, the reservation table is shown in Figure 5–12. To detect

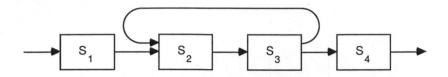

Figure 5–11. **A Pipeline with a Cycle**

conflicts in the use of the pipeline's stages, the reservation table is shifted by one cycle time and superimposed on the original table. If two Xs occupy the same slot, there will be a conflict in the stage indicated if the new data is shifted in on the next cycle. Conflicts further down the line can also be checked by shifting the table by the number of cycles that the next data will appear in the pipe and performing the superimposition. For the example of figure 5-12, two consecutive items may be shifted into the pipeline, whereas three may not. Delays of four cycles or more are acceptable.

Let's now return to the problem of keeping the pipe full as much of the time as is possible. Earlier we mentioned two areas of difficulty, data reference dependencies and the branch problem, and stated that data reference problems could be solved by delaying input of the affected data. The conditions that cause data dependencies in pipelined instruction streams have been

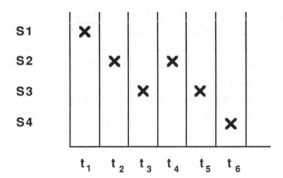

Figure 5–12. **Reservation Table for the Pipeline of Figure 5–11**

generalized in [Ramamoorthy77]. In that work, any pair of operations that may exist simultaneously within the pipe, which access the same data and which contain at least one write, have the potential for causing inconsistent data accesses. This is a result of the existence of several instructions that are in various stages of completion. The combinations, then, are read after write, write after write, and write after read. The write after write problem occurs when writes to a location can happen out of sequence and can be avoided by maintaining a serial write buffer. The write after read problem can be significant if an initiated read does not complete before a write to the same data occurs. This problem is avoided by maintaining the proper read/write synchronization. The read after write problem, referred to earlier, occurs when a later instruction uses the results of an earlier instruction that may not have completed. As stated earlier, this problem can be solved by delaying the start of the reading instruction. Another solution that is sometimes pursued, at the cost of increased control complexity, is to allow the out-of-order execution of instructions. In this case, the dependent instruction is delayed, but subsequent instructions are allowed to enter the pipe (as long as they do not contain dependencies themselves). The dependent instruction is then fed in at a later time, and the proper result sequence is reconstructed after the calculations are complete. In this way, the pipeline is kept as full as possible, and a higher throughput is achieved.

The branch prediction problem is essentially an instance of the read after write problem, in which the write is the result of a branch test and the read is the instruction stream fetch. The branch problem occurs when the execution of a branch condition causes a change in the pattern of instruction fetches. When this happens, all of the partially completed instructions that are in the pipeline after the branch condition must be discarded. The solution to this problem comes in two general forms: predicting the outcome of the branch instruction and incorporating recovery mechanisms to minimize the impact of a branch that is taken. We will discuss the latter solution method first.

All branches, even n way branches, can be decomposed into a series of two-way branches that can be fed into two separate pipelines, one of which fetches the next sequential instruction and the other the branch target. When the branch condition is resolved, the appropriate pipeline can be selected for further execution. The entire pipeline need not be replicated here, only enough to determine the target of the branch. This approach, however, requires twice the number of memory fetches until the branch is resolved. Also, this approach does not take advantage of a common program structure, that is, loops.

When loops are used in an application program, they almost always run for a number of iterations before proceeding to the next code section. The branch at the end of the loop, then, has a much better probability of being taken than not. A solution, then, is to provide a high-speed memory that can hold the loop sequence so that the fetch of instructions can proceed from there. Also, after the branch has been encountered once, it can be identified as such, and the next instruction can be fetched from the beginning of the loop. The loop buffer is not absolutely necessary here, although it will substantially improve performance due to the faster-than-memory speed of the loop buffer. Instructions are sequentially loaded into the loop buffer as they are brought into the pipeline, so that the buffer contains the loop instructions when a branch is encountered. The size of the loop buffer is determined by analysis of the intended system applications to determine the expected loop length and hence the buffer size.

Several methods exist that perform a function similar to the replicated pipeline approach with a smaller cost than for the dual pipeline approach. One mechanism duplicates only the stage that calculates the branch address. The branch target address is then used to fetch the branch target in addition to the next sequential instruction. The branch target is held in a special buffer, and if the branch condition indicates a branch to be taken, the target is fed into the pipe.

A software solution to the branch problem provides a prepare to branch instruction in the instruction stream, along with the address of the branch target before the actual branch instruction. The target is then used, in the same way as for the prefetch mechanism, to get the branch target instruction. A variation on this scheme, called delayed branching, causes all branches to be effective not on the next sequential instruction after the present instruction p, but rather on the $(p + k)$th instruction. Here, k is greater than or equal to the number of pipeline stages that a datum will travel before the resolution of the branch condition is complete. This option appears attractive except for two drawbacks: that it may be difficult for programmers to adjust to the effects of the delayed action of the branch instruction and that the program structure may hinder its use. These problems could be handled by an intelligent compiler that would rearrange the instruction stream by moving all possible branch instructions ahead while ensuring the maintenance of a correct instruction stream.

A final set of strategies deal with predicting the behavior of branch instructions, based upon past performances. Two general methods exist:

history saving and branch target buffers. History saving involves attaching extra bits to the instructions stored in cache memory. The bits are set or reset, based upon the branch history of the instruction. For example, two extra bits could be used: one to hold information on whether the last jump was taken or not (taken/not taken bit) and one to save whether or not the previous prediction was correct (wrong bit). The taken/not taken bit is examined to determine whether to fetch the next sequential instruction (i.e., previous branch not taken) or the branch target (i.e., previous branch taken). When the actual condition of the branch is computed, the wrong bit is updated to reflect whether or not the guess was correct. If the last prediction and the current prediction were both incorrect, then the jump bit is negated, to indicate the change in prediction strategy.

A method that incorporates both prediction and prepare to branch characteristics is the use of a branch target buffer. Here, in addition to the prediction mechanism, an address is also saved that points to the target of the branch. When a branch is predicted, the target address contained in the branch target buffer is used to fetch the target instruction, thereby saving the time necessary to perform the effective address calculation. As long as a branch instruction remains in cache, then, the calculation of the target's effective address will have to be calculated only once, when the branch is first encountered. The strategy used for predicting the status of the next branch is crucial to the success of these, or any, prediction schemes. [Lee84] gives a good account of strategies for prediction and branch target buffer design, based upon the analysis of computer instruction sets and application program behavior.

As mentioned earlier, pipelining has been successfully used in many computer designs, both in initial designs and to improve the performance of existing designs. One design that has achieved popularity in many supercomputers is that of vector pipelines. Vector machines, as defined in the previous section, achieve their speed by operating on sets of data simultaneously. Often, however, several operations on a vector may occur sequentially, using several of the functional vector processing element sets shown in Figure 5–4. The sets of functional processing elements, then, can be arranged as a multifunction pipeline. The action of routing the results of one vector operation to another or the same set of processing elements is called vector chaining. In addition to chaining, the operation of each individual PE can be pipelined, using the methods described earlier. [Ramamoorthy77] discusses pipelining in the context of two vector machine architectures.

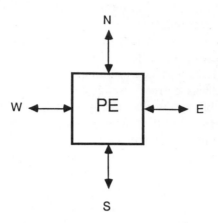

Figure 5-13. **An Array Processor Element**

Array Processors

An array processor is defined as a rectangular grid, each intersection de-noting a processing element, and the lines between intersections denoting communication paths. Each node in the array has the appearance of Figure 5–13 and can communicate with its neighbors on the four compass points: north, south, east, and west. The PEs are interconnected in this regular pattern by a communication system that consists of serial or parallel, point-to-point links. In addition, an array computer typically contains a controlling processor and some array memory to store the array data. A typical array computer architecture is shown in Figure 5–14. We will discuss each of the major elements in the architecture.

The processing power of this type of computer arises from the summation of processing that occurs in the processor array. Each PE in the array is essentially a conventional SISD computer, complete with its own instruction repertoire, local memory, and I/O subsystem. The PEs may be only single-bit machines (i.e., the operands consist of one bit only) or may be as large as 32 bits, or larger. Memory on a PE may be used to store local programs and data or to store the results of calculations or communications with neigh-boring PEs. A PE's I/O subsystem is special-purpose, containing interfaces for its neighbor connections, the control unit and possibly for external (or array memory) data I/O. Each PE must be capable of accepting data on one

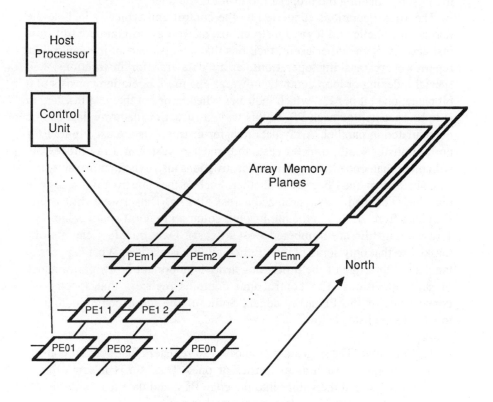

Figure 5–14. **Array Computer Architecture**

of its interfaces, operating on that data through a series of local instructions and releasing the result on one of its interfaces. On each one of these cycles, the PE will be instructed by the control unit over the control unit interface as to what it is to perform. Commands on how to accept and reroute data are also provided in this way. The control unit of the array is usually a fairly powerful conventional computer. Its functions include indicating what operations are to be performed by which PE during a cycle; enforcing an interconnection pattern among the PEs so that the array data is properly routed; controlling the transfer of data to and from the array memory planes; and providing access to the array processor by the outside world through a host computer interface. It also functions to collect the results of certain array operations. The control unit synchronizes the transfer of data between the PEs, by enabling the proper PE transfer commands.

The array operations supported by the control unit typically include the normal arithmetic and logical instructions, as well as program control flow instructions. Some other useful facilities that are also part of the controllers repertoire are masking operations, array data transfer instructions, and special indexing or loop control hardware. The mask operation consists of a bit plane, one bit per PE, which indicates whether or not the next instruction is to be executed on each PE. In this way, a subset of the array data can be manipulated in parallel. Array data transfer instructions are usually transfer north, transfer south, transfer east, and transfer west. For array processors with more than one processing array, instructions also exist to move an entire data plane from one PE array to another. Each of these instructions takes one machine cycle and is synchronized across all PEs. Thus a west shift would shift data from all PEs in the north-south column i to north-south column i − 1 (assuming PEs are numbered west to east). Data transfers can also be masked so that only some of the PEs actually transmit data. What happens to the data at the edge of the processing array is important in the performance of shift operations. The control unit contains registers that specify the connections of the PE array edges. Some of the more common routing topologies are listed below.

1. *Unrouted*: The edges are connected to registers that contain constant values, such as all zeroes or ones. Data shifts in from the registers load the values into the edge PEs, and data that is shifted out of the edge PEs is lost or collected as results.

2. *Cylinders*: If the first and last PEs of row i are connected, we have a vertical cylindrical pattern. Connecting the columns in the same way creates a horizontal cylinder.

3. *Spirals*: By skewing the connections for a cylinder by one or more PEs, we get a series of PE strings. A shift of one connects all PEs in one long string, a shift of two creates two strings with half of the PEs each, etc.

4. *Torus*: If we connect the east-west and north-south edges simultaneously in cylindrical and/or spiral patterns, we will get a variety of torus shapes describing the PE interconnections.

The type of edge interconnection to be used depends upon the application to be programmed. The edge connections are also used to get memory data into and out of the processing array. Typically, data is shifted one row or column at a time (in Figure 5–14, a row at a time).

Memory in an array processor comes in two forms. The first is attached to each PE and serves as local memory to hold intermediate results and/or operands. The second, called the array memory, reflects the structure of the processing array in that there is one n bit memory cell for each PE in the processing array. The memory content maps to the PE in such a way that one memory array plane (a horizontal slice through the three-dimensional memory) contains a complete set of PE data. To allow for the simultaneous transfer of a whole row or column of data, the array memory is usually organized into independent banks that form vertical planes along the north-south axis of Figure 5–14.

The function of the host processor in an array computer is to provide the user's development and execution interface and environment. It is here that the user develops the application program in whatever low- or high-level languages are supported. Support for program compilation and debug are also provided on this machine. In order to execute user programs, facilities also exist for loading and reading the controller's program memory, the array memory, and other special-purpose control parameters.

Array processors are situated in the organizational space as shown in Figure 5–15. The granularity of the processing elements ranges from single-bit to whole-word, and their instruction set typically does not include program control instructions or sophisticated memory addressing mechanisms. Rather, these jobs are performed by the controller unit processor. The PEs themselves, then, are relatively special-purpose and are therefore considered finely grained processors.

The topology of interconnection between the PEs is fairly dense and highly synchronized. It takes at most $2(n-1)$ cycles to exchange data between any two PEs in an $n \times n$ array. Also, if multiple PE arrays exist, the interconnection topology increases in density to allow interarray data transfer. The PEs in this arrangement would each have one or two more I/O ports for data exchange. For each PE, then, there could be four to six separate I/O paths. These factors combine to make an array processor heavily interconnected.

As mentioned earlier, the operation of all PEs is synchronized so that a single operation is performed on all data at once. The control for this action resides within the control unit at all times and is always synchronized with the main processor clock. Similarly, data transfers between PEs must be

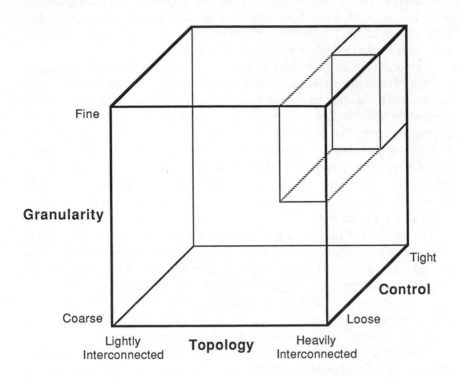

Figure 5-15. **Array Processor Region in the Organizational Space**

orchestrated in such a way that all PEs release and receive their data simultaneously to avoid access conflicts. For these reasons, array processor control is defined as tight. In terms of Flynn's classifications, array processors are SIMD machines, because instructions issued by the controller are worked on simultaneously by all PEs in the array.

In order to program an array machine, extensions to traditional programming language constructs are necessary. Presented here are several of these constructs and their usage.

Naturally, arrays are the basic data type that we are concerned with for array processor applications. Most of the language extensions presented here are aimed at manipulating, storing, and otherwise using array variables.

Although a Pascal-like syntax is presented for the language extensions, no particular base language is assumed. The extensions could apply to any high-level language with the appropriate syntax changes. The extensions here are based upon those for the Pascal language found in [Potter85].

Defining an array for storage in the array memory is important to ensure the proper physical arrangement of the data when allocated to the PEs. For this we define a new key word, *parallelarray*, which indicates the above relationship.

type dataarray = parallelarray[indices] of datatype;

The indices on the array may indicate a multidimensional array. Dimensions of up to three may be physically represented in the array memory by using a number of array planes. Dimensions greater than three, however, would be better handled by breaking them up into several subarrays. The definition of parallel array types also indicates that these arrays may be operated on in parallel, thereby allowing language expressions such as:

$$A := B * C$$

which, in standard Pascal, is equivalent to:

    For i = lowi to highi
      For j = lowj to highj
        A[i,j] = B[i,j] * C[i,j];

for appropriately defined matrices A, B, and C (i.e., the matrices A, B, and C must have the same structure). Some other standard array assignment statements are also augmented to allow their parallel execution. For example, some languages permit array subset assignment operations such as row assignment. A parallel extension to do the same thing would allow the compiler to recognize this fact and assign the array memory locations accordingly. Similarly, it should be possible to move a range of data from one array to the next. This action is useful for working with arrays of the same number of dimensions and the same size in each dimension but with different offsets in the ranges.

Several other statements that are useful for array manipulations are functions to transpose a square array, to shift array elements, to perform logical and arithmetic operations along the elements of an array dimension, and to rotate data in a circular shift manner. All of these functions could be performed with standard programming language operations, but they are specified as special operations in some array processors in order to take advantage of the array-processing hardware and memory organization. To facilitate conditional processing, Boolean array operations are also useful. For example, the expression:

if A < B then (statement using array indices);

compares each element of A and B and, if the condition is met, performs the statement using only the values of the array for which the condition is met.

To perform such functions as the masking of operations and the specification of edge connection topology, special definitions must be provided. These could be provided as reserved array types, with elements for each PE or connection, which map to special-purpose hardware registers or arrays for these functions.

Systolic Processors

All computations involving computers can be classified as compute bound or I/O bound. In I/O bound applications, there is not enough I/O bandwidth to keep the processing elements busy. This is a characteristic of either a poor I/O structure or very large volumes of data. Another factor that can contribute to this problem occurs in applications in which a slight amount of computation is done for every input data item and the results stored away for later use. Thus a variable or its derivative is passed through the I/O system several times, compounding the problem. For compute bound problems, there are not enough computational resources to keep pace with the incoming flow of data, and so I/O must wait. But a compute bound computation can become I/O bound if its implementation exhibits the input-compute-output behavior just described. One approach to solving the I/O (actually memory) bandwidth problem, referred to as the von Neumann bottleneck, is to perform many calculations on the data before returning the results to memory. The implementation of this goal has led to processing architectures referred to as systolic, because they have the characteristic of pumping operands in one end, operating on them for a while, and then pumping them out the other end. Systolic architectures can be thought of as extensions of the concept of pipelining. The extensions occur in two areas: pipelines generally have one-dimensional, unidirectional flow, whereas systolic architectures can have multidimensional and multidirectional flows; and while only partial results flow in traditional pipeline architectures, both partial results and the original data move within the systolic architecture.

Systolic architectures, unlike many of the parallel processing architectures discussed in this chapter, do not have a standard or generic
representation that is common to processors in this class. They do, however,
exhibit certain characteristics that make them unique. The four major factors
[Kung82] are listed below:

1. Each input data item is operated on or used in operations several
   times before returning to memory

2. Many data items are operated on concurrently

3. The operations performed at each step in the system are relatively
   simple, and the PEs used at each step are of a simple, regular design

4. The flow of control and data within the architecture is regular and
   consistent across the PEs

Two systolic architectures are shown in Figure 5–16. The first architecture will perform the convolution computation given a sequence of
weights $\{w_1,w_2,...,w_n\}$ and an input sequence $\{x_1,x_2,...,x_n\}$ to produce the
outputs $\{y_1,y_2,...,y_n\}$. Each y_i is computed by:

$$y_i = w_1 * x_i + w_2 * x(i+1) + ... + w_n * x(i+n-1)$$

In Figure 5–16(a), the values $z(i+1)$ are equal to $z_i + w_i * x_i$, and z_1 is simply
the input stream. The results of the convolution exit at the z_n output. The
weights are input once before the computation begins, and then they stay
throughout at the same cells. During each cycle, an x value is input from the
right, is multiplied by the weight at that cell, and is stored for addition to the
previous cell's result on the next cycle. Thus the x values propagate straight
through to the left and the y values accumulate to the right and exit on the
right. The x values are entered in alternate cycles to allow time for the y
values to accumulate. Thus after a startup time, a y value appears on every
other cycle of the array.

Figure 5–16(b) shows part of a systolic array for matrix multiplication.
This example multiplies a $2 \times n$ matrix by an $m \times 2$ matrix to produce an $m \times
n$ result.

$$A[2 \times n] \times B[m \times 2] = C[m \times n]$$

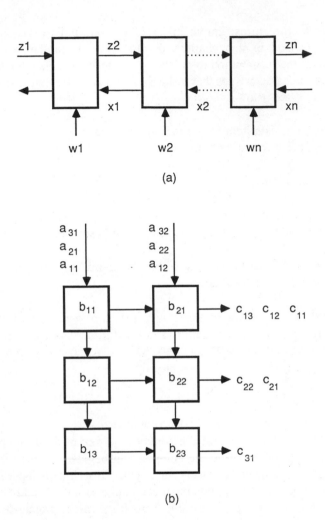

Figure 5–16. **Systolic Architectures for (a) Convolution and**
(b) Matrix Manipulation

The columns of the B matrix are stored across the array elements and remain there until completion. The rows of the A matrix are fed in through the top row of array elements. The results appear on the right, with the columns of the C matrix appearing skewed in time. On each cycle of the array, a row of products is formed and then summed to form an element of the result matrix.

The additions propagate from the left as a kind of wave to force the result out. Thus the next cycle of multiplications cannot begin until the addition wave is completed.

Because of their regular structure and interconnection patterns, systolic architectures have become popular topics in the area of VLSI design. The technology makes the achievement of systolic processors with large numbers of cells realizable. Therefore, any application that is characterized by a regular computation and communication structure and that is compute bound is a candidate for a systolic, VLSI solution.

The region occupied by systolic architectures in the organizational space is shown in Figure 5–17. Because each processing element performs only a few simple operations and because there are many of these elements to implement a given function, systolic architectures are classified as having a fine granular structure.

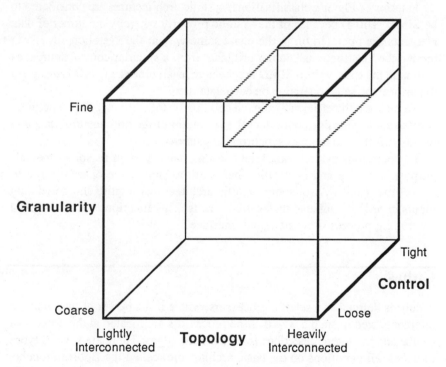

Figure 5–17. **Systolic Architecture Region in the Organizational Space**

Indeed, the use of VLSI to implement the elements of a systolic architecture will contribute to this even further, as it becomes more feasible to build special-purpose solutions in hardware. [Kung82] gives several systolic processing examples and a general discussion of systolic architectures.

Within a systolic processor there may be hundreds of connections between the individual cells. Usually, the transfers that occur over these connections are highly synchronized. Also, the transfer of data is seldom more than a word or byte at a time. The topology of the elements, therefore, is referred to as heavily interconnected.

Control in a systolic processor is defined as tight. This is the result both of the synchronization that is required between the processing cells and of the required setup of the data values at specific cells for some application solutions.

In terms of Flynn's classifications, systolic architectures are considered to be SIMD. This is because of the systolic property whereby a number of data elements are operated on in the exact same way at the systolic cells. Even though the "instructions" do not originate from a singular control source, as is usually the case with an SIMD architecture, each processing cell is designed to perform the same operation on each data item.

To increase the efficiency of each cell in a systolic architecture, pipelining is often used. This does not effect the operation of the architecture; data and results still flow in regular, synchronous patterns.

In operation, systolic implementations usually require some special-purpose interface and controlling hardware to supply the operands and to collect the results. Also, some systolic architectures require staggered data inputs in order to achieve the desired results. This function is provided by a controlling processor or intelligent interface.

Cubes

A cube is defined as a set of n processors, where n is a power of two, that are interconnected in such a way that the processors are located at the corners of a cube and the interconnections form the cube edges. There are several types of cubes, all variations on the basic architecture, called the Boolean n cube, or binary cube. For the Boolean n cube, as shown in Figure 5–18, each of the n nodes contains log n connections to its neighbor nodes. Each node is numbered in such a way that there is a one binary digit difference between any node and its log n neighbors. (Note that the logarithms are all base 2.) This

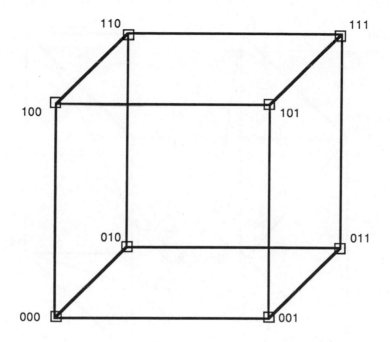

Figure 5–18. **Boolean n Cube Architecture for n = 8**

relationship is given by the following expression, which states that two nodes a and b, numbered by the binary sequences a1,a2,...,a(log n) and b1,b2,...,b(log n), are adjacent to each other if and only if:

$$\text{sum}(\text{lai} - \text{bil}: i = 0 \text{ to } \log n) = 1$$

The distance, in number of arcs that must be traversed to communicate between any two nodes, is bounded by log n.

Cubes with dimensions (i.e., log n defines the dimension) greater than three are generally called hypercubes. Figure 5–19 shows a hypercube with dimension 4 (i.e., it has 16 nodes). A hypercube is still a binary cube and retains all of the binary cube properties. Hypercubes are formed by duplicating three-dimensional binary cubes, such as in Figure 5–18, and then

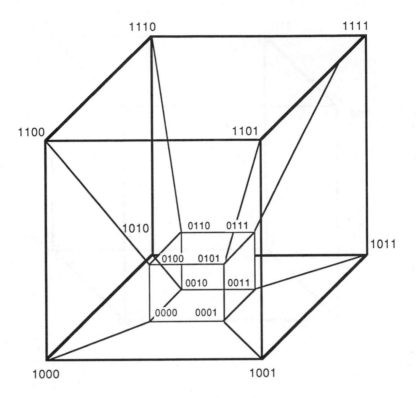

Figure 5–19. **Hypercube with n = 16**

connecting the corresponding corners of every cube. The corners are then renumbered to preserve the adjacency relationship discussed earlier. The processing power of the nodes of a cube are typically on the order of today's midrange microprocessors. Some implementations have slightly less-capable machines that perform only basic operations, while others have high-performance processors. Memory at the cube corners corresponding to the processing elements tends to match the capability of the local node processor. The more simple versions require only limited amounts of RAM, while the more sophisticated ones can contain entire memory management systems.

Interconnection between the nodes in a cube are necessarily point-to-point and may be serial or parallel. The connection scheme of a cube is robust,

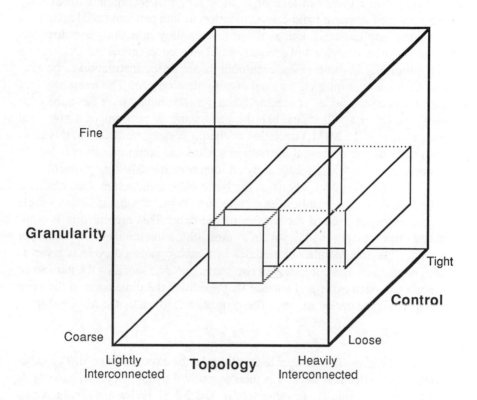

Figure 5–20. **Cube Architectures in the Organizational Space**

because there are several different paths that exist between any two nodes in the cube.

Figure 5-20 places cube architectures in the organizational space. Because the node processors are usually capable of performing a full range of operations and are often as powerful as some 16- and 32-bit microprocessors, we consider cube architectures to be fairly coarse-grained. The complexity of the interconnection at each node in a cube architecture grows slowly (log n) as the number of nodes grows. Also, the communication between nodes does not have to be synchronized, as we will see later. The topology of a cube, therefore, is of medium interconnection complexity.

Control in a cube can take on a wide range of techniques, from fully synchronized operation and communication to independent nodal activities. For some applications, such as those that employ inherently synchronous solutions such as divide and conquer, an SIMD, cube-connected architecture is appropriate. In those cases, each node receives the instruction to be executed from a controller via a global communication path. The interchange of data between the nodes is accomplished synchronously over the cube connections. Other applications, like the processing of portions of a graphical image, call for the MIMD operation of the processing elements. In this case, each node has its own local instruction stream and communication is locally controlled, either by buffering or by an internode handshaking protocol.

There are several variations on the basic cube architecture. One of these, called the cube-connected cycles architecture, contains what is called a cycle of processors at each of the corners of the cube. This architecture is composed of processing modules with, at most, three interconnection points per module. The total number of modules in a cube-connected cycle is given as 2^k. The quantity k is composed of two parts, one that specifies the number of modules in each cycle and another that specifies the dimension of the cube along which the cycles are held. The quantity k is given by the relationship:

$$k \leq r + 2^r$$

where r is the smallest integer that will make the expression hold. The cube-connected cycles architecture is then composed of $2^{(k-r)}$ cycles, each cycle containing 2^r modules. In other words, the $2^{(k-r)}$ cycles are arranged in a binary cube architecture of dimension k–r. A few examples (shown in Figure 5–21) will make this clear.

The introduction of the cube-connected cycles architecture is an attempt to retain a constant interconnectivity value for each node (also called module here) and to create structures that are more suitable for VLSI implementation.

In operation, a cube-connected cycles architecture typically executes in a pipelined fashion within the individual cycles and exchanges data along the cube edges when a pipelined round of computations is complete. The operation of an arbitrary dimension hypercube can be emulated on the cube-connected cycles architecture. Thus this architecture can solve the same kinds of problems as can binary cube or hypercube architectures, at the cost of having some extra processing nodes. This liability is offset by the limit on the interconnection complexity of each node and the resulting VLSI applicability.

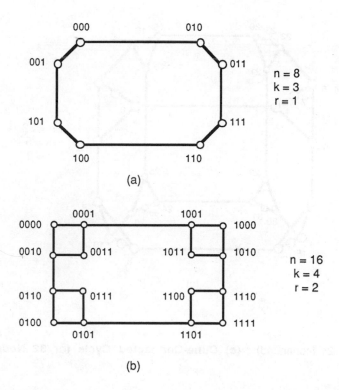

Figure 5–21. **Cube-Connected Cycles for (a) 8 nodes and (b) 16 nodes**

Cube architectures are versatile in that a host of other interconnection patterns among processing elements can be embedded into a cube structure. For the regular n dimensional cube (or hypercube), graphs such as trees, arrays, shuffles, and others can be emulated. For cube-connected cycles architecture, the above graphs, as well as a pipelined operation mode, can be implemented in the cycles.

For further information on cube architectures, the VLSI issues associated with cube implementation and the embedment of other interconnection schemes, see [Preparata81], [Asbury85], [Wu83], and [Sahni81].

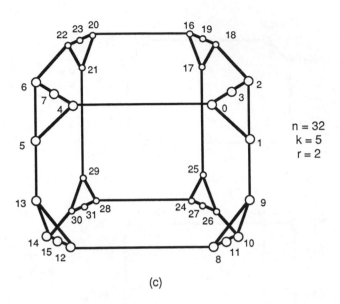

(c)

Figure 5–21 (continued). **(c) Cube-Connected Cycle for 32 Nodes**

Associative Processors

An associative processor is generally characterized by the fact that stored data is content-addressable and that operations can be performed on many of the stored data items in parallel. *Content-addressable* means that the physical or logical address of a word in memory is not necessary to retrieve that word. Instead, it can be retrieved by specifying the contents or part of the contents of the word that can uniquely identify it as the one that is desired. In fact, several items or sets of items that are stored in associative memory can be retrieved in this way. The operations that may be performed on the identified data encompass all of the traditional arithmetic and logical data transformations and some additional ones that are unique to associative processors.

A typical architecture for an associative machine is shown in Figure 5–22. Let's look at each of the major components shown.

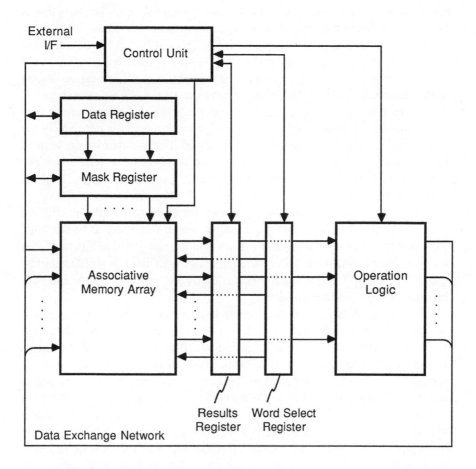

Figure 5–22. **Typical Associative Machine Architecture**

The data register is used to hold the pattern by which the associative memory is to be searched. Its width corresponds to the width of the words stored in the associative memory array, and its contents may be broken into fields of varying lengths. Its contents are loaded from the control unit at the start of an operation cycle, and it may be read back to the control unit or fed into the associative memory array. The data register may also be loaded from the data exchange network as the result of a previous operation. On each operation cycle, its contents are fed, through the mask hardware, to the associative processing hardware in the associative memory array. The data that is conveyed in this step is used to select memory data for operation.

The mask register enables or disables individual bits in the data register when they are passed through to the associative processing hardware in the memory array. If a mask bit is set to a 1 (on) state, then the corresponding bit in the data register is used in the associative memory array's processing. A 0 (off) state in a mask bit indicates that the corresponding data register bit is to be ignored in the associative processing. The mask register is necessarily the same width as the data register. Its contents are fed in either by the control unit or from the data exchange network as the result of a previous operation. Also, its contents may be returned to the control unit or fed into a location within the associative memory array.

The word-select register contains one bit for each word in the associative memory array. These bits are used to select which words are to be searched for a match with the data register bits. A one in a bit position indicates that the word is to be included in the search, a 0 indicates that this word should be ignored. The word select register is loaded by the control register and may be read back into the control unit.

The result of an associative search is reported to the results register, which also contains one bit for each word in the associative memory array. After an associative search, a bit in the result register is set if the corresponding word matched the conditions given in the data word and mask registers, and if the corresponding enable bit was set in the word-select register. This register is read by the control unit to get information on which memory words correspond to the given pattern. The bits in the results register are also used to gate result data from the associative memory array to the operation logic. If a prespecified set of memory words is to be gated, the results register can be loaded by the controller, and memory data can be forced to the operation logic. This process could be coupled with a mask register value of all zeroes so that all data patterns match. The normal matching process could also be used. Also, the loading of the results register by the associative memory array would have to be inhibited to allow the controller-deposited values to remain for the whole cycle. The various combinations of values at the data, mask, results, and word-select registers enable sophisticated word-selection procedures to be performed.

Given that a set of data words has been selected from the associative array memory by the methods just described, the operation logic then can perform the required data manipulations. The operational logic contains two major parts: the data manipulation part and the data switch part. The data manipulation portion consists of an ALU suite that performs the same operation on each data item that passes through. There may not be as many ALUs as there are words in the associative memory array, in which case some data routing must occur. This part of the operation logic is not always present or may appear in a greatly reduced form. The second part of the operation logic, the data switch, serves to route data from one data path to another, essentially allowing the reordering of many memory words in one cycle. Again, the data switch may not always exist in its full-blown form but may merely imply some kind of rudimentary swapping capability. The output of the operation logic unit is routed back to the appropriate word locations in the associative memory array along the data exchange network.

At the heart of the operation of such a machine is the associative memory array. Basically, this unit has the capability to search for matches between its contents and the pattern specified by the data register, according to some matching strategy. The memory array has the property that every word in its contents is searched for a match, simultaneously in a single cycle. This implies that some level of computational power be associated with each and every word location in the memory. This is in fact true and is the basis for parallelism in associative processors. Some typical matching conditions that may be imposed by the control unit include equal to, greater than, less than, not equal to, maximum value, minimum value, between limits, outside limits, and next in sequence. Notice that some operations would require two matching data items, in which case two data registers are supplied. An alternative method would be to perform two searches and then combine the results indicated in the results register. In addition to these conditions, the associative memory array is controlled by the various mask and select inputs described earlier.

As has been intimated in the descriptions of the other portions of an associative processor, the control unit provides matching data, indicates the matching strategy, controls which operands get performed, handles the switching of data connections, enables and masks the search operations, and retrieves results. It also functions as a link to the outside world, responding to operation requests and supplying the results. Built into the control unit and distributed among the processor's elements are the various timing and control circuits necessary for the proper operation of a machine cycle. Also, the control unit may have its own instruction set and CPU to assist in performing control-related calculations and result-melding operations.

As an example of associative processor operation, suppose we had the memory contents indicated in Figure 5–23.

Entry	Employee	Years Service	Salary
1	Employee 1	03	10K
2	Employee 2	13	25K
.	.	.	.
.	.	.	.
.	.	.	.
n	Employee n	17	33K

Figure 5–23. **Example of Associative Memory Array Contents**

We wish to give all employees with 10 to 15 years of service a 10% raise. First we load the data, mask and select registers as shown in Figure 5–24, and perform a greater-than or equal-to match operation. The results appear as shown in the results register of Figure 5–24.

Next, we move the contents of the results register contents to the word-select register and perform a less-than or equal-to search, using the data of Figure 5–25. In this same cycle, the result data words are routed to the operation logic unit. The salary values are upgraded by 10% and the results routed back to the memory.

Obviously, much detail has been left out of this scenario, such as the operation logic control for the first match operation. These questions are part of an individual machine design and would only serve to complicate a description at this level. The general method of operation, however, is illustrated.

[Yau77] classifies associative processor architectures into five categories: fully parallel word-organized, fully parallel distributed-logic, bit-serial, word-serial, and block-oriented. Each of these classes will be discussed briefly.

A fully parallel word-organized associative memory is one that has comparison logic associated with every bit of every word in the associative memory array. When a search is made, the bits of the data register are fed to the corresponding bit logic of each word in the array. A bit-by-bit operation is then performed on every bit in a parallel or cascaded fashion, depending upon the operation. There are also interconnections between the bit logic elements to permit the propagation of results along the word. Note that the

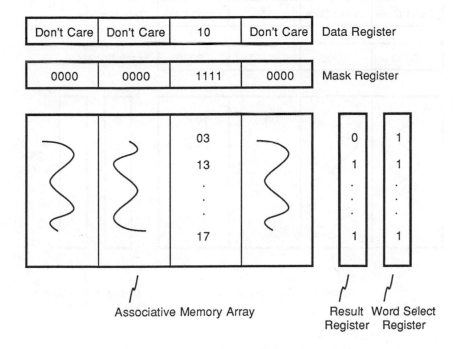

Don't Care	Don't Care	10	Don't Care	Data Register

0000	0000	1111	0000	Mask Register

Associative Memory Array

Result Word Select
Register   Register

Figure 5–24. **Setup and Results for Greater-Than or
Equal-To Match**

comparison operations also occur in a word-parallel mode; that is, each word
is operated on simultaneously by the bit-comparison logic contained within
each word. The term *fully parallel* refers to this fact. Fully parallel word-
organized associative processors are the fastest implementations of this
architecture because of the high degree of parallelism that can be achieved on
every search. They are also the most costly in terms of hardware, however,
because of the replication of the bit logic.

In an effort to reduce the amount of bit-computational logic required for
fully parallel word-organized associative processors while retaining the par-
allel-by-word search feature, fully parallel distributed logic associative
processors were developed. Instead of having the comparison logic incorporated at the bit level of every word, distributed logic associative processors
employ comparison circuitry for groups of bits within words. The groups
are referred to as characters and may range in size from several bits to an

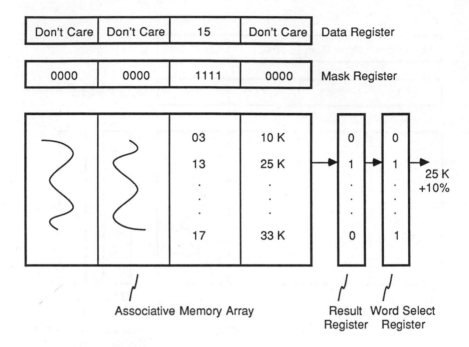

Figure 5–25. **Setup and Results for Less-Than or Equal-To Match and Add 10% Operation**

entire word. The idea is that the individual bits within a character are acted upon sequentially by the distributed logic versus a completely bit-parallel operation. Thus the "distribution" comes about because the single-bit-comparison logic is repetitively used over a string of bits in a character. An n bit word may be divided into m characters so that there are m (versus n) bit-comparison logic elements, a savings of n – m. Of course, the comparison over an entire word will now be slowed by a factor of m, so that if the original, fully parallel word-organized comparison speed was given as s, the fully parallel distributed-logic comparison speed will be m/n × s (assuming the same speed at the bit-comparison logic level). Also, we must add back some complexity to handle the cycling of the character bits through the single bit- comparison logic. This will in turn introduce more delay, so that the speed cited above represents an upper bound on distributed logic performance. These types of associative processors are, however, fully parallel in that all words in memory are acted upon simultaneously in the manner just described. Fully parallel distributed-logic associative processors, then, do not match the performance of fully parallel word-organized processors, but they may be more economical to implement because of the decreased hardware requirements. Note that in order for these machines to be more cost effective than a word-organized machine, we assume that the bit-routing and synchronization circuitry will be less costly to implement than the bit-comparison logic itself. With the maturation of VLSI technology, the cost differential may become insignificant when compared to the total fabrication cost, thus making word-organized architectures more feasible.

If we extend the concept of distributed-logic architectures to the point that the entire word is a character and there is only one bit-comparison logic element per word, then we have what is known as a bit-serial associative processor. The mode of operation is exactly like that described for distributed-logic associative architectures, except that there are no parallel operations that occur within words. The speed of this type of processor, then, is $1/n$ times the original word-organized speed.

Some improvement in distributed-logic and bit-serial architecture speed can be achieved by using multiple-bit-comparison logic (byte at a time, for example). Thus, for a l-bit-wide comparison logic element, of which there are m per word, the speed versus a word-organized machine is bounded by $(1 \times m)/n \times s$. These solutions do slightly increase complexity, however, because an l-bit data path and synchronization logic are now required.

Word-serial associative processors contain only one set of n bit-comparison logic elements. Comparisons on the entire array of words must occur one at a time through the entire memory array. Thus, if we have k words in our array, this architecture will perform at $1/k$ of the word-organized speed. Note that this architecture is nothing more than the hardware implementation of a software loop that sequentially compares each memory word.

The combination of several word-serial associative units that share control and data inputs and outputs within a single memory array create what is called a block-associative memory. Conceptually, these processors work on subsets of the entire memory set, each word-comparison logic element working serially on a block of data. If we segment the total memory into b blocks, each with its own word-comparison logic, we will achieve a comparative speed of $b/k \times s$. Originally, this architecture was proposed for use with rotating mass storage devices, where a comparison logic unit was associated with each track on the medium.

Granularity of processing in an associative processor is very fine-grained. Processing is on the bit or word level and is highly replicated, at least for the

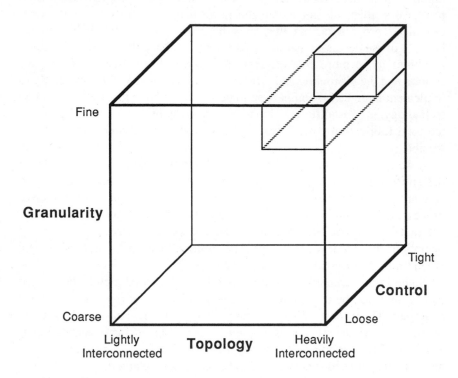

Figure 5–26. **Associative Processor Region in the
Organizational Space**

fully parallel cases. This is shown, in relation to the other classifying traits, in figure 5-26. The topology of an associative processor is fairly heavily interconnected, because of the requirement to route the comparison data to each memory cell and to the collection of the necessary outputs.

Since each search or comparison operation in an associative processor requires detailed setup and timing among the major elements, as well as within the associative memory array, control must be tightly exercised. Also, the programming and operation of the operation logic components must be synchronized with the data transfers to and from the associative memory array. Control, therefore, is tight in an associative processor.

In operation, an associative processor is strictly an SIMD machine. Instructions emanate from the control unit and are simultaneously performed at the various compare logic units.

As mentioned earlier, the heart of an associative processor is the associative memory array and its related setup and result hardware. Often, this portion gives the machine in which it is contained the characteristic of being an associative processor. In this section, we have presented some additional circuitry, the operation logic unit, to represent a form of an associated computational unit. Because of the SIMD nature of the associative memory array, the computational portion (or operation logic) often takes the same form. It is fairly common, then, to see associative processors that are actually combinations of associative memory arrays and vector processing units. This is the basic form pictured in Figure 5–22.

One final important characteristic of the associative memory array is that it can usually be accessed by conventional addressing means, in addition to the associative method that has been described. This feature is essential for loading and unloading blocks of data from other memory sources. Also, some associative memory arrays allow selected bits of a column of words to be extracted, operated on, and returned to memory. Those types of associative memory arrays are often referred to as multidimensional access (MDA) memories. They have the address, data paths, and bit compare logic that allows them to be accessed vertically (e.g., as columns of bits) or horizontally (e.g., word-organized).

This section has present associative processors in terms of their generic architectures and capabilities. More details on specific associative architecture implementations can be found in [Yau77], [Thurber75], [Batcher74], [Goodyear84], and [Batcher82].

Interconnected Network Processors

This section deals with processing systems whose processing elements are interconnected with some kind of data-routing network, with the capacity to transfer many data items simultaneously. These types of networks come in various forms known as shuffle networks, augmented data manipulator networks, and butterfly switches, among others. The processors that use these types of data exchanges are collectively referred to here as interconnected network processors. The types mentioned above will be discussed.

A number of application problems require solutions that have the individual data items in the problem data set interacting with each other in a regular way to produce results. For example, the fast Fourier transform forms the weighted sums of time-sampled data pairs to produce new pairs that are then shuffled and combined again. The architectures to be examined in this section are made to suit these classes of problems.

One of the most well-known interconnection networks is the so-called shuffle-exchange, or perfect shuffle, network. The interconnection pattern for an 8-processor perfect shuffle system is shown in Figure 5–27.

The perfect shuffle is so named because the processors, split into two equal "piles," are shuffled as cards in a deck. The interconnections result because the processors will alternate after a perfect shuffle. The connection

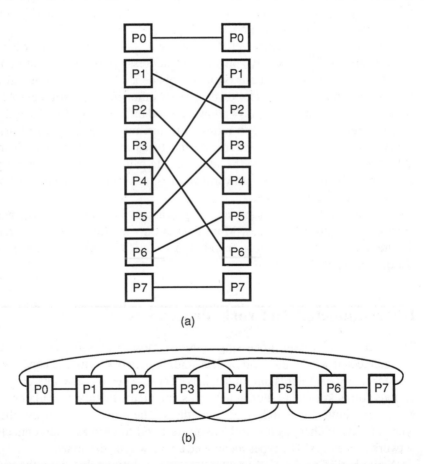

(a)

(b)

Figure 5–27. **(a) Perfect Shuffle Organization; (b) Interconnections for an 8-Processor System**

pattern for the shuffle is given by the following relationship, where i is the number of the present processor and P(i) is the processor that is encountered next in the interconnection:

$$P(i) = 2 \times i \qquad \text{for } 0 \leq i \leq (n/2) - 1$$
$$= (2 \times i) + 1 - n \qquad \text{for } n/2 \leq i \leq n - 1$$

The perfect shuffle interconnection can be used in conjunction with special-purpose processing elements to effect hardware solutions to specific application problems. One such application is the fast Fourier transform. Others include solutions for polynomial evaluation, sorting, and matrix transposition. The use of the perfect shuffle for these applications is illustrated in [Stone71]. We will not present any of these solutions in detail here, but we will highlight the operation of the shuffle for the fast Fourier transform. The basic mechanism of the fast Fourier transform is the iterative calculation of weighted sums. The architecture for this process is shown in Figure 5–28. The boxes labeled L are latches that hold the data on each cycle of the processor. The P boxes are simple processors that perform transformations on the data. For the fast Fourier transform, the processors are simple and perform weighted sums of the two input items, to produce the two output items that are used on the next cycle. On each cycle, data is shifted back into the latches. For a fast Fourier transform of n data samples, this process is repeated log n times to produce the results.

Another use for the perfect shuffle, which is frequently associated with parallel processing and other interconnection schemes, is the hookup between sets of processors and memory. The goal here is not so much to effect a certain data permutation but rather to allow any processor to communicate with any memory. We have already seen, in the crossbar matrix switch, one instance of an interconnection scheme that allows this. One of the major difficulties with the crossbar, however, is the rapid growth rate of the number of connections that must be made when new processors and memories are added (the crossbar has a complexity of n^2 connections). Also, large crossbar switches are difficult to build and expand. As a solution to this problem for large n, multistage switching networks are used.

A multistage switching network consists of a series of switching elements, as shown in Figure 5–29, and the associated connections between the switches. The switches accept a set of inputs and, based upon the state of control line signals, perform a permutation on the order of the input to produce an output. The different switch configurations are used to route incoming data to the desired output path. A series of these switching elements arranged in several columns and connected with a shuffle or other

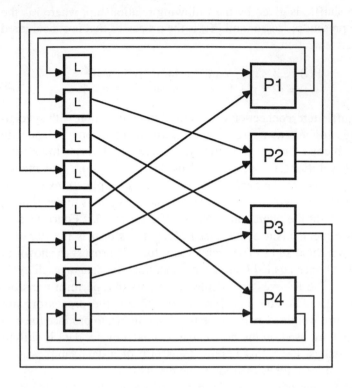

Figure 5–28. **Shuffle Architecture for Fast Fourier Transform**

interconnection network, forms a routing network. One such network, called
a baseline network, is shown in Figure 5–30 for 16 processors and 16
memories. In this network, any processor can communicate with any
memory, with the proper switch settings. Each switch in Figure 5–30 is of
the type shown in Figure 5–29. This type of connection network offers an
improvement in that it has n(log n) complexity versus n^2 for the crossbar.
Addressing of memory modules in Figure 5–30 is accomplished by
providing a string of four controlling bits, one bit for the control line of each
switch in the path. The pattern selects a number of switches to configure a
path to the desired memory. For example, Figure 5–30 shows the switch
settings required to establish a path between processor 3 and memory 11. The
path address is "carried" along the connections with one bit being "used" at
each switch. With this scheme, the path address can propagate with the data.

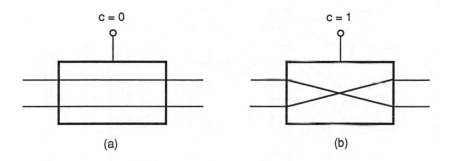

Figure 5–29. **A 2 x 2 Switching Element with (a) c = 0 and (b) c = 1**

Switches for these types of interconnections, sometimes called butterfly connections, can be built to handle 2^k inputs switched to the same number of outputs. In these cases, there are k control lines for each switch.

One drawback of these interconnection networks is that there may be path conflicts among a set of processors and memories that are attempting to use the network concurrently. For example, if in addition to the processor 3 to memory 11 connection in Figure 5–30 we have a need for a processor 7 to memory 10 connection, we will have a conflict at the third and fourth switch columns. Switch conflicts are generally resolved in one of two ways: by an arbitration method with blocking, or by queuing connection requests. The first is normally used in systems that require the establishment of dedicated channels for the duration of a processor-to-memory exchange. The arbitration can be any based on an ordering scheme (e.g., first come first serve, priority, etc.) that causes one request for a path connection to be granted and one to be denied. Other more complex mechanisms involving preemption and path control can be built upon this scheme. The other general solution involves the queuing of communication data units (called messages or sometimes packets) and the related path control bits at the switches themselves. This method does not establish dedicated paths, but it also does not cause blocking of a communication request. These kinds of interconnection networks are referred to as packet-switched. A third method requires different switches that have additional connections that can be controlled independently. These switches allow the rerouting of messages around blocked switches. This is the basis of the next topic, data manipulation networks.

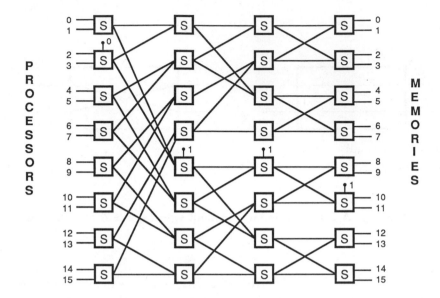

Figure 5–30. **Baseline Network for 16 Processors and 16 Memories**

Another class of interconnection scheme is comprised of various forms of what are called data manipulator networks. Several versions of this class have been proposed, based on different size switching elements and inter-connection patterns. One example, the inverse augmented data manipulator network, is shown in Figure 5–31. In this network, there are 2^n switches in each column, and three input and three output connections on each switch. There are n columns, or stages, of switches, and the connections between stages are as follows:

1. output 1 of switch j in stage i connects to one of the inputs of switch
   $(j - 2^i)$mod n in stage $(i + 1)$mod n

2. output 2 of switch j in stage i connects to one of the inputs of switch
   i in stage $(i + 1)$ mod n

3. output 3 of switch j in stage i connects to one of the inputs of switch
   $(j + 2^i)$mod n in stage $(i + 1)$mod n

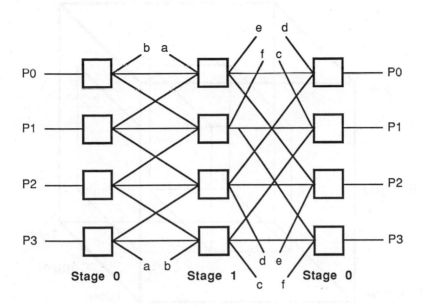

Figure 5–31. **Inverse Augmented Data Manipulator for Four Processors**

This interconnection scheme is called plus-minus 2^i (PM2I), because for stage i, the switches connect to switches in stage i + 1 which are plus and minus 2^i away (as well as having a straight-through connection). Note also that the connections are modulo, or end around, so that there are no special switch configurations at the ends. Routing occurs much as described for the other interconnection networks. [Feng74] provides the basis for much of the work on data manipulator networks.

In the organizational space, interconnected network processors appear as shown in Figure 5–32. Granularity ranges from fairly simple fine-grained processors, such as those used in Figure 5–28, to more sophisticated, general-purpose processors. The topology is relatively lightly interconnected; each processor directly connects to at most several switches. Control in these types of systems varies greatly, from SIMD-type operation, with synchronized data transfers between network stages, to MIMD-type operation, where the interconnections are packet-switched and communication occurs asynchronously.

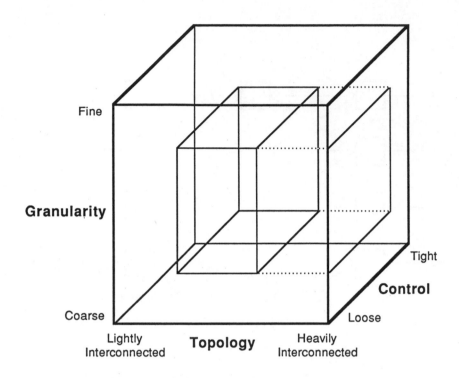

Figure 5–32. **Interconnected Network Processor Region in the Organizational Space**

Data Flow Computers

A somewhat unique kind of parallel processor is called a data flow computer. It is different because it is based upon the notion that a sequence of data, not instructions, should control the execution of the machine. In a data flow architecture, operations on data occur when the operands themselves are ready to be operated on. This is in contrast to more-traditional von Neumann architectures in which the sequence of instructions determines when an operation is to be performed. The concept of data flow is usually represented by data flow program graphs. A graph of this type contains two basic entities, actors and links. An actor consists of an operation and a firing rule. The operation can be almost anything: for example, the addition of two numbers or a conditional test to produce a Boolean value (see Figure 5–33).

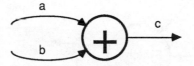

Firing Rule: When a and b are
present, output a+b.

(a)

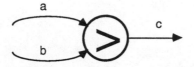

Firing Rule: When a and b are
present, output T if
a>b, F otherwise

(b)

Figure 5–33. **Actors and Firing Rules for (a) Addition and
(b) Comparison**

Actors may also be constructed to implement conditional data flow, as seen
by the switch and merge actors in Figure 5–34. Actors are interconnected by
arcs that are simply data paths that carry operands from point to point. The
operands on an arc are sometimes called tokens. Tokens are consumed and
produced by the actors.

As can be seen by the definition of an actor, the only precondition on the
execution of an operation is that its firing rule is satisfied. This allows operations to take place in arbitrary orders and, provided there are enough
computational resources available, allows operations to occur in parallel. For
example, the instruction sequence in Figure 5–35(a) is implemented by the
graph of Figure 5–35(b). The forks in the data paths imply the duplication of
operands that may be done by additional actors that are not shown.

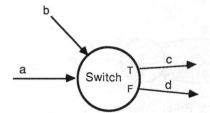

Firing Rule: If a and b are present and b is T,
route a to output c. If a and b are
present and b is F, route a to output d.

(a)

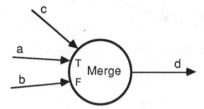

Firing Rule: If c and a are present and c is T,
output a. If c and b are present
and c is F, output b.

(b)

Figure 5–34.   **Actors and Firing Rules for (a) Conditional
Switch and (b) Conditional Merge Operations**

The basic architecture of a data flow computer is shown in Figure 5–36. This architecture is often referred to as a circular pipeline, because of the simultaneous operation of each unit and the routing of data. The instruction execution unit does precisely that: It executes the operations specified by an actor on its associated input data. It is evident, however, that the abstract form of the data flow program graph does not provide a good mechanism for physical implementation. For this reason, most data flow architectures utilize packaged units that contain the operation to be performed, the data to be used as operands, and the destination process for the result. These packages are sometimes referred to as cells and look as shown in Figure 5–37. The operation and operands fields are self-explanatory. The control information field indicates such things as the data types of operands, whether acknowledged operand communication is required, error control information — in short, everything that makes the process of firing an actor complete. The destination information is necessary to identify where the results of this operation are to be sent. With this structure, we can continue to discuss the basic data flow architecture.

Within the instruction execution unit, a cell is assigned to a processing element that performs the required operation to produce the results. The instruction execution unit may contain a multiplicity of PEs of varying capa-

```
if x>y
then
   a = b + x * y;
   c = b / y
else
   a = b / y;
   c = b + x * y
```

(a)

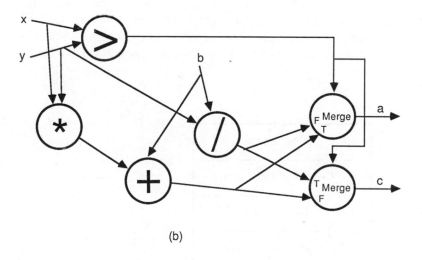

(b)

Figure 5–35.   (a) Instructions and (b) the Data Flow Graph
                Representation

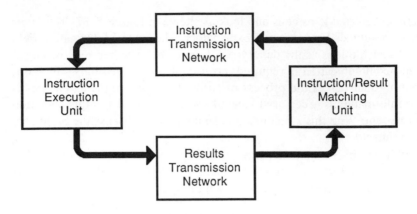

Figure 5–36. **Basic Data Flow Computer Architecture**

bilities. One approach provides n identical PEs that can each perform all of the operations that are specified for the particular data flow computer. In this case, an incoming cell is assigned for execution to any available PE in the instruction execution unit. Other approaches segment the n PEs into k partitions, with the PEs in each partition capable of performing some subset of the operation suite of the data flow computer. The extreme of this arrangement has special-purpose PEs that perform only one operation. These may also be replicated to provide a number of special purpose PEs, possibly based on the

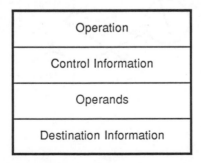

Figure 5–37. **A Typical Cell in a Data Flow Architecture**

complexity of the given operations or the frequency of their occurrence. Parallelism in a data flow computer results from this multiplicity of PEs in the instruction execution unit.

After a cell has been operated on by a PE in the instruction execution unit, it is repackaged and sent out on the results transmission network. The repackaging essentially attaches the operation results to the destination information. The network itself can be of any form. Existing designs have used networks ranging from token ring local area networks to multistage interconnection networks, as described in the previous section.

After the results transmission network, the results enter the instruction/result matching unit. Here, the destination information identifies the cells into which the results are to be deposited as operands. It is within this unit that the data flow between actors in a program graph (such as in Figure 5–35) is coordinated. Thus the destination information specifies the actor cell for which the result is destined, as well as the operand field into which the result will be deposited. The construction of a cell is completed and released to the instruction transmission network when its firing rule is satisfied. The firing rule is part of the cell's control information field. The instruction/result matching unit is sometimes implemented using an associative memory to speed the correlation of results with cells.

Cells that are ready for execution are released to the instruction transmission network. This network is usually of a form that is similar to the results transmission network. Routing techniques that are appropriate to the network type can be used to direct cells to idle or special-purpose PEs.

Queuing of cells and results occurs at the instruction execution and instruction/results matching units. The location and control of the various queues, as well as the interconnection network control, is architecture-dependent.

Programming a data flow computer generally takes one of three forms: graphical, single-assignment, or functional.

The graphical form essentially provides a graphics interface by which the programmer can draw and connect actors, much as illustrated earlier. Capabilities also exist that allow the specification of data types for operands, results, and links, and for the expression of actor operations and firing rules. The graphs that are developed in this way are translated into specifications for the number and types of cells in the instruction/results matching unit.

The single-assignment approach states that a data item cannot be used as both an operand and result within the same program instruction. Programs in this case refer to the more traditional statement approach versus the graphical methods. This is in contrast to multiple-assignment approaches, which imply the existence of a centrally controlled location to store the referenced variable, an assumption that is not followed in data flow computers. Single-assignment programming, then, ensures the independence of each cell's operation so that it may be executed at any time and in any sequence. The crux of the problem is that reference-type data variables are not allowed; only values are circulated and operated upon. Thus an identifier is always associated with a value and not with a variable. If the value changes, we must reassign an identifier for it. Note, however, that the concept of binding an identifier with a value is not mandatory; we do not need to name all data if we do not wish to. Instead, the source and destination paths for values give them identity. An example of this language form, VAL, is discussed in [McGraw82].

The third form of programming for data flow architectures does away with assignment expressions altogether. Called functional programming, this method consists only of expressions to be evaluated and used as input for other expressions. This is somewhat analogous to the single-assignment situation, because only values are produced and worked with. Functional programming languages are discussed in detail in [Backus82].

In terms of Flynn's categorizations, data flow architectures are MIMD machines (when there are multiple PEs present). Also, multiple instructions may be "matching" concurrently, thereby allowing multiple independent processes to run concurrently. Data flow processors are placed in the organizational space, as shown in Figure 5–38.

Granularity of the PEs varies from the utility type that can perform any operation to the simple type that is limited to operations of only one kind. Even the single operand types, however, are word width processors (versus single-bit processors) and must contain enough sophistication to handle cell-type inputs and outputs. The PEs are not, however, as capable as general-purpose machines, because they do not have and do not need special memory addressing capabilities or program control flow logic. Therefore the granularity of data flow machine PEs is classified as medium.

Since the interconnection networks of a data flow machine can vary from local area networks to multistage interconnection networks in complexity, their topology ranges from lightly to moderately interconnected. Also, synchronization between multiple-data transmissions is not maintained; indeed cells or results in the processor are transferred independently of other cells or results. Control in data flow architectures is defined here as loose. This is attributed to the very nature of a data flow computer in that data, not control,

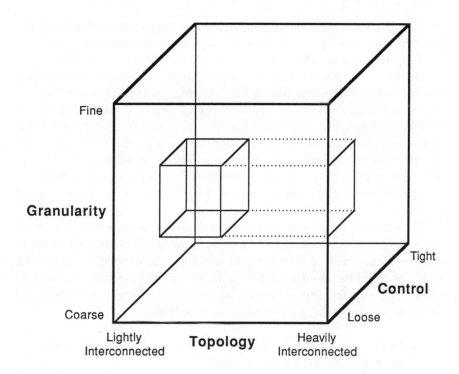

Figure 5–38. **Data Flow Architecture Region in the Organizational Space**

drives execution. Hence, the PEs operate independently, as do the various instruction/result matching processes.

Additional information on data flow architectures in general can be found in [Dennis79], [Dennis80], and [Lerner84]. The programming of data flow architectures is discussed in [McGraw82] and [Backus82].

Very Long Instruction Word (VLIW) Architectures

Most of the parallel and multiprocessor architectures that we have examined thus far produce parallelism by replicating processing resources that are of a relatively conventional nature. VLIW architectures, on the other hand, take an approach that attempts to stretch one aspect of a conventional architecture to achieve parallelism. The aspect of concern here is the widening of the instruction processing portion of a computer to handle instructions that are at least an order of magnitude wider than an ordinary instruction. Essentially, a VLIW machine can be thought of as a multiprocessor system with very tight control and synchronization over each processor's execution and communication. A major difference, however, is that control is not replicated in a VLIW machine; one controller handles the operation of the series of processing elements. Thus instructions for each of the PEs come from portions of the same very long instruction word in the same cycle, but each PE may execute a different instruction. Indeed, each PE may be different or specialized by a specific instruction set. Figure 5–39 shows the conceptual VLIW machine architecture.

The existence of a very long word instruction may suggest a single, wide memory to accommodate the instruction. In reality, however, the memory may be constructed of several banks and allocated to specific processing elements. The PEs are connected by some sort of interconnection network to allow data transfer during instruction execution. Fisher ([Fisher82] and [Fisher84]) characterize a VLIW machine as follows:

1. There is no duplication of control in the machine; a single control unit issues the very long instructions

2. Every very long instruction word contains many operations to be performed on the various PEs

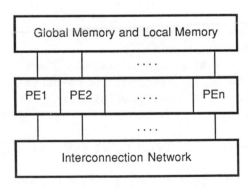

Figure 5–39. **General VLIW Machine Architecture**

3. Each operation performs on the PEs in a small, known number of subinstruction cycles and completes before the next very long instruction cycle

VLIW machines have been mainly conceptual to date, because of the difficulty encountered in programming such architectures. Advances in compiler technology, however, are making it more feasible to program in a high-level language and to take advantage of implicit parallelism within programs. One technique that has been the focus of much research is called trace scheduling. Trace scheduling is the process of compacting a series of normal, high-level language instructions into a very long instruction word. Code compaction, as performed by a trace scheduling compiler, essentially guesses at the probable states of all condition statements within a particular piece of code. The guesses are often based upon the outcome of a conventional compiler, which gives a starting point for guessing the conditional outcomes. Once a likely instruction stream (a trace) is recognized, as much of it as possible is compacted into a single long instruction word. During the trace scheduling process, code is moved about to allow it to be compacted into the instruction word. This necessitates the insertion of new code to maintain the proper execution state after compaction. This code is placed before and after the scheduled trace, as necessary.

Once one trace has been completed, a second is initiated, using the next likely instruction execution path. The new trace scheduling and compaction iteration also works on the added code from the last iteration. The process continues until all code has been compacted. The addition of the state preserving code decreases the efficiency of the end result somewhat, but the justification is that the amount is small compared to the benefits of compaction. The result of this process is the formation of a set of very long instructions that, when executed along with the appropriate operands and correction code, produce the same results as the original program would have.

In operation, VLIW machines are of the MIMD type, but not as usually seen in a multiprocessor. Here, instruction execution is tightly synchronized, and the processing elements are not general-purpose. The topology of the interprocessor connection network is typically a multistage network, as described earlier, thereby forming a moderate interconnection pattern. Figure 5–40 shows the VLIW region in the organizational space.

VLIW machines have not yet become widely accepted as popular parallel processors. Much of the work in this area has concentrated on the develop-

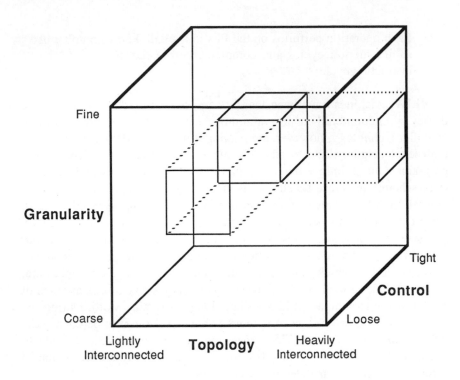

Figure 5–40. **VLIW Architecture Region in the Organizational Space**

ment of high-level language compilers that can uncover enough parallelism to take advantage of the VLIW architecture. The maturation of VLSI technology, however, is assisting efforts to actually build a programmable VLIW machine by allowing several PEs to be fabricated together.

This completes our survey of existing parallel machines and architectures. As we can see from the variety, there are no set rules that must be followed when designing a parallel machine. Often, the intended application suggests a structure for the machine organization. Usually, then, the implementation of parallelism in a computer results in performance gains for the intended applications, at a cost of some performance lost for many others. There is, therefore, no one "best" parallel or multiprocessor organization; each must be judged on its benefits and weaknesses relative to the intended application.

6. PERFORMANCE ANALYSIS

Once we have an idea, design, and/or implementation of a given parallel architecture, we often wish to analyze its performance at various levels. There are three general tools or methods that are traditionally used to accomplish this: analytical modeling, simulation, and benchmarking.

This chapter deals with several aspects of solutions for queuing network models of computing systems. We will cover general queuing model solutions, open and closed network solutions, and the operational analysis technique. After that, we will deal with the subject of simulation, followed by a brief discussion of the practice known as benchmarking.

Analytical Modeling

Analytical modeling involves the mathematical description of a system's operation and the subsequent analysis. Typically, queuing networks are used in conjunction with probability and statistics to form the analytical models. This chapter will discuss the use of queuing theory to evaluate the performance of computer systems. We will not, however, provide rigorous derivations or in-depth analyses, as there are many texts available that do a far superior job to what can be accomplished in a single chapter. Also, a basic background in probability and statistics is assumed for the discussions. Probability and statistics background information can be found in many texts, including [Walpole78], [Papoulis84], and [Trivedi82]. A number of excellent references that cover the material of this chapter in depth exist, notably [Trivedi82], [Lavenberg83], [Lazowska84], and [Kleinrock75,76].

Why should we be interested in analyzing systems? One obvious answer is to be able to judge whether or not a design will meet the expected performance goals. Another is to be able to find system bottlenecks that limit the total effectiveness of the system and to explore alternatives for improvement. We will, therefore, explore some of the methods that are commonly used to achieve these ends.

Most often, we are interested in two types of measures of a system's effectiveness: response time and throughput. Response time refers to the interval between the request for the performance of a unit of work and the subsequent completion of the work. There are many subtleties involved in this definition such as where we begin and end the measurement, and whether we count certain delays that are not actually part of the job processing but contribute to the overall time (e.g., whether we include context switch times in a multiprogrammed system). This measure is also referred to as turnaround time, which implies that all delays are included. In any case, this quantity is a measurement of delay.

Throughput refers to the amount of work that can be accomplished per unit of time. Typical measurements include operations per second, jobs per day, and characters per second. This quantity gives the capacity of a system over time but does not specify how hard the system is working to maintain that rate. For the latter, we refer to the utilization of the system, a measurement of what percentage of a system's total capability is being used at any given time. Often, the utilization measure is applied to a single resource within a computer system. It is typically defined as the ratio of total time to busy time.

Preliminaries

A queue is simply a waiting line in which customers wait for service by some servicing entity. A common example is the line of customers at a bank waiting for a teller. The queue and its associated server(s) together form a queuing model. Note the possible multiplicity of servers. Also, the combination of several simple models (i.e., one queue and its server or servers) also constitutes a queuing model, which is often referred to as a queuing network. Queuing network models are based upon the study of probabilities and are generally not suitable for modeling transient behavior in a system. They are quite suitable, however, for the steady-state analysis of a system, and this is where the majority of queuing models are applied.

Since the study of queuing systems is based upon probabilities, we use random processes to model the parameters we need to characterize the queuing model. The processes with which we are concerned here are called stochastic processes. A stochastic process is defined as any function of time $f(t)$ whose value at any point in time $f(t^i)$ is a random variable. As an example, let $M(t)$ be the sum total of the rolls of a dice taken over time; the value $M(t^i)$ for time ti is a random variable, and $M(t)$ is a stochastic process.

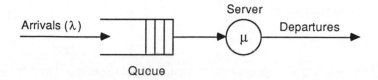

Figure 6–1. **A Simple Queuing Model**

Stochastic processes are important in the study of queuing systems and are used to represent the various parameters of the queuing model.

Consider the simple queuing model of Figure 6–1, with one server. Shown on the drawing are the four characteristics that are important for any queuing model. The arrivals are signified by an arrival process (which is stochastic) with parameter lambda. This process is used to generate arrivals (e.g., customers, etc.) over time for the queuing model. The queue is, as described earlier, a waiting line that develops when the server is busy. Associated with a queue is a queuing discipline that orders the entries in the queue according to some characteristic of the entries in the queue. Examples include priority order, first in first out (FIFO), and last in first out (LIFO). Here, for simplicity, we will use the FIFO queuing discipline. The server is a mechanism that performs the required task on or for the queue entries and produces results. The service time is also characterized by a stochastic process with parameter mu. After servicing, results or serviced entities exit from the model. In the case of a queuing network in which there are a series of cascaded queues and servers, there may be a routing function that determines where the results will go next.

The following discussions consider single-customer-class queuing systems. For an extension to multiple-class models, see [Lavenberg83]. Also, results for different queuing disciplines are given in the references cited earlier.

The arrival and service processes are typically based upon either discrete or continuous probability distributions. One that is commonly used to describe the arrival process in a queuing model is the Poisson arrival process. It is based on a discrete Poisson probability distribution (i.e., its values can only assume discrete values) with parameter lambda given by:

$$P\{N(t) = i\} = \frac{(\lambda t)\, e^{-\lambda t}}{i!} \qquad i = 0, 1, \ldots \qquad (6.1)$$

The parameter lambda represents the arrival rate or number of arrivals per unit time in such a way that

$$E[N(t)] = \lambda t \tag{6.2}$$

This process has the property that the interarrival times are statistically independent random variables, each with parameter lambda. These factors give the Poisson process the property that the probability of the next arrival does not depend upon when the last one occurred; this is called the memoryless, or Markovian, property. This property will become important when we discuss Markov processes.

Another distribution commonly used to represent the service time is the exponential distribution:

$$F(t) = 1 - e^{-\mu t} \tag{6.3}$$

The expected service time is given by:

$$E(s) = \frac{1}{\mu} \tag{6.4}$$

where μ is referred to as the service rate of the server. The exponential service distribution also has the memoryless property.

The choice of which arrival process and service distribution we use for a queuing system depends upon the actual system being modeled. For most computer modeling applications, however, the Poisson process for arrivals and the exponential distribution for servers have been shown to be sufficient.

Queuing Models

Now that we have discussed the basic parts of the simple queuing model shown in Figure 6–1, we will present the standard queuing model notation and analyses for several simple queuing models. This will prepare us for the discussion of queuing systems later in the chapter.

The standard notation for specifying queuing models is given as A/B/C/K/M/Z. This notation is called the Kendall notation, and the elements have the following significance:

A — The interarrival time distribution for arrivals into the queue

B — The service time distribution for each server in the model

C — The number of servers that are servicing the customers in the queue

K — The maximum number of customers that are allowed in the system at any one time

M — The size of the customer population that may enter the system

Z — The queuing discipline used to order customers in the queue

Normally, the shorthand notation A/B/C is used, and the other parameters are assumed to have the default values of infinity for K, infinity for M, and FIFO for Z. The possible definitions for A and B are as follows:

G — General interarrival or service time distribution

D — Deterministic interarrival or service time distribution

M — Exponential interarrival or service time distribution
(M for Markovian)

Also, queuing models may admit a number of different classes of customers with different service requirements. For discussions of these systems, consult the references cited earlier. This chapter will consider only single-customer-class systems.

The notations given in Figure 6–2 are fairly common when dealing with queuing theory and will be used in the discussions of this chapter. The items in parenthesis indicate the units on the quantities.

We will examine two queuing models, the G/G/m and M/M/1 models. The G/G/m model has general interarrival and service time distributions, and can therefore be analyzed only at a high level. The M/M/1 system has specific (exponential) distributions that enable the calculation of more specific results.

The G/G/m model has general distributions for the service and inter-arrival times, and has m servers for the single queue. Because of the generality of the service and interarrival distributions, only a limited number of quantities may be calculated. These are the values for the upper bounds on the average response time and average number of customers in the system for the steady-state solution case. *Steady-state* here means that the system in question has been in operation for a long enough period of time for all transient behavior to have ceased. The formulas for calculating the quantities for the G/G/m model are given as:

$E[w]$ = expected response time

$$= E[s] + \frac{\lambda \, [\, var[t] + var[s]/m]}{2(1 - \lambda \, E[s]/m)} \qquad (6.5)$$

$E[n]$ = expected number of customers in model

$$= E[s] + \frac{m \, \lambda \, E[s] + \lambda^2 \, (var[t] + var[s]/m)}{2(1 - \lambda \, E[s]/m)} \qquad (6.6)$$

If we introduce more specific distributions for interarrival and service times, we can obtain more results on the performance of a given queuing structure. One well-known model is the M/M/1 model. This system is very popular because the process for the interarrival times (a Poisson process) accurately models real-world arrival patterns for many systems, and because the service time distribution (exponential) also reflects many actual service time distributions. For the M/M/1 model, the interarrival process is given by

---

λ – Arrival rate of customers at the queue (customers/unit time)

T – Interarrival time for customers at the queue (unit time)

μ – Service rate of the server(s) attached to the queue (customers/unit time)

n – Number of customers in the model at steady state (customers)

n_q – Number of customers in the queue at steady state

u – Utilization of resources in the model (%)

p – Throughput of model (customers/unit time)

w – Total wait time in the system at steady state, also called response time

w_q – Queue wait time in system at steady state

Figure 6–2. **Notation Used in this Chapter**

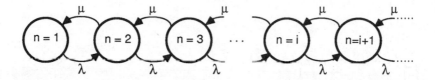

Figure 6–3. **State Transition Diagram for the M/M/1 Model**

(6.1) with an average of lambda customer arrivals per unit time. The service time distribution is as given in (6.3), with average service time given by (6.4). The memoryless property of the interarrival process means that the arrival of a new customer does not depend on the number of customers already in the system. This model, then, fits into the category of a birth-and-death process, which can be represented by a state transition diagram in which the states indicate the number of customers in the system (see Figure 6–3). The state transition diagram shown in Figure 6–3 is a continuous time birth-and-death process that can be solved by finding the so-called flow balance equations for the process. The flow balance equations simply equate the probability of being in a particular state times the rate values of the state's incident edges with the neighboring states and edges for a steady-state process. Thus the flow balance premise says that, for a system in steady state, the flow into a state equals the flow out of that same state. For any state P_i, then, the relationship is given as:

$$\mu P_i = \lambda P_{i-1} \quad \text{or} \quad P_i = (\lambda/\mu)P_{i-1} \quad i > 0 \tag{6.7}$$

where $P_i = P[n=i]$, the probability that there are i customers in the system. At state $n = 0$, we have:

$$\mu P_1 = \lambda P_0 \quad \text{or} \quad P_1 = (\lambda/\mu)P_0 \tag{6.8}$$

Substituting for successive states yields:

$$P_i = (\lambda/\mu)^i P_0 \quad i > 0 \tag{6.9}$$

We know from the axioms of probability theory that

$$\sum_{i=1}^{\infty} P_i = 1 \tag{6.10}$$

so,

$$\sum_{i=1}^{\infty} P_0 \, (\lambda/\mu)^i = P_0 \sum_{i=1}^{\infty}(\lambda/\mu)^i = 1 \tag{6.11}$$

For a stable system, the average arrival rate must be less than the average service rate, else the queue will build to infinity. With this condition, the summation in (6.11) is a geometric series, so we have:

$$P_0 \sum_{i=1}^{\infty}(\lambda/\mu)^i = \frac{P_0}{1 - \lambda/\mu} = 1 \tag{6.12}$$

$$P_0 = 1 - \lambda/\mu \tag{6.13}$$

Thus the probability that there are i customers in the queue is given by:

$$P_i = (\lambda/\mu)^i \, (1 - \lambda/\mu) \tag{6.14}$$

The quantity lambda/mu is called the server utilization and represents the fraction of time the server is busy. The expected number of customers in the system for the M/M/1 model is:

$$E[n] = \sum_{i=1}^{\infty} i \, P_i = \sum_{i=1}^{\infty} i \, (\lambda/\mu)^i \, (1 - \lambda/\mu) \tag{6.15}$$

This can be reduced to:

$$E[n] = [\frac{\lambda/\mu}{(1 - \lambda/\mu)^2}] \, (1 - \lambda/\mu) = \frac{\lambda/\mu}{1 - \lambda/\mu} \tag{6.16}$$

The average amount of time a customer must wait in the queue, assuming there are customers ahead of him, is given as the number of customers ahead of him divided by the average service time (6.17). The expected wait time in the queue is given in (6.18).

$$E[w_q \mid n = i] = i/\mu \tag{6.17}$$

$$E[w_q] = \sum_{i=1}^{\infty} (i/\mu)\, P_i = (1/\mu)\, E[n] = \frac{\lambda/\mu^2}{1 - \lambda/\mu} \tag{6.18}$$

The total expected waiting time for a customer in the system is the sum of the queue waiting time and the time to get serviced:

$$E[w] = E[w_q] + \frac{1}{\mu} = \frac{1}{\mu - \lambda} \tag{6.19}$$

The two previous results can also be obtained by using Little's result, which states that, for a steady-state system, the average number of customers in the system equals the product of the arrival rate times the average waiting time:

$$E[n_q] = \lambda E[w_q] \quad \text{(Little's result)} \tag{6.20}$$

and

$$E[n] = \lambda E[w] \tag{6.21}$$

The expected number of customers in the queue and in service, given in (6.21), is as found in (6.16).

The results for the G/G/m and M/M/1 queuing models, along with other models using different arrival and service parameters and queue characteristics, are useful when modeling the characteristics of an isolated portion of a computer system. For example, the M/M/1 model is often used to represent the queue of jobs and their execution on the CPU of a computer.

Networks of Queues

Although the previous queuing models are useful for analyzing the performance of single elements of a computer system, we need more encompassing methods to deal with combinations of these models to allow the analysis of entire systems. One way of accomplishing this is through the use of networks of queues that, in combination, characterize the total operation of a system. There are generally two forms of queuing networks: opened and closed. Open queuing networks allow entries (arrivals) from and departures to the world external to the queuing network. For example, Figure 6–4 shows an open queuing network, consisting of a queue and server for both the CPU and the I/O subsystem. The arrival process is Poisson, and the two servers are exponential with the indicated service rates. The steady-state solutions for this type of system can be found using Jackson's theorem, which states that if we have Poisson arrivals into the network, if the servers at each queue are exponential servers (assuming that they are identical, if there are multiple servers for each queue), and if there is no delay between the completion of service and the entrance into another queue or departure from the system, then the arrival rate at each queue is given as [Jackson57]:

$$A_i = \lambda_i + \sum_{j=1}^{k} P_{ji} A_j \qquad (6.22)$$

where P_{ji} is the probability of the customer going from server i to queue j, and there are k servers in the network. Also, the expression for the number of customers in each of the queues is given as:

$$P(n_1, n_2, ..., n_k) = P_1(n_1)\, P_2(n_2), ..., P_k(n_k) \qquad (6.23)$$

where $P_i(n_i)$ is found from the steady-state solution for the number of customers in the queue for an M/M/k system with the following:

$$A_i = \text{arrival rate into queue i} \qquad (6.24)$$

$$\mu_i = \text{service rate for server i} \qquad (6.25)$$

$$E[n_i] = \text{average number of customers in a M/M/k model}$$

where

$$\lambda = A_i \text{ and } \mu = \mu_i \qquad (6.26)$$

Thus, for Figure 6–4, we have the following:

$$A_{CPU} = \lambda_{CPU} + A_{I/O} = \lambda_{CPU} + pA_{CPU} = \frac{\lambda_{CPU}}{1-p} \qquad (6.27)$$

$$A_{I/O} = pA_{CPU} = \frac{p\lambda_{CPU}}{1-p} \qquad (6.28)$$

The utilizations of both servers are given as:

$$U_{CPU} = \frac{A_{CPU}}{\mu_{CPU}} \tag{6.29}$$

$$U_{I/O} = \frac{A_{I/O}}{\mu_{I/O}} \tag{6.30}$$

and the throughput of the system is the number of jobs leaving per unit time or:

$$p = (p-1)A_{CPU} \tag{6.31}$$

The average number in the system is the sum of the number in each queue and server, and the average wait time is given by Little's result.

By (6.16): $$E[n_{CPU}] = \frac{A_{CPU}/\mu_{CPU}}{1 - A_{CPU}/\mu_{CPU}} \tag{6.32}$$

By (6.16): $$E[n_{I/O}] = (A_{I/O}/\mu_{I/O})\,(1 - A_{I/O}/\mu_{I/O}) \tag{6.33}$$

$$E[n] = E[n_{CPU}] + E[n_{I/O}] \tag{6.34}$$

by (6.21): $$W = \frac{E[n]}{\lambda_{CPU}} \tag{6.35}$$

Next we will look at an example of a closed queuing network called the Boyse and Warn Straightforward model [Boyse75] [Allen78]. In the model, shown in Figure 6–5, we allow k programs to be active at one time as well as k I/O servers, which handle the reading of memory pages into main memory. The CPU and I/O servers are both assumed to have exponential or constant service time distributions, and the terminals each have think times given by a general distribution. The solution for this model's interesting quantities is given in the Pascal code shown in Figure 6–6. By putting the calculations for such a model into a program, we can easily alter the quantities for the various system parts to determine appropriate improvements. The notation for the calculated quantities is given in the program. Exponential service times for the CPU(s) and I/O device(s) are used.

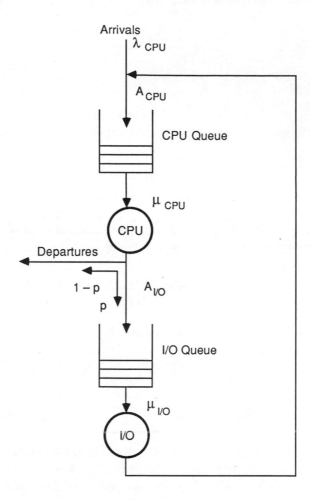

Figure 6–4. **Simple Open Network Model of a Computer**

Other models, in addition to the Boyse and Warn model of multiprocessing, can be constructed using the simple queuing models discussed earlier. Several classical models are summarized nicely in the appendix of [Allen78].

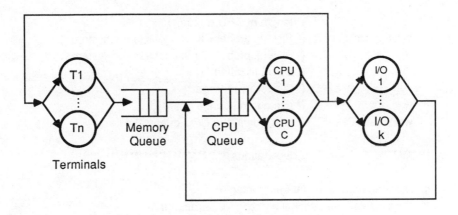

Figure 6–5. **The Boyse and Warn Closed Queuing Network Model**

Figure 6–6. **Pascal Program for the Network of Figure 6–5.**

program Boyse_and_Warn (input,output);

    (* This program is an implementation of the Boyse and Warn straightforward model [Boyse75]. The values for the model parameters are read in and the model statistics are calculated.
    *)

(*************** variable declarations ************************)
var
    i,   (* loop counter *)
    c,   (* number of CPUs *)
    k,   (* multiprogramming level *)
    m,   (* number of CPU quantums *)
    n:integer;   (* number of terminals *)

    e_of_o,   (* E[o], mean service time for each I/O server *)
    e_of_s,   (* E[s], mean service time for each CPU *)
    e_of_t,   (* mean think time at the terminals *)
    lambda,   (* arrival rate at the CPU *)
    lambda_t,   (* average throughput *)

```
    lq,                   (* length of CPU queue *)
    p_of_zero,            (* P[N=0], probability of 0 jobs in the system *)
    p_of_h,               (* P[N=h], probability of h jobs in the system *)
    rho,                  (* CPU utilization *)
    sum,                  (* temporary storage *)
    w,                    (* average response time *)
    wq : real;            (* wait time in the CPU queue *)

(*************** function declarations ***********************)

function factorial(num : integer) : integer;
    (* calculates the factorial of the input parameter *)
var
    fact , j : integer;
begin
    fact := 1;
    for j := 1 to num do
        fact := fact * j;
    factorial := fact;
end;


function power(base : real; exponent : integer) : real;
    (* This function calculates the value of base raised to the exponent power *)
var
    j : integer;
    basetemp : real;
begin
    basetemp := base;
    for j := 2 to exponent  do
        basetemp := base * basetemp;
    power := basetemp;
    if exponent = 0 then power := 1;
end;



function ratio(j : integer) : real;
    (* This function calculates the ratio p_of_n/p_of_zero for
    the values of j from 1 to k
    *)
begin
```

```
    if j <= c then
        ratio := factorial(k)/(factorial(j) * factorial(k-j))
                * power(e_of_s/e_of_o,j)
    else
        ratio := factorial(j)/(factorlal(c) * power(c,j-c))
                * factorial(k)/(factorial(j) * factorial(k-j))
                * power(e_of_s/e_of_o,j);
end;

(******************** main program ***************************)

begin
    writeln;  writeln;
    writeln('***** Boyse and Warn Straightforward Model *****');
    writeln;

(* read input values for model parameters *)
    writeln('enter the model parameters');
    write('number of terminals ?');                         readln(n);
    write('number of CPUs ?');                              readln(c);
    write('multiprogramming level ?');                      readln(k);
    write('number of CPU quantums required per job ?');     readln(m);
    write('mean terminal think time (sec), E[t] ?');        readln(e_of_t);
    write('mean I/O service time (sec), E[o] ?');           readln(e_of_o);
    write('mean CPU service time (sec), E[s] ?');           readln(e_of_s);
    writeln;   writeln;

(* calculate the model output statistics *)

(* calculate sum of ratio P[n]/P[0] for (1 <= i <= k) *)
    sum := 0;
    for i := 1 to k do
        sum := sum + ratio(i);

(* probability of no jobs in the system *)
    p_of_zero := 1/(1 + sum);
    writeln(' probability of no jobs in the system = ',p_of_zero);

(* probability of h jobs in the system and average CPU queue length *)
    lq := 0;
```

```
      for i := 1 to k do
          begin
              p_of_h := ratio(i) * p_of_zero;
              writeln(' probability of ',i,' job(s) in the system = ',p_of_h);
              if i > c then
                  lq := lq + ((i - c) * p_of_h)
          end;
      writeln(' average queue length = ',lq,' jobs');

(* average wait time in the CPU queue *)
      wq := lq * (e_of_o + e_of_s)/(k - lq);
      writeln(' average CPU queue wait time = ',wq,' seconds');

(* arrival rate at the CPU *)
      lambda := k/(e_of_o + wq + e_of_s);
      writeln(' arrival rate at the CPU queue = ',lambda,' jobs/second');

(* the CPU utilization *)
      rho := lambda * e_of_s/c;
      writeln(' CPU utilization = ',rho,' %');

(* the average throughput *)
      lambda_t := c * rho/(m * e_of_s);
      writeln(' average throughput = ',lambda_t,' jobs/second');

(* average response time of the system *)
      w := (n * m * e_of_s/(c * rho)) - e_of_t;
      writeln(' average response time = ',w,' seconds');

end.
```

Operational Analysis

The preceding section deals with queuing systems that are solved by assuming that the important model quantities can be characterized as stochastic processes. The underlying assumption is that the values of the quantities of interest in the model can be accurately represented by known functions of these quantities. This process is arguably imprecise, for we cannot know for sure whether or not the chosen functions are accurate representations of the quantities or processes of interest. An alternative approach to the stochastic modeling presented previously is called operational analysis. This discipline uses the same basic mechanisms to model a system, namely networks of queues and servers. The major difference, then, is how we characterize the parameters that determine the behavior of the model. Operational analysis does just that; it utilizes operationally measured or estimated data to analyze a queuing network. Thus, whereas stochastic models use general distributions to characterize the system parameters over time, operational analysis uses measured quantities that are valid for the specific modeling period. Another important feature of operational analysis is that the hypotheses about system quantities can be tested, so that the analyst knows whether or not the model accurately reflects reality. Thus operational analysis appears more intuitive and does not require extensive background in probability and stochastic processes. Let us now look at some of the techniques for evaluating a queuing model using this method. The following material is largely summary in nature; much more depth can be found in [Denning78] and [Lazowska84].

The operational analysis discipline was popularized in a landmark paper by Denning and Buzen, which collected and presented a great number of practical tools and methods for analyzing queuing systems [Denning78]. The material is this section, and all other works on operational analysis, for that matter, are heavily influenced by the work of Denning and Buzen.

For the basic queuing model of Figure 6–1, there are the following quantities:

T — The interval of time for which the system is to be modeled

A — The total number of arrivals that occur during the period T

C — The total number of customers that have completed service

B — The amount of time a server is busy during the interval

The importance of these quantities is that we can obtain them from the system to be modeled or from estimates of the system environment. These basic quantities are used to calculate the derived quantities for arrival rate, throughput, utilization, and average service time.

$$\text{Arrival rate} = \lambda = A/T \quad \text{customers/second} \tag{6.36}$$

$$\text{Throughput} = P = C/T \quad \text{customers/second} \tag{6.37}$$

Utilization $= U = B/T\%$ (6.38)

Average service time $= \mu = B/C$ seconds/customer   (6.39)

We can work these expressions to obtain the following identity:

$U = P\mu$ (6.40)

which states that the utilization of a system server is a function of the throughput and the average service time. This expression can be applied to individual servers to determine their utilizations if we use the values for the throughput and service time for the server in question. We can also derive Little's law in a similar manner, if we define the following:

T_C — Total customer seconds accumulated in the system

then:

Number of customers in the system $= n = \dfrac{T_C}{T}$ (6.41)

Average response time $= w = \dfrac{T_C}{C}$ (6.42)

We can manipulate these quantities together with (6.37) to obtain Little's law:

$n = Pw$ (6.43)

As with utilization, Little's law and the other derived quantities [(6.36) – (6.39)] can be applied to specific servers in the system by using server-specific quantities. The problem we encounter here is how to obtain the server-specific quantities. An important law that helps us out here is called the forced-flow law. It states that the proportional visit ratio for a server during a particular period is defined by the ratio of customer completions at the device to the total number of system completions.

Visit ratio for device $k = V_k = \dfrac{C_k}{C}$ (6.44)

Thus we have:

$$P_k = V_k P = \frac{C_k}{T} \qquad\qquad\qquad\qquad (6.45)$$

the so-called forced-flow law. This, in combination with the other expressions, can be used to derive server-specific expressions through suitable algebraic manipulations.

One more assumption that facilitates the analysis of networks of queues is the job flow balance assumption. This states that, for suitably long periods of observation, the total number of arrivals is approximately equal to the total number of completions.

$$A = C \qquad\qquad\qquad\qquad (6.46)$$

from the above, we can deduce that:

$$\lambda = P \qquad\qquad\qquad\qquad (6.47)$$

This assumption is equivalent to the flow balance assumption of the previous section on queuing analysis, and it suggests the same kinds of analytical calculations. The advantage of the operational analysis method, however, is that it enables the testing of the flow balance assumption and the quantification of errors that may result from an approximate application of the assumption.

The definitions and expressions given above form the basis for all of the operational analysis techniques for queuing networks. The general techniques are upper and lower bound analysis, mean value analysis, and the flow equivalence technique. These are all discussed in depth in [Lazowska84] and are not covered here.

This concludes the section on analytical evaluation of computer systems using queuing networks. The two general approaches, stochastic modeling and operational analysis, are useful for the general evaluation of a system's performance. We can see, however, that more complex queuing networks become increasingly difficult to analyze using these techniques. To supplement this form of analysis, then, we introduce simulation as a tool for obtaining more detailed analyses of performance measures.

Simulation

We often wish to obtain information on the dynamic behavior of a system under consideration. When using analytic models as described above, certain quantities are difficult to model and complex to calculate. For example, in the queuing models described earlier, it is difficult to analyze the transient behavior of a system or to evaluate conditions such as the interaction of customers in a system. Indeed, these problems are often overlooked in these models by making simplifying assumptions that ease the problem of solution complexity. Thus the previous methods are useful mainly for predicting the steady-state behavior of a system. Simulation models, on the other hand, can effectively characterize detailed system activities within a model that can be evaluated on a computer. A simulation model, then, defines the states and the operators that cause state transitions in such a way that the dynamic behavior of a system can be analyzed.

This is not to imply that the analytical modeling used earlier should be discarded in favor of simulation; each has its place. In a typical scenario, an analytical model is the first step in performing an overall system assessment to find trouble spots and to indicate large-grained changes to a system's structure. After the significant problems have been identified, simulation is appropriate to obtain more detailed analyses of the dynamic behavior of system components.

In a simulation model, we typically characterize the system under question by a set of state variables and by operators that manipulate the state variables. A state implies reference to some underlying independent variable, usually time. There are two basic types of simulation models, discrete and continuous. In a discrete model, changes to the simulation-state variables can be made only at specified (discrete) times. Time management is performed either by continually advancing the simulated time clock or by jumping to the time of the next scheduled simulation event. At each event time, simulation routines are executed. These routines implement the actions that are necessary to model the system at the desired level. In either the continually advancing or jump-to-next-event time management schemes, the simulated state of the system changes at specific times by a prescribed amount.

An example of a discrete event would be the arrival of a customer at a service queue. At time t^-, these are n customers in the queue. At time t, there are n + 1 customers. Thus the arrival of a customer happens "all at once," and the number of customers changes in a discrete manner.

Continuous modeling uses an integration process to maintain the values of the simulation-state variables. Actual changes to the variables are made in such a way that the changes appear to have happened continuously with relation to the independent variable (time). The rise and fall of the voltage level on a conductor is an example of a continuous process, because the value of the simulation variable at time t would be given by a continuous function.

The type of simulation to be run, discrete or continuous, is dependent upon the characteristics to be modeled and the desired results. In general, if the arrival and service characteristics of the system of interest are countable (e.g., number of customers entering and having completed service), then the process is discrete. Otherwise, the process is continuous and simulated accordingly.

Note, however, that combined discrete and continuous modeling is also possible for systems with combined characteristics. In the context of this book, the quantities of interest are mainly discrete (e.g., messages, jobs, bytes, etc.), and so we will concentrate on discrete simulation methods.

Once we have decided on the type of simulation, we can construct a model that represents the processes of interest in our system. The model contains the following:

1. Representative queues and service centers, and their characteristics for the parts of the system under consideration

2. Information about the routing of customers in the system

3. Specification of the simulation variables, data to be collected, and statistics to be recorded

4. Mechanisms for stimulating the model

5. A method for managing the independent simulation variables (e.g., time)

The actual implementation of a simulation model is greatly simplified by using a simulation language or development package. These tools provide built-in support for the definition and characterization of networks of queues and for the gathering of statistical information. They typically also allow the customization of the tools for special-purpose simulation functions. Most popular simulation tools provide the user with several arrival and service time distributions that the user can parameterize for the specific application, a time management function, and a basic statistical collection and analysis package.

Figure 6–7 shows a simulation representation for the simple computer model of Figure 6–4. The representation is that of the SLAM (Simulation Language for Alternative Modeling) language developed by Pritsker and Associates, Inc. [Pritsker79]. The language defines about two dozen symbols

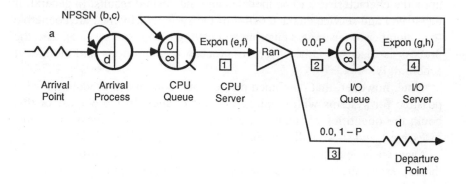

Figure 6–7. **Simulation Model for the Network of Figure 6–4**

that are used to construct system models. We will not discuss them all here, only those shown in Figure 6–7. In the model, arrivals are generated by a create node, labeled "arrival process" in the diagram. The parameters indicate that there should be a total of d customers created at the node and that they should arrive according to a Poisson distribution, with a mean arrival time of b time units. A random number stream, labeled c, is used to generate arrivals from the Poisson distribution, with the first arrival being delayed by the number of time units indicated by a (at the arrival point).

The CPU queue is defined to initially contain no entries and to have an infinite capacity. Entries in the queue are defined in the default ordering, which is FIFO. Arrivals to the CPU queue come from the arrival process and from the I/O server.

After the CPU queue, customers are serviced by the activity labeled CPU server. The number 1 in a box identifies this as activity number one. The service time distribution is defined to be exponential, with mean of e and with entries based upon the random number stream f. The CPU server activity can service one customer at a time. When service of a customer is completed, a new customer is drawn from the CPU queue. If no customers are waiting in the CPU queue, the server remains idle until one appears.

Serviced customers from the CPU server flow to the select node labeled RAN. This node is used to implement a branching point, at which a customer may take one of several paths. Various branching rules may be specified here, including round robin, priority, largest busy time, and longest idle time (of the following server). In Figure 6–7, the label RAN indicates that the branch is based upon a random probability that is identified at the activities. Customers at the branch, then, go to the I/O queue with a probability of P via service activity 2 or to the departure point with a probability of (1 – P) via service activity 3.

The I/O service queue is like the CPU queue, in that it is initially empty, has infinite capacity, and is FIFO-ordered.

The I/O server (activity 4), has exponential service time with a mean of g drawn via the random number stream h. Notice that activities 2 and 3 have zero service times, so that there is no delay for a customer passing through these paths. These activities, then, are used to direct customers to the appropriate downstream nodes.

Customers leaving the model do so at the departure point. The parameter d indicates that the simulation should be stopped after that many customers have exited. Note that this value is the same as for the total number of creations at the create node, so that the simulation will not end until all of the customers have departed. Other values may be used for this parameter, or combinations of parameters, such as ending the simulation after n customers or k seconds, whichever occurs first.

Each graphical representation of a node type translates directly to an SLAM language statement. The sequence of statements, along with some simulation setup, control, and reporting parameters, are then "executed" by an interpreter to actually run the model.

The significance of the random number streams are twofold: to enhance the random nature of the simulation and to ensure repeatability of a simulation's circumstances. The random issue results from the nature of random number generation for simulators on digital computers. Actually what we use are pseudo-random numbers that are generated by a deterministic equation that generates the next random number by using the previously generated one as a seed value for the calculation. Thus we have a stream of pseudo-random numbers that are related by the generating function. We use different pseudo-random streams to drive different distributions so that they are "random" with respect to each other. For example, if we had an arrival and a service distribution that were identical and based upon the same pseudo-random stream, we would have a strict correspondence between the arrival and service times. By using different streams, however, we introduce randomness between the numbers picked from the distributions. If a stream is initialized using a known seed value, the stream is completely reproducible. This is essential in simulation in which we wish to control all model parameters except those in which we are interested. Without this property, we could never be sure whether the obtained results were perpetuated by changes in the model parameters or by variations in the random number streams used in the model's distributions. More information on this and related topics, as well as a full description of the SLAM modeling language, are available in [Pritsker79].

The simulation model discussed above is quite simple in nature and could have been analyzed just as easily using the earlier analysis methods. The real benefits of simulation, then, are seen when we must develop complex models or when we must represent situations that are not easily described by formal mathematical means. For example, suppose we had the structure of Figure 6–7 but that the CPU service distribution had an increasingly large mean service time because of a tiring server. Suppose also that the server reverted back to the original service speed and began decaying again at regular intervals (like a bank teller after lunch). This situation could easily be simulated by defining the service time as EXPON (i + 1, f), where i is the mean value of the previous service time whose value is reset to the original service mean value e at regular intervals by special purpose simulation code.

Benchmarking

A computer benchmark is defined here as a program that, through a series of computations, operations, and actions, produces a relative figure of merit of a system's performance. A benchmark program is typically written in a high-level language, and the frequency and type of statements that appear reflect the characteristics of the intended application. Thus the benchmark is usually not the application code itself but a representative program. Because benchmark programs are typically written in a high-level language, they are as much a test of the efficiency of compiler-generated code as of the system upon which they are executed. A report of a benchmark program's performance on a particular system, then, is much more meaningful if it is accompanied by a statement of the language in which the benchmark was written and a description of the compiler used to generate the executable code. We will discuss the desirable characteristics of a benchmark program and then touch upon some of the more popular benchmark programs.

The construction of a "good" benchmark program can be achieved by using some broad guidelines and some common sense. To this end, we define and discuss several points that are germane to the practice of benchmarking. The points discussed below are based on those in [Purdum86].

Before we pick a benchmark program to run on the system of interest, the exact measurements that we are interested in must be identified. This identification is directly tied to the characteristics of the intended application to be run on the system. It is absolutely necessary, therefore, to have a thorough understanding of the intended application before choosing or developing a representative benchmark. As an alternative to using a single benchmark to rate the system's performance, several benchmarks, each emphasizing different aspects of performance, can be used. In this case, a weighting system is appropriate to determine an overall figure of merit for the system under study.

Another aspect of benchmarking involves determining precisely what each benchmark program tests. Because they are usually written in a high-level language, benchmark programs indirectly measure the efficiency of the compiled code of the compiler used to create them. Once this determination has been made, we can select one or a set of benchmark programs as may be appropriate. Also, we must temper our results with the knowledge that the compiled code efficiency may vary with different compilers. Also, the implementation of programs in the libraries that may be linked with the benchmark code may be a factor in determining the benchmark's performance.

The final two characteristics of a benchmark program are that it should produce a known result and that it should be absolutely repeatable. The production of a known result verifies that the benchmark program at least ran correctly and that no major, undetected errors occurred that could have an impact on the benchmark's execution time. Repeatability is, of course, important for verification of the obtained results.

Thus far, we have been discussing mainly single-program benchmarks. These are defined as single programs that test several aspects of a computing system through the use of certain types or sequences of high-level language statements and subprogram calls. The fact that these benchmarks are single programs is significant because there will be none of the overhead associated with operating system functions (such as context switching) included in the measurement. Another common characteristic of these types of benchmarks is that they often test several aspects of a language's capabilities at the same time.

Benchmarks also exist that test only very specific features of a language. These are constructed in such a way that the language features of interest are isolated as much as possible. These types of benchmarks should also satisfy the conditions outlined above.

Moving out of the realm of single program benchmarks to perform a more comprehensive system test presents additional problems. With multiple program or multiple task benchmarks, the efficiency of the operating system's context switching mechanism, as well as the compiler and hardware efficiency, is tested. Although several "standard" single program benchmarks are available, there has not been much activity in the way of multiple program benchmarks.

As mentioned earlier, several single program benchmarks exist, notably those to test integer and floating-point computations, high-level language statements based on "typical" statement frequencies, and looping and conditional branch constructs. One of the most widely used benchmark programs, called the Whetstone program, was first proposed in [Curnow76] and was originally developed in Algol 60. A Pascal version of the program appears in Figure 6–8, and an Ada version is given in [Harbaugh84]. This

Figure 6–8.   WHETSTONE Benchmark Program, Pascal Version.

```
program WHETSTONE (input,output);

type
    array_dim    = 1..4;
    vector       = array [array_dim] of real;
var
    x1,x2,x3,x4,x,y,z,t,t1,t2 : real;
    e1 : vector;
    i,j,k,l,n1,n2,n3,n4,n5,n6,n7,n8,n9,n10,
    n11,no_of_cycles,cycle_number : integer;

(* benchmark procedures *)

procedure pa(var e : vector);
label
    label_1;
var
    j : integer;
begin
    j:= 0;
    label_1:   e[1] := (e[1] + e[2] + e[3] - e[4]) * t;
               e[2] := (e[1] + e[2] - e[3] + e[4]) * t;
               e[3] := (e[1] - e[2] + e[3] + e[4]) * t;
               e[4] := (-e[1] + e[2] + e[3] + e[4])/t2;
```

```
    j := j + 1;
    if j < 6  then
        goto label_1;
end;

procedure po;
begin
    e1[j] := e1[k];
    e1[k] := e1[j];
    e1[l] := e1[k];
end;

procedure p3(x,y : real; var z : real);
begin
    x := t*(x + y);
    y := t*(x + y);
    z := (x + y)/t2;
end;

begin                        (* main program *)
    no_of_cycles := 10;
    i := 10;
    t := 0.499975;
    t1 := 0.50025;
    t2 := 2.0;
    n1 := 0;
    n2 := 12 + i;
    n3 := 14 * i;
    n4 := 345 * i;
    n5 := 0;
    n6 := 210 * i;
    n7 := 32 * i;
    n8 := 899 * i;
    n9 := 616 * i;
    n10 := 0;
    n11 := 93 * i;

(* here must be code to initialize and start the system timer *)

    for cycle_number := 1 to no_of_cycles do
```

```
begin
(* module 1 - computations with simple identifiers *)
   x1 := 1.0;
   x2 := -1.0;
   x3 := -1.0;
   x4 := -1.0;
   for i := 1 to n1 do
      begin
         x1 := (x1 + x2 + x3 - x4) * t;
         x2 := (x1 + x2 - x3 + x4) * t;
         x3 := (x1 - x2 + x3 + x4) * t;
         x4 := (-x1 + x2 + x3 + x4) * t;
      end;

(* module 2 - computations with array elements *)
   e1[1] := 1.0;
   e1[2] := -1.0;
   e1[3] := -1.0;
   e1[4] := -1.0;
   for i := 1 to n2 do
      begin
         e1[1] := (e1[1] + e1[2] + e1[3] - e1[4]) * t;
         e1[2] := (e1[1] + e1[2] - e1[3] + e1[4]) * t;
         e1[1] := (e1[1] - e1[2] + e1[3] + e1[4]) * t;
         e1[1] := (-e1[1] + e1[2] + e1[3] + e1[4]) * t;
      end;

(* module 3 - using an array as a procedure parameter *)
   for i := 1 to n3 do
   pa(e1);

(* module 4 - conditional jumps *)
   j := 1;
   for i := 1 to n4 do
      begin
         if j = 1 then
            j := 2
         else
            j := 3;
         if j > 2 then
```

```
            j := 0
        else
            j := 1;
        if j < 1 then
            j := 1
        else
            j := 0;
    end;
```

(* module 5 is omitted from the program as it is not run *)

(* module 6 - integer arithmetic *)
```
  j := 1;
  k := 2;
  l := 3;
  for i := 1 to n6 do
     begin
        j := j * (k - j) * (l - k);
        k := l * k - (l - j) * k;
        l := (l - k) * (k + j);
        e1[l-1] := float(j + k + l);
        e1[k-1] := float(j * k * l);
     end;
```

(* module 7 - trigonometric functions *)
```
  x := 0.5;
  y := 0.5;
  for i := 1 to n7 do
     begin
        x := t * arctan(t2 * sin(x) * cos(x)/(cos(x + y) + cos(x - y) - 1.0));
        y := t * arctan(t2 * sin(y) * cos(y)/(cos(x + y) + cos(x - y) - 1.0))
     end;
```

(* module 8 - procedure calls with simple parameters *)
```
  x := 1.0;
  y := 1.0;
  z := 1.0;
  for i := 1 to n8 do
```

```
        p3(x,y,z);

(* module 9 - array references and procedure calls *)
   j := 1;
   k := 2;
   l := 3;
   e1[1] := 1.0;
   e1[2] := 2.0;
   e1[3] := 3.0;
   for i := 1 to n9 do
      po;

(* module 10 - integer arithmetic *)
   j := 2;
   k := 3;
   for i := 1 to n10 do
      begin
         j := j + k;  k := j + k;
         j := k - j;  k := k - j - j;
      end;

(* module 11 - computations with standard math functions *)
   x := 0.75;
   for i := 1 to n11 do
      x := sqrt(exp(ln(x)/t1));
end;(* cycle loop *)
(* here must be code to read the final timer value, calculate a delta time and
calculate thousands of Whetstone instructions as1000 * no_of_cycles/delta
time
*)
end.
```

---

benchmark program deals mainly with floating-point, integer, and array element calculations, as one might expect to find in a scientific program. Looping constructs and subroutine calls are also tested in the program.

After a decade of programming and computer advances, the Whetstone benchmark may have outlived its usefulness as a "typical" program (although it is still widely used to benchmark floating-point and transcendental applications). For this reason, a new benchmark, dubbed the Dhrystone, was developed [Weicker84]. This benchmark reflects a high-level instruction mix that is representative of more recent statistics on instruction frequency. Included in the program are sections on pointer manipulation and record element access, array referencing, and string manipulation. A Pascal version of the Dhrystone benchmark program is given in Figure 6–9.

Both of the benchmarks mentioned above involve instruction mixes and subprogram activations to achieve a composite rating. Another simple benchmark program, called the Sieve of Eratosthenes, is sometimes used to rate basic instruction speed without the overhead of any procedure calls [Gilbreath81] [Gilbreath83]. The program is based upon Eratosthenes's algorithm for calculating prime numbers, and it finds them all up to 16,000. The program is given in Figure 6–10.

The execution of a benchmark gives a result in high-level language instructions per second (Whetstone or Dhrystone instructions per second). On a single CPU machine, this number reflects both the efficiency of the compiled code and the speed of the underlying machine hardware. On computers with multiple processors, the results of these benchmarks will be highly dependent upon the compilers used to generate the executable code. To date, there has been little effort in the area of developing benchmark programs for parallel and multiprocessor computers. Some applications do exist, however, that are sometimes used as benchmark programs. These include programs for the solution of a set of linear equations using Gaussian elimination and other matrix-oriented applications. More comprehensive parallel computer benchmarks will require tests on the communication speed between processing elements, compiler tests for finding implicit parallelism, efficiency tests of the processor's control software (which controls the different portions of a parallel program), and methods for testing architectures with varying numbers of processing elements. The benchmarks discussed earlier, however, do provide a starting point for evaluating parallel systems with traditional programs.

Figure 6–9. **DHRYSTONE Benchmark Program, Pascal Version**

```pascal
program DHRYSTONE (input,output);

type
    enumeration = (ident_1,ident_2,ident_3,ident_4,ident_5);
    one_to_thirty = 1..30;
    one_to_fifty = 1..50;
    capital_letter = 'A'..'Z';
    string_30 = packed array[one_to_thirty] of char;
    array_1_dim_integer = array[one_to_fifty] of integer;
    array_2_dim_integer = array[one_to_fifty,one_to_fifty] of integer;
    record_pointer = ^record_type;
    record_type = record
        pointer_comp:record_pointer;
        case discr : enumeration of
            ident_1:            (enum_comp : enumeration;
                                int_comp : one_to_fifty;
                                string_comp : string_30);
            ident_2:            (enum_comp_2 : enumeration;
                                string_comp_2 : string_30);
            ident_3..ident_5:   (char_comp_1,
                                char_comp_2:char)
        end;

var
    bool_glob : boolean;
    int_glob:one_to_fifty;
    char_glob_1,
    char_glob_2,
    char_index:char;
    array_glob_1 : array_1_dim_integer;
    array_glob_2 : array_2_dim_integer;
    pointer_glob,
    pointer_glob_next : record_pointer;
    int_loc_1,
    int_loc_2,
    int_loc_3 : one_to_fifty;
    char_loc : char;
    enum_loc : enumeration;
    string_loc_1,
    string_loc_2 : string_30;

procedure proc_3(var pointer_par_out : record_pointer);    forward;

procedure proc_6(enum_par_in : enumeration;
                    var enum_par_out : enumeration);    forward;
```

```
procedure proc_7(int_par_in_1,int_par_in_2 : one_to_fifty;
                 var int_par_out : one_to_fifty);   forward;

function func_3(enum_par_in : enumeration) : boolean;   forward;

procedure proc_1(pointer_par_in : record_pointer);
begin
   with pointer_par_in^.pointer_comp^ do
      begin
         pointer_par_in^.pointer_comp^ := pointer_glob^;
         pointer_par_in^.int_comp := 5;
         int_comp := pointer_par_in^.int_comp;
         pointer_comp := pointer_par_in^.pointer_comp;
         proc_3(pointer_comp);
         if discr = ident_1 then
            begin
               int_comp := 6;
               proc_6(pointer_par_in^.enum_comp,enum_comp);
               pointer_comp := pointer_glob^.pointer_comp;
               proc_7(int_comp,10,int_comp);
            end
         else
            pointer_par_in^ := pointer_par_in^.pointer_comp^;
      end
end;

procedure proc_2(var int_par_in_out : one_to_fifty);
var
   int_loc : one_to_fifty;
   enum_loc : enumeration;
begin
   int_loc := int_par_in_out + 10;
   repeat
      if char_glob_1 = 'A'  then
         begin
            int_loc := int_loc - 1;
            int_par_in_out := int_loc - int_glob;
            enum_loc := ident_1;
         end
   until enum_loc = ident_1;
end;

procedure proc_3;
begin
   if pointer_glob <> nil then
      pointer_par_out := pointer_glob^.pointer_comp
   else
      int_glob := 10; proc_7(10,int_glob,pointer_glob^.int_comp);
end;
```

```
procedure proc_4;
var
    bool_loc : boolean;
begin
    bool_loc := (char_glob_1 = 'A');
    bool_loc := bool_loc or bool_glob;
    char_glob_2 := 'B';
end;

procedure proc_5;
begin
    char_glob_1 := 'A';
    bool_glob := false;
end;

procedure proc_6;
begin
    enum_par_out := enum_par_in;
    if not func_3(enum_par_in) then
        enum_par_out := ident_4;
    case enum_par_in of
        ident_1:  enum_par_out := ident_1;
        ident_2:  if int_glob > 100 then
                      enum_par_out := ident_1
                  else
                      enum_par_out := ident_4;
                      ident_3: enum_par_out := ident_2;
        ident_4: ;
        ident_5:  enum_par_out := ident_3;
    end
end;

procedure proc_7;
var
    int_loc : one_to_fifty;
begin
    int_loc := int_par_in_1 + 2;
    int_par_out := int_par_in_2 + int_loc
end;

procedure proc_8(var array_par_in_out_1 : array_1_dim_integer;
                 var array_par_in_out_2 : array_2_dim_integer;
                 int_par_in_1,int_par_in_2 : integer);
    var
    int_loc,int_index : one_to_fifty;
```

```
begin
    int_loc := int_par_in_1 + 5;
    array_par_in_out_1[int_loc] := int_par_in_2;
    array_par_in_out_1[int_loc+1] := array_par_in_out_1[int_loc];
    array_par_in_out_1[int_loc+30] := int_loc;
    for int_index := int_loc to int_loc + 1 do
        array_par_in_out_2[int_loc,int_index] := int_loc;
        array_par_in_out_2[int_loc,int_loc-1] :=
                        array_par_in_out_2[int_loc,int_loc-1] + 1;
        array_par_in_out_2[int_loc+20,int_loc] :=
                        array_par_in_out_1[int_loc];
        int_glob := 5;
end;

function func_1(char_par_in_1,char_par_in_2:capital_letter):enumeration;
var
    char_loc_1,
    char_loc_2 : capital_letter;
begin
    char_loc_1 := char_par_in_1; char_loc_2 := char_loc_1;
    if char_loc_2 <> char_par_in_2 then
        func_1 := ident_1
    else
        func_1 := ident_2;
end;

function func_2(string_par_in_1,string_par_in_2 : string_30) : boolean;
var
    int_loc : one_to_thirty;
    char_loc : capital_letter;
begin
    int_loc := 2;
    while int_loc <= 2 do
      if func_1(string_par_in_1[int_loc],string_par_in_2[int_loc+1])=ident_1 then
        begin
            char_loc := 'A'; int_loc := int_loc + 1
        end;
    if (char_loc >= 'W') and (char_loc < 'Z') then
        int_loc := 7;
    if char_loc = 'X' then
        func_2 := true
    else
        if string_par_in_1 > string_par_in_2 then
            begin
                int_loc := int_loc + 7; func_2 := true
            end
        else
            func_2 := false;
end;
```

```
function func_3;
var
    enum_loc : enumeration;
begin
    enum_loc := enum_par_in;
    if enum_loc = ident_3 then
        func_3 := true;
end;

begin                                   (* main part of program *)

(* initialize variables *)

    new(pointer_glob_next);
    new(pointer_glob);
    pointer_glob^.pointer_comp := pointer_glob_next;
    pointer_glob^.discr := ident_1;
    pointer_glob^.enum_comp := ident_3;
    pointer_glob^.int_comp := 40;
    pointer_glob^.string_comp := 'DHRYSTONE PROGRAM, SOME STRING';
    string_loc_1 := 'DHRYSTONE PROGRAM, 1"ST STRING';

(* here must be inserted some code to initialize and start the system timer *)

    proc_5; proc_4;
    int_loc_1 := 2; int_loc_2 := 3;
    string_loc_2 := 'DHRYSTONE PROGRAM, 2"ND STRING';
    enum_loc := ident_2;
    bool_glob := not func_2(string_loc_1,string_loc_2);
    while int_loc_1 < int_loc_2 do
        begin
            int_loc_3 := 5 * int_loc_1 - int_loc_2;
            proc_7(int_loc_1,int_loc_2,int_loc_3);
            int_loc_1 := int_loc_1 + 1
        end;
    proc_8(array_glob_1,array_glob_2,int_loc_1,int_loc_3);
    proc_1(pointer_glob);
    for char_index := 'A' to char_glob_2 do
        if enum_loc = func_1(char_index,'C') then
            proc_6(ident_1,enum_loc);
    int_loc_3 := int_loc_2 * int_loc_1;
    int_loc_2 := int_loc_3 div int_loc_1;
    int_loc_2 := 7 * (int_loc_3 - int_loc_2) - int_loc_1;
    proc_2(int_loc_1);

(* stop the timer and read the results, calculate the delta time and
 DHRYSTONE instructions per second by 100/delta time *)
end.
```

Figure 6–10.   **Sieve of Eratosthenes Benchmark Program,
Pascal Version**

```pascal
program SIEVE (input,output);

const
    size = 8190;
var
    flags : array[0..size] of boolean;
    i,prime,k,count,iteration : integer;
begin
    writeln('program runs for ten iterations');

(* here should be code to start the system timer *)

    for iteration := 1 to 10 do
        begin
            count := 0;
            for i := 0 to size do
                flags[i] := true;
            for i := 0 to size do
                if flags[i] then
                    begin
                        prime := i + i + 3; k := i + prime;
                        while k <= size do
                            begin
                                flags[k] := false; k := k + prime
                            end;
                        count := count + 1;
                    end;
        end;

(* here should be code to record the timer value and report
 the elapsed execution time
*)

end.
```

Section III:
Case Studies

In this section, we will examine several examples of parallel and multiprocessor systems. The examples are drawn both from the commercial and research environments, and were chosen based upon their acceptance or upon their architectural advances. Some of the systems we will look at are of a historical nature and have had a great influence upon the current generation of computer architectures. Others are new, exploratory efforts that attempt to advance the state of the art in computer architecture design. A few represent the commercially available systems of today.

For some of the architecture types discussed in Chapter 5, case studies will be presented. Whenever possible, details on software support and applications will be included in the discussions.

This section is organized as two chapters. Chapter 7 deals with several systems that have had impact on the design of today's parallel and multiprocessor systems. Chapter 8 deals with efforts of the last decade or so that have produced products that either were or still are commercially available, as well as with a few current development and research efforts that are attempting to establish the future direction for various forms of parallel and multiprocessor systems.

7. Historical Parallel Architectures

Over the course of computing history, there have always been examples of successful or novel computers that become standard reference points when discussing computer architecture. This is true not only for traditional von Neumann architectures but for parallel and multiprocessor organizations as well. Here, we will examine some of those systems and discuss their significance. One may feel that the examination of "old" architectures is fruitless, especially in today's age of rapid advancement in semiconductor technology. It is often remarkable, however, how the architectural ideas of these systems are continually reborn and reapplied with new technology. The age of an architecture is not the only factor in deciding whether it is historically significant; its influence on subsequent architecture designs is also important. Thus some of the computers discussed in this section are of a relatively recent vintage (within the past decade), but they have either significantly contributed to current computing practices or have become landmark efforts.

The Illiac IV

In any historical discussion of computing, a section on the Illiac IV array processor is a necessity. The Illiac IV project was active in the early 1970's at the University of Illinois, under a grant of the United States Department of Defense's Advanced Research Projects Agency (DARPA). An implementation of an Illiac IV machine was built by the Burroughs Corporation, with help from Texas Instruments and Fairchild Semiconductor, and delivered to the NASA Ames Research Center in California. The Illiac IV machine (only one was built) allowed the performance of computations that were either too complex to perform by hand or on existing machines.

The realization of the Illiac IV architecture required the use of many state-of-the-art components and the development of some new ones. The Illiac IV is the classic form of an array processor, with an array of processors composed of 64 processing elements logically arranged in an 8 x 8 square. It should be noted here that a 64-PE array represents one fourth, or one quadrant, of the originally conceived Illiac IV computer. The quadrants were to be similar, each with 64 PEs, and their combination made up the total machine. Because of technological and cost constraints, however, only one quadrant was implemented. The interconnection between PEs is nearest neighbor, with edge connections as shown in Figure 7–1(a) The connection pattern, assuming a location i, is defined as follows:

$$\text{East neighbor} = (i + 1) \bmod 64$$
$$\text{West neighbor} = (i + 63) \bmod 64$$
$$\text{North neighbor} = (i + 56) \bmod 64$$
$$\text{South neighbor} = (i + 8) \bmod 64$$

Each PE is a 64-bit processor that can perform floating-point, logical, and other arithmetic operations. The 64-bit data items may be operated on as whole words or in subsets of equal-length word parts. Each PE has a set of six registers, which are used for holding operands, for communicating words with neighboring PEs, and for controlling PE operation. The registers are listed below.

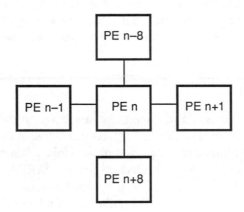

Figure 7–1(a) **Illiac IV PE Interconnections**

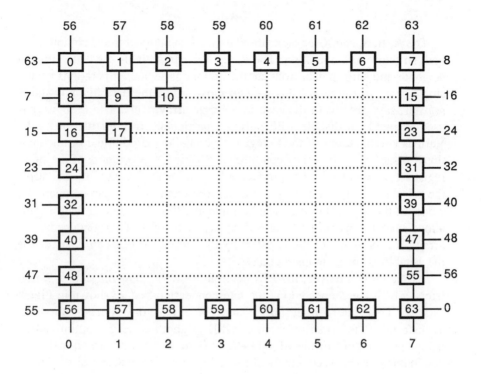

Figure 7–1(b)   **Illiac IV Edge Connections**

A register: 64-bit wide accumulator that holds operands and results

B register: 64-bit register that holds operands

R register: 64-bit routing register that is used to transmit and receive
information from neighboring PEs

S register: 64-bit register used for holding temporary results

X register: 16-bit index register

D register: 8-bit mode register used to control PE operation

The A, B, S, and X registers are like those found in a typical computer, in both structure and operation. The R register can shift its contents out to a neighbor and shift in data from another, either as separate operations or in a single-array instruction. Thus we can move all of the data items in the R register, say, one PE to the east, in a single-array cycle. The D register is used to enable or disable a PE during a particular array instruction cycle. Various combinations of the D register's bits allow conditional or unconditional disabling of PEs. For conditional masking, the contents of the other register can be compared to produce a logical result, which in turn controls the activity of the PEs during that cycle. For example, we can compare the values of the A and B registers and disable the PE if A is greater than B. This allows selective operations to take place on subsets of the data contained in the array. Access to any of the registers by the individual PEs can be made via the usual load and store instructions.

As mentioned before, the PEs communicate via their respective R registers, which are connected via the interconnection system shown in Figure 7–1(b). This interconnection system is called the routing network. Transferral of information from one PE to another can be optimized by using combinations of the +1, −1, +8, −8 routing paths described earlier. A communication between any two PEs in the array can be accomplished in no more than seven steps, where a step consists of a point-to-point, inter-PE transfer. In addition to the routing network, there are three other connections between the various PEs and the control unit. The array and control unit configuration is shown in Figure 7–2. The mode line is used to transmit one of the eight D register bits between the control unit and the PEs, or vice versa. Thus the control unit can interrogate all PEs for their D register status. There are a total of 64 mode lines in the array, one for each PE, so that the mode information can be transferred simultaneously for all PEs. The control data bus is a broadcast connection from the control unit to each PE in the array. This connection is used to give all PEs the same data or instruction address for an array cycle. The transmission of data on the control data bus is useful for enabling an identical operation on all PEs, such as adding a constant value to each individual data item. The broadcast of addresses is the mechanism that gives the Illiac IV its SIMD characteristic. In this case, however, an instruction is not actually transmitted; instead its address within each PE's memory (labeled PEM in Figure 7–2) is broadcast. The combination of the PEM and the control unit bus is used to load PE instructions and data from the control unit and to return data to the control unit. Thus the PEM holds the instructions for the PE to execute, and the

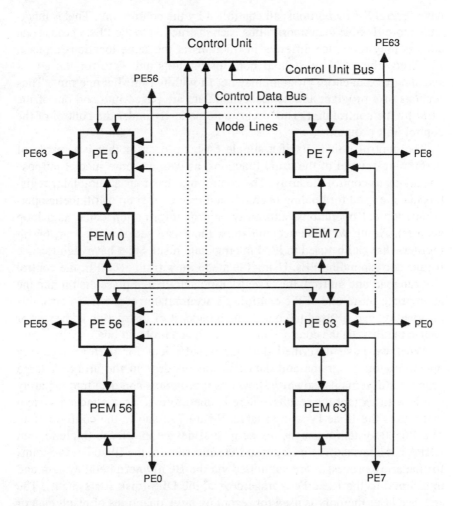

Figure 7–2.   **Illiac IV Array and Control Unit Configuration**

addressing of each PEM is globally controlled by the control unit. The combination of the broadcast address and the X register contents can also be used to address the PEM.

Each PEM contains 2K 64-bit words contained in semiconductor RAM. In operation, the PEMs can transfer data in blocks of eight 64-bit words to and from the control unit. Remember that these transfers can be enabled or disabled by the D register contents. Thus we could load part of the array with one program and another part with a different program. In this way, we can have several SIMD portions, all controlled by the control unit. This is inherently more flexible than transmitting each instruction to the PEs, because one address may reference different instructions at the same locations on each PE. Since the PEM must hold both instructions and data for the corresponding PE, an entire program may not fit within a PEM at one time. Thus sections of a program and its associated data are paged into and out of the PEM by the control unit. This occurs automatically under the control of the control unit program.

The control unit is itself a simple 64-bit processor that is capable of performing several of the usual functions, as well as some special-purpose operations to control the array. The control unit has four accumulator registers that are used for holding operands and results of simple arithmetic operations, logical operations, and array control information (such as a loop counter). Along with the accumulators, there is a set of sixty-four, 64-bit registers that can be used to hold intermediate results that have significance for the corresponding PEs. Using the mode lines from each PE, the control unit can read one bit from the D register of each PE and place the bit into the appropriate bit in one of the controller's accumulator registers. In turn, this information can be used to control the broadcast of instruction addresses or data to the PEs via the control data bus and the control unit bus.

What we have described thus far is sufficient for performing array operations on programs and data that are resident in the array. A large problem still remains, however: how to get programs and data into the array and how to extract the results. There is, therefore, a large attached system that makes the Illiac IV array usable. Figure 7–3 shows the configuration. The B6500 system manages the peripheral device interfaces (including an ARPA net interface), as well as the I/O subsystem of the Illiac IV. Programs for the array processor are submitted via the B6500 peripheral system and transferred to the Illiac IV storage device, the DFS (disk file system). The attached laser memory is used for recording large quantities of result data or user programs. Its capacity is 10^{12} bits of write once memory. A laser is used to burn holes (i.e., bits) into a rotating surface, which can be read back later. The major Illiac IV peripherals are the DFS, the control descriptor controller (CDC), the buffer I/O memory (BIOM), and the I/O switch (IOS). The BIOM buffers program and data transfers between the B6500 and the DFS. Buffering is required for speed matching and also to convert the B6500's 48-bit words to the 64-bit format of the Illiac IV array. The DFS holds programs and data for use on the array. This information is transferred through the IOS to the PEMs in the array. The IOS transfers 1024-bit wide words at a time, which can be distributed to 16 PEMs at once. The CDC

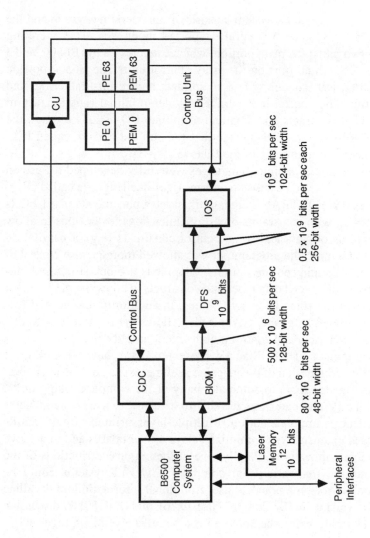

Figure 7–3. The Illiac IV Environment

controls the actions of the BIOM, DFS, and IOS, and responds to requests from the array control unit for instruction or data transfers from the I/O subsystem.

Software on the Illiac IV system consists of the operating system and the programs written in one of several supported languages. The operating system is in two parts: the main portion, which executes on the B6500, and a small kernel OS, which runs on the array control unit. The B6500 portion controls all I/O, job scheduling and setup, data and results gathering, and program setup. The control unit kernel provides minimal functionality to load and unload programs and data and to initiate I/O actions through the CDC. An Algol-like control language that runs on the B6500, called ICL, facilitates system programming of the Illiac IV.

Two high-level programming languages were fully developed for use on the Illiac IV: a FORTRAN extension and an Algol-like language called Glypnir. The Illiac IV FORTRAN language is based upon the standard FORTRAN language, with constraints on array dimensions, extensions to allow vector operations on data and some control constructs (e.g., a parallel do statement). In Glypnir, the programmer was allowed more precise control of the individual PEs and routing options. Glypnir is a block-structured language that contains special data types and constructs to allow the programmer full control over the Illiac IV array features. In addition to the normal features of a high-level language, Glypnir also allows the programmer to differentiate between array and control unit instructions and data.

The development of the Illiac IV presented many new technological challenges. First, the design of the machine itself necessitated the use of computer resident design tools to automate many of the complex design tasks. Next, the Illiac IV computer was the first to extensively use semiconductor for main memory implementation. Multiple-layer printed circuit boards were also used extensively to minimize delays on the boards and to achieve the desired interconnectivity. Finally, one of the major contributions of the Illiac IV was the realization that complex, powerful systems could be achieved and put to some practical use. Additional information on the Illiac IV project is available in [Bouknight72], [Falk76], and [Baer80]. A discussion of an Illiac IV predecessor, the Solomon computer, is given in [Gregory63].

STARAN

The STARAN computer is an associative processor that was developed and implemented by Goodyear Aerospace around 1970, with support from

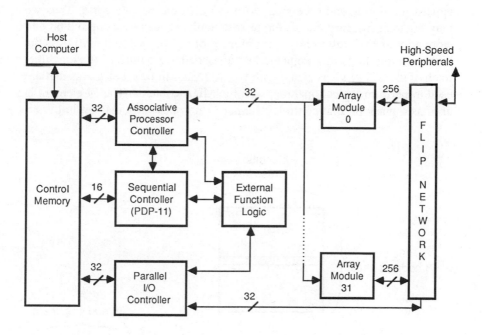

Figure 7–4.   **STARAN Basic Block Diagram**

company R&D funds and the United States Navy. STARAN is a bit-serial associative processor, as described in chapter 5. The basic system block diagram is shown in Figure 7–4. The heart of the STARAN processor is the collection of array modules and the "flip" network. We will discuss these two components first.

Up to a maximum of 32 array modules can be configured in a STARAN system. Each array module consists of a 256×256 bit multidimensional access memory (MDA), a vector of 256 simple processing units, and a flip network. The MDAs consist of 64K storage cells that are logically arranged in a 256×256 square pattern. Access to the memory can be done in two ways, by bit position and by word position. Bit position access is used when performing associative operations upon the data in the array. Word position access is used for performing parallel I/O into and out of the MDA. Figure 7–5 shows this concept. Both bit and word accesses can be masked so that only a specified subset of the addressed bits will be used in a transfer. The memories can also be segmented differently so that part of the bit I/O section is used for storing and accessing word information, or vice versa. Thus we may organize memory into different rectangular shapes by using the bit and word address lines differently; see Figure 7–5(c). Coupled to the MDA is the bit-processing logic that implements the associative nature of the machine. Each of the 256 PEs associated with the MDA has three bit elements that are used to perform logical operations on the MDA contents. The M element is used as a mask bit that controls whether or not that particular bit in the bit

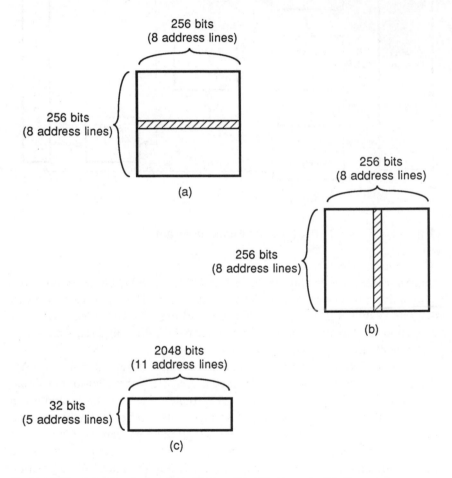

Figure 7–5. (a) Word Access Mode, (b) Bit Access Mode, and (c) Hybrid Access Mode

slice is written in a masked write operation. The X and Y elements each contain one bit that can be used as an operand in a logical bit operation. The other operand comes from the output of the flip network, which gets its data from an MDA. The 256 M, X, and Y bit elements can be thought of as three 256-bit registers, which, along with the Boolean operation logic, perform the array's associative processing.

The flip network is used to perform permutations on the bits of the MDA output, thereby allowing communication of bits among the 256 PEs in the module. Note that the flip network described here is located within each array module. The flip network shown in Figure 7–4 is an additional network that allows communications and permutations between array modules. The array module flip networks allow permutations on the 256 bits in groups of powers of two. Thus the entire 256-bit slice can be permuted at once, or bits can be permuted two at a time, as well as the other values in between (4, 8, 16, 32, 64, and 128). The allowable permutations include shifts and rotations in either direction, swapping of groups, and straight-through operation. To achieve a desired permutation on the MDA data, several iterations through the flip network may be required. This capability is supported within each array module. Thus we have a composite view of an array module, shown in Figure 7–6. Note that the X, Y, and M values can also be run through the flip network and that the flip output can be redeposited in any of these registers, as well as in the MDA.

Returning now to Figure 7–4, we see that a STARAN computer may have up to 32 of the array modules just described. These array modules are also interconnected through a flip network that performs permutations using the 256-bit array module outputs. This flip network is not required on all STARAN implementations. Instead, a parallel I/O system could be placed there for high-speed peripheral data transfer to and from the array modules.

The operation of the flip network is controlled by the parallel I/O controller. It is also responsible for loading data into the MDA memories and can associatively address each MDA memory to accomplish this. If high-speed devices are attached to the flip network, their interfaces are also controlled here.

The associative processor controller instructs the PE logic and flip networks within each array module for each machine cycle. Data can be loaded to the array modules by the array processor controller. Although this data path is only 32 bits wide, the array module flip network allows these bits to be directed to any part of the MDA memory.

The sequential controller, implemented with a Digital Equipment Corporation PDP-11, handles peripheral control and diagnostics. It is also used to

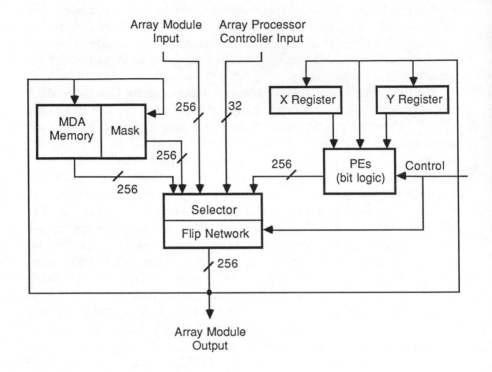

Figure 7–6. **STARAN Array Module**

load STARAN programs into the control memory, and it handles the communication with the attached host computer (if there is one).

External function logic refers to the implementation of external machine control. This unit performs the synchronization of events that access the array modules. The commands to start and stop the associative array modules, to transfer data in or out of the memories, and to control the parallel I/O interfaces are performed through the external function logic.

Programming on the STARAN is performed using assembly language programs for the PEs and control units. Programs are loaded into the control memory, which contains a section for user programs and a section for system routines.

Several applications using the STARAN hardware have been developed, including fast Fourier transform analysis, sonar processing, and data base searching. Improvements were made in the STARAN hardware to increase the MDA memory size to 9216×256 bits. Successors of STARAN were also developed, namely, the Massively Parallel Processor and the Airborne Associative Processor [Batcher82]. More information on STARAN and its applications is given in [Batcher74]. Also see [Yau77] and [Thurber75].

The Safeguard System

As far back as the 1950's, Bell Laboratories was involved in designing and developing computer systems for defense applications. An early work, called the Zeus System, consisted of digital computers and special, high-reliability components that, together with special-purpose software, were designed to perform the operations necessary to detect and intercept ICBMs. It consisted of several computers, each assigned to perform a specific task such as acquisition, tracking, and guidance. It was deployed in the early 1960's and was a pioneer effort in this area. Another defense system for tracking radar targets, called the Parallel Element Processing Ensemble (PEPE), consisted of two processor subsections that worked cooperatively. One section consisted of a general-purpose digital computer that was used for controlling the tracking process, maintaining the large program and data memory, and performing the sequential processes necessary for radar processing. The other section consisted of an indefinite number of special-purpose computers, each of which was assigned to track a single target in real time. Each of the special-purpose computers was itself a small digital computer with its own memory, CPU, and special-purpose correlation unit. It was developed in the late 1960's and early 1970's.

The Safeguard system, developed in the early 1970's, contains concepts found in both the Zeus system and the PEPE computer. Its intended application was for a ballistic missile defense system. The architecture of the Safeguard system is both interesting and historic, in that it represents one of the first practical applications of a multiprocessor architecture, and in that it successfully developed and used real-time system programming and execution techniques within this environment. In addition, the goal of achieving a fault-tolerant system resulted in some interesting architectural features that are not usually seen in a typical multiprocessor.

A basic block diagram of the Safeguard system central logic and control section is shown in Figure 7–7. The emphasis on fault tolerance is evident from the figure, redundant data paths exist between the controlling and processing units, and the essential components are all replicated. The interconnection network is actually implemented in sections, with each major component (e.g., processor unit, variable store, program store, time and status unit, and I/O controller) supplying a piece of the interconnect. In this way, the system can be expanded incrementally and can tolerate the loss of a module, because the failure affects only a portion of the switching network. The system itself employs n + 1 redundancy. This means that, if n units of a particular type are required to perform the application, then at least one redundant spare is provided for backup. Thus we see that there are two time and status units and two I/O control units, even though only one of each is required for the system to function at any given time. The mechanisms by which units are reconfigured will be discussed later.

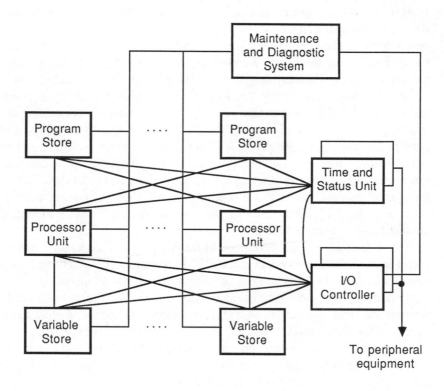

Figure 7–7.   **Safeguard System Central Logic and Control Unit**

Up to ten processor units may be included in a single Safeguard central logic and control unit. Each processor in a processing unit is a 32-bit machine that uses a three-stage pipeline to overlap the instruction fetch, operand fetch, and instruction execution. Also, two separate instructions are fetched: the next instruction and the branch target, whenever a conditional branch instruction is encountered. When the condition is evaluated, the correct instruction is fed into the pipe, as described in Chapter 5. Addressing by the processor is absolute for both the program and variable stores. An instruction stack of four double words (eight instructions) is used to buffer instruction fetches, and short loops that fit entirely within this buffer are executed without refetching the loop instructions (see the section on loop buffers, under pipelined processors, in Chapter 5) The processors each contain thirty-five, 32-bit registers, organized as 5 A registers, 15 B registers, and 15 Z registers. The A registers are used as general-purpose accumulators, and they are the source and sink for operands, in addition to the variable store. Single (32-bit) or double (64-bit) word operations may take place in the A registers. The B registers are used for the storage of memory addresses or index values. The information contained in the A and B register banks may be exchanged via register move operations. The Z register set contains special locations for interrupt addresses and returns, a time-keeping location, and memory protection bits (for the variable store). The processor also supports a read-modify-write operation to the variable store: A memory word is fetched, its upper two bits are modified, and it is returned to memory. The processor then checks the two bits to determine whether it obtained a lock on the data word. This is essential for a shared memory system.

As shown in Figure 7–7, there are separate program and variable stores. The processor can access each memory independently and simultaneously, thereby increasing the overall memory bandwidth. The variable store memory is arranged in modules of 16K double words (i.e., 16K × 64), with parity on each 16-bit quantity. A Safeguard implementation may have up to 16 of these modules. Each module, through the attached switching network, has an independent path to each processor in the system. Thus each variable store module is accessible by each processor. This makes it necessary to implement a contention resolution scheme at the memory, to order access by the processors. For this, a priority resolver is placed at each memory switch, as shown in Figure 7–8. Operand fetches to the variable store are made in double word (64-bit) increments, and the memory cycle time is 500 nsec.

The program stores are constructed of the same basic memory components as the variable store. Each program store, however, consists of two

8K × 64 memory modules (see Figure 7–8). The addresses of a program's instruction are set up in such a way that sequential addresses reside in separate memories. This effectively decreases the cycle time for sequential instruction fetches to 250 nsec, thereby doubling the instruction fetch rate. Up to 16 of these double-module program memories can be placed in a Safeguard system, and each program store is accessible by every processor. Note the separate data paths for each program store memory module and the presence of the priority logic at the switch. Accesses to a program store are also made on a double-word basis.

Each of the aforementioned elements (processor, program store and variable store) are independently operable in one of two states, labeled green and amber. A third stated, isolated, is also possible for disabled units. The elements may be partitioned into these states in any combination; there is no implied pairing of processors with memories, etc. Elements in the green state may work only with other elements in the green state; the same is true for the amber elements. Exceptions to this are the memory units, which can be shared between the green and amber partitions. Thus the system is parti-

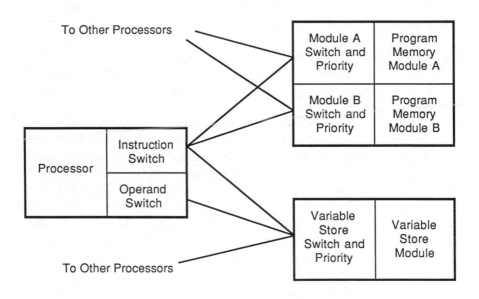

Figure 7–8.   **Safeguard Memory Organization**

tionable into two independent multiprocessors, each with its own job stream. Alternatively, the amber portion can be configured as spares, with the green partition using them as necessary because of failures or increased processing demands. Thus green partition components have priority over amber portion ones.

As with the other elements, the time and status unit and the I/O controller are also partitionable, although the green state has priority if only one unit of either type is operational. The time and status unit has two major functions: the provision of accurate timing information to the processor units, and the maintenance of the operational status of each element in the system. Timing information is provided in two forms: a general time-of-day counter and a time-driven event generator. The event generator contains a list of events (processes to be scheduled) and the associated time at which they are to be run. When the current time-of-day counter reaches an event time, the process is initiated. Status in the unit is kept in a partition matrix. The matrix state can be changed manually upon the detection of a fault in the system, under software control, or upon a change in the job load on the system. The partition matrix can be read by the processors to get information on the other elements that are within the same partition. The information between the green and amber timing status units is somewhat redundant, and it is kept consistent through special purpose software on the unit's controller.

As seen in Figure 7–7, the timing and status unit interfaces to each program and variable store, as well as to the processing units through a switch network. This interface is used to load both programs and data to the respective stores, as well as to control each processing unit's partition state. Thus the timing and status unit is the primary controller for the elements in the Safeguard system.

The I/O controller provides the interface to the outside world and controls the transfer of information into and out of the Safeguard central logic and control unit. As seen in Figure 7–7, it is also connected, through the switch network, to each element. Therefore transfers with the external world are initiated and controlled here. There are two of these units and, as with the other elements, they may operate in either the green or amber state.

Now that we have examined the basic hardware elements of the Safeguard central logic and control unit, let's examine some of the software aspects of the system. We will first briefly discuss the Safeguard implementation language, called CENTRAN, and then examine the operating system and tasking mechanisms used to support real-time programs.

During the early stages of the Safeguard system development, it was decided that the programmer productivity that could be provided with a high-level language was necessary to meet the code development requirements. It was also felt, however, that assembly level programming would still be required for some functions in which code execution efficiency was critical. Rather than adopt an existing high-level language, augment it to provide the necessary multiprocessing constructs, and interface it with the assembly language routines, it was decided to develop a tailored language that provided all of these facilities. Thus the CENTRAN language was developed, and it was designed to be extendable and to have several levels (i.e., high-level, intermediate, and assembly) that could be freely intermixed. The language has the following basic features: a low-level cadre of instructions that allow direct machine control; modern program flow control constructs such as those found in PL/1; high-level data structures; and intermediate level constructs, such as based variables, and word and partial word operations.

The Safeguard central logic and control operating system consists of a set of tasks that execute on the processing units. The OS provides real-time execution control of the tasks that make up a job stream. The operating system has two modes of operation: process execute mode and support mode. The support mode is used for debug and utility operations, and is not discussed here. The process execute mode provides the services and control for the execution of tactical process code. Real-time operating systems generally use one of two methods of processor management to ensure the real-time execution of the current process load, event-driven or time-driven. Event-driven systems are characterized by the predominance of interrupts that initiate actions in response to external world events. Time-driven systems allocate and schedule the processor's time in such a way that all tasks receive enough CPU time to complete before their deadline requirement. The Safeguard OS is time-driven, although it does have provisions for responding to external events. Before discussing the OS further, let's discuss the structure of tasks in the system.

Tasks in the Safeguard system are of three varieties:

1. *Synchronous*: Enabled by time events, of a specified duration, and guaranteed to have data available for processing

2. *Asynchronous*: Enabled by external events at random times

3. *Mixed*: Can be scheduled or invoked by an external event

Because the Safeguard system is a multiprocessor, some processes may be performed more than once at the same time. The question arises, then, whether or not to replicate the program code or allow sharing of the same code. In Safeguard, both approaches were allowed, depending upon the response requirements of each task. Ultimately, it was found that only those tasks that required the best possible response times were replicated.

Load balancing in the system consists of allocating tasks to processors to achieve the best response time for all tasks involved. The Safeguard designers identified two main factors of importance here, jobs that required immediate response, and those that could be run over a longer term. The allocation of immediate response tasks was performed dynamically (at run time), based upon processor loading data. Even with this capability, however, the long-term tasks turned out to be statically balanced, as their response time requirements could be met without dynamic load balancing. Related to load balancing is the job of allocation of resources to tasks as they execute. There are two extremes: do all allocations dynamically or statically. Again, a compromise position was chosen, to perform an initial static allocation that could be changed as tasks were executed.

Returning now to the issue of a time-driven OS, we are still faced with the problem of how to regain processor control in order to perform a task switch. One method is to generate periodic interrupts based upon an interval timer. This method is unattractive, however, because of the overhead and the added complexity of handling the interrupts. An alternative method, used in Safeguard, is to ensure that all tasks execute within a maximum specified time. Thus tasks are written in such a way that they always finish execution within the prescribed time limit. Typically, this time allotment is on the order of several milliseconds. If a task cannot be written in such a way that it fits within the specified interval, it is broken up into smaller subtasks that do. A problem arises, however, in ensuring the proper sequencing of the subtasks to perform the overall task job. This is ensured by establishing predecessor rules that state that, for instance, task B may run after task A completes. Thus, on any available processor, the OS schedules the task of the highest priority that has had its preconditions satisfied. The task queue, which holds ready tasks, is held in a fixed table that is accessed by the operating system when performing a scheduling operation. It should be restated that, in order to meet the real-time response requirements, all tasks, including those of the operating system, must utilize this same mechanism.

In retrospect, the Safeguard effort has provided us with many good techniques for designing and implementing real-time, multiprocessor systems. Redundancy in both components and interconnection, coupled with effective hardware management programs, form a good model against which to judge real-time architectures. Also, the hand-in-hand cooperation between the executable tasks and the operating system form a realistic approach to achieving real-time response and control. More details on these and other aspects of the Safeguard system can be found in *The Bell System Technical Journal, Safeguard Supplement*, 1975.

Cm*

The Cm* system is a distributed multiprocessor that uses packet-switched communication between a hierarchy of processing ensembles, called clusters. Developed at Carnegie Mellon University in the mid-1970's, Cm* was intended to answer some of the questions that were beginning to arise because of the advancement of processor fabrication technology and the subsequent proliferation of small, inexpensive, and powerful processors. The focus of the Cm* project was markedly different from that of the Safeguard effort. In Safeguard, the emphasis was on real-time fault tolerance in a tightly controlled environment, with few or no cost constraints. For Cm*, the economical usage of large numbers of loosely coupled processors formed the central issue. The Cm* project, as does Safeguard, provides some valuable experience in designing and building multiprocessor systems. Many of the ideas that were nurtured by Cm* were adopted by later projects, both for hardware and software.

Perhaps the one characterizing feature of the Cm* architecture is that all of its processors shared a single virtual memory address space. This does not imply that there existed a single, large memory store managed by a virtual memory access system; rather, the converse is true. Each processor has associated with it a portion of the total system memory.

The architecture of Cm* is organized as a three-level hierarchy: module, cluster, and system. At the module level resides a processor, memory and other devices, and a local switch, all hooked onto the module processor's bus. The module processor, an LSI-11 manufactured by Digital Equipment Corporation, is a 16-bit machine that is program-compatible with DEC's PDP-11. The LSI-11 has a 64-Kbyte address space that is used to map into Cm*'s 2^{28} byte segmented, virtual address space. A typical computer module, or Cm, is shown in Figure 7–9.

Each Cm is connected, via the local switch, to a cluster of Cms. The cluster consists of the attached Cms; a cluster bus, called the Map bus; and a controller called the Kmap. Clusters are interconnected via intercluster buses to form the total system. Figure 7–10, illustrating two clusters, shows the overall system architecture. Notice that a cluster may have up to 14 Cms on the Map bus. An arbitrary number of clusters may hook together on the intercluster buses to form a Cm* system. The Kmaps do not all have to reside on the same intercluster buses; the system can be arranged into cluster groups.

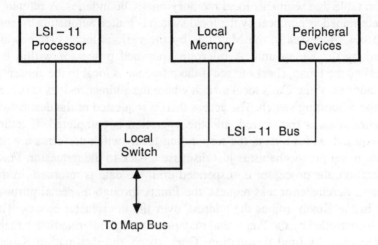

To Map Bus

Figure 7-9. **Cm* Computer Module Structure**

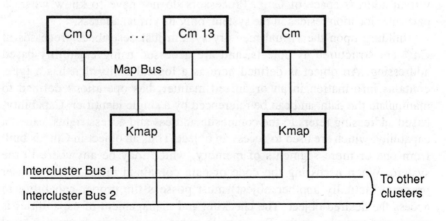

Figure 7-10. **Cm* System Architecture**

Two features of Cm* make it an attractive vehicle for multiprocessing: the addressing mechanism, and the process structure and communication. First is the implementation of the virtual address space. Each LSI-11, through its own 64K address space, accesses its own local memory via the local switch. The local switch maps local addresses by using an internal relocation table that segments local memory on 4K boundaries. A reference that is determined as nonlocal by the local switch is routed automatically onto the Map bus. Accesses to the Map bus by the various local switches are arbitrated by the Kmap unit. A microprogrammed processor within the Kmap, called the Pmap, checks to see if the reference is local to the cluster. If it is, the address of the Cm's local switch where the address resides is passed back to the requesting switch. The access then is requested of the destination local switch, data is transferred, and the operation is completed. If return data is required, as for a read, the responding local switch performs a write operation, using the mechanisms just discussed, back to the requestor. For a read operation, the processor is suspended until the data is returned. In the case of an intercluster access request, the Pmap, through a special purpose element in the Kmap, routes the address over the intercluster busses. The routing is controlled by the Pmap, and may pass through intermediate Kmaps before reaching its final destination. Once there, the destination Kmap, through its own Pmap, performs the operation through the appropriate local switch. A reply containing the requested data or a completion status is sent back to the requesting Kmap. All of the above mechanisms provide the virtual address space of Cm*. Processors do not have to know where a particular location resides in the system, only its virtual address.

Building upon the virtual memory system just described, processes in Cm* are structured as objects, and are accessed using capability-based addressing. An object is defined here as a logical entity that has a type, contains information in an organized manner, has operations defined to manipulate the data, and can be referenced by a single identifier. Capability-based addressing refers to the composite address and access rights, called a capability, which are used to access an object. Thus an object in Cm* is built from one or more segments of memory, which may be anywhere in the system. When accessing the code or data contained in an object, a user program (actually another object) must possess the proper capability to access the desired object. The checking and management of capabilities is performed mainly by the Pmap, with some support given by the local operating system of the LSI-11. The combination of the virtual addressing mechanism, object structures, and capability-based addressing, provide a good environment for the execution of transparent multiprocessor software.

More information on object structures and capability-based addressing can be found in [Linden76]. The Cm* system is presented in greater detail in [Jones76], [Swan77], and [Siewiorek77].

This concludes our discussion of some of the past architectures that continue to have a profound influence on current efforts in the area of parallel and multiprocessing systems. Chapter 8 discusses more recent systems that have many of the characteristics of the architectures presented in this chapter.

8. RECENT SYSTEMS

This chapter discusses some recent parallel and multiprocessing architectures. Most of the machines discussed are currently available or have been within the past several years. They range from microprocessor-based systems to supercomputers. We begin with an architecture that, although never commercially successful, illustrates that many of the multiprocessor concepts developed in the Cm* project could be applied in an integrated system that supports transparent multiprocessing.

The iAPX432

The 432 project was begun in the late 1970's by Intel Corporation. The goal was to provide 32-bit processing power in an extendable multiprocessor system, with hardware support for the operating system. In this machine, the use of object structuring and capability-based addressing is so ingrained in the architecture that it must be discussed before looking at the overall system. In the 432 architecture, everything, from programs to processors, is represented as an object. An object is defined as a logical structure that:

1. Contains information in an organized manner

2. Has a set of operations defined to manipulate the information

3. Can be referenced with a single identifier

4. Has a type associated with it

The definition given above is used in the Intel literature that describes the iAPX432 processor system [Intel80]. This system implements objects as memory areas and uses them to define the particular functional parts that make up a software system and user program. The object types and their characteristics that are supported by the 432 system are:

Processor object: information on processor status, diagnostics, machine state

Process object: process state, scheduling information, reference for current image (context)

Context object: information for instance of procedure, instruction pointer, stack pointer, return link, references for objects accessible in this context

Instruction object: instructions, only object that can be executed

Data object: data

Communication port object: for interprocess communication, any object can be a message

Domain object: organizes objects into modules, static list of instruction, data, procedure objects that work together

Objects on the 432 are implemented as protected areas of memory that are accessible via a segmented address translation scheme. Memory segments are not restricted to single size chunks, as with paged memory, but their size must be static and defined. That is, memory may be segmented into variable-sized chunks, but the sizes of the chunks are not dynamically alterable. Each memory access is first passed through an access segment that contains the access environment for the module (i.e., a table of exactly what objects in memory the process can access and the type of access that is supported). Next, the address is sent to the segment mapping table that performs the virtual to physical address translation (see Figure 8–1). The key to object implementation in the 432, then, is the combination of segmented memory, the two-level mapping process to check capabilities and perform the address translation, and the hardware support for the two-level mapping (the 432 has a cache for storing the mapping and access tables).

The 432 has a virtual address space of 2^{40} bytes, arranged as up to 2^{24} segments, each of up to 2^{16} bytes. The memory protection mechanism that performs type checks on intended operations operates on a segment-by-segment basis so that we may have up to 2^{24} "protected" areas, or objects, in a system.

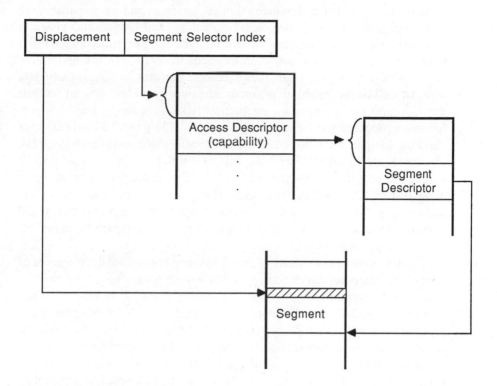

Figure 8–1. **iAPX432 Addressing Scheme**

Capabilities in the 432 system are implemented in four fields within a word: directory index, access rights, segment index, and type rights. The directory index is to a systemwide object table directory that contains an entry for each process object table. A process may have several process object tables that together form a process. The segment index then selects an object descriptor from the process object table. The object descriptor contains information about the location of the object in segmented memory, as well as a type field to identify the object. The access rights and type rights from the capability are checked against the desired operation and the type of the referenced object descriptor before the operation can proceed.

The instructions of the 432 are coded in variable length format according to their frequency of use. They range from 6 to 344 bits in length, and they may be stored anywhere in memory (i.e., they need not be on byte or other boundaries). Included in the instruction set are fixed and integer arithmetic and floating-point operators, logical operators, and branch and program control instructions. Also included are operators to perform character and ordinal manipulations, as well as instructions to create, control, and define capabilities, manage the segmented memory, perform locking on any data type, as well as for interprocess communication. From this we can see that the 432 supported many more instruction types than the typical high-performance processors of the day. In addition, the 432 provided hardware type checking of operations on its defined data types, which include integer, real, character, port, ordinal, and access descriptors. Thus the iAPX432 instruction set provides a semantic level that is suitable for use by an operating system. That is, the basic instruction set incorporates several of the features (e.g., segmented memory control, object type checking) that would normally have to be implemented as special-purpose software functions for the operating system to use.

The extensive use of objects in the 432 system enables the development of logical interprocess communication (IPC), which further paves the way for transparent multiprocessing. To understand why this is so, we must introduce two specific 432 objects, the processor object and the dispatching port. The processor object is a hardware-recognized memory structure that contains the processor's state and access descriptors for other related objects (such as the dispatcher port object). The dispatcher port object contains descriptors for processes that are waiting for service by a processor. As mentioned before, communication ports transmit and receive interprocess communications (which are objects also). The basic mechanism is relatively simple: When a processor becomes idle, it uses its access descriptor to reference the dispatch port and obtain another process. Each process that is "waiting" in the dispatch port specifies the policy by which it is to be scheduled. Typical scheduling policies indicate how long a process is to run each time it is dispatched, and how many times it can be dispatched before the operating system must reevaluate its progress, and its priority. These scheduling policies determine how the processor's resources are split up between processes. Higher-level scheduling functions (e.g., FIFO, shortest job first, etc.) are performed by the operating system.

The policies mentioned above are carried out by the processing hardware itself, one example of the raised semantic level of the 432. With the presence of a single dispatching port and logical interprocessor communication, it is evident that a process can effectively run on any available processor.

In the 432 system, there are two types of processors: the general data processor (GDP) and the interface processor (IP). So far, we have been discussing mostly the GDP capabilities, although the IP also is an object-based machine that has the same type of scheduling and memory access mechanisms. Thus there is a dispatching port for each type of processor in the system, usually one for the GDPs and one for the IPs. There may be up to six processors in the system, with each processor either a GDP or an IP. A notional system that shows a typical use of the components is displayed in Figure 8–2. In the figure, one of the GDPs is shown with a "checker." This is a built-in feature of the GDPs: By applying the appropriate signal level to the control pin, a GDP can act as a redundant processor that does not actively control any of its external GDP interfaces. If an error is detected by the checker, it can disable the main GDP, thereby providing run time fault detection. The presence of two IPs is not a necessity, merely an illustration of a possible configuration. All processors on the 432 bus have access to the memory modules. Special contention resolution and bus control circuitry are

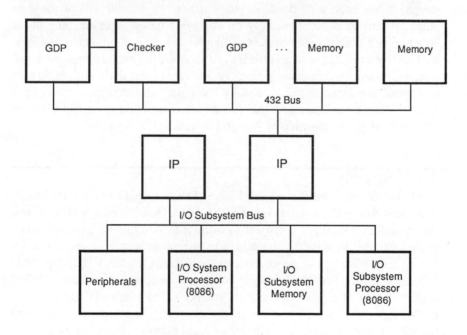

Figure 8–2.   **iAPX432 Organization**

placed at the processor interface points, to arbitrate and facilitate memory accesses. On the I/O subsystem, standard microprocessors and peripherals are utilized to form an independent I/O system. Thus 432 processing and I/O processing can be completely overlapped. Also, the IP facilitates this by providing special capabilities, such as memory windowing for outside access, and automatic DMA transfers to and from the 432 memory space.

We have already discussed some of the features of the 432 architecture that can be used to help implement software on the machine. Two forms of software were developed for use by the 432: the iMAX operating system and the Ada programming language. The iMAX operating system is an object-based operating system, in that the primary entity that it manages are objects. It is responsible for such things as establishing process-scheduling policies, creating and maintaining the various access descriptor and segment tables, and providing some multiprocessor support software [Kahn81].

For the 432 project, Ada was adopted as the primary application language. It has been well-documented that the implementation of the Ada language can be done effectively on an object-based machine. The block structure and strong typing of Ada demands modular and protected memory, such as that provided with an object system. Also, the mechanisms by which Ada implements information hiding (i.e., private types) and multiple threads of control (i.e., tasking) are aided by the object structure as well as by a multiprocessor environment. The 432 architecture is described in detail in [Intel81] and the relationship of Ada and objects in [Desrochers84].

The Butterfly

Under the sponsorship of the United States Department of Defense's Advanced Research Projects Agency (DARPA), Bolt Beranek and Newman, Incorporated, undertook a project to build a large-grained, generally connected parallel processor. The machine is representative of the interconnected network class of processors described in Chapter 5. The Butterfly processor is an MIMD machine in which the processing elements (called nodes) consist of a processor, a local memory, and a connection to a high-performance switch. Each node in the Butterfly consists of a Motorola MC68000 processor, up to 4 Mbytes of local memory, an Advanced Micro Devices AMD2901 processor which implements the processor node controller (PNC) function, and a memory management unit. Also available is a small daughter board to replace the 68000, which contains a MC68020 processor, as well as a floating-point coprocessor (the MC68881). Figure 8–3 shows a node's configuration. A Butterfly system may contain from one to 256 of these nodes, all interconnected with a switching network.

The aspect of a node that makes it work in the parallel environment is the processor node controller (PNC). The processor's access to the Butterfly switch is accomplished through the virtual memory interface. A 68000 virtual address is interpreted by the PNC to determine if the reference is to local memory or destined for a remote node. If it is a local reference, the memory management unit translates the virtual address into a physical memory location. For a remote access, the PNC sends a message through the switch to the remote node, where the reference is satisfied and a reply is sent, if necessary. The message contains a physical memory address for the remote memory, and the remote node's address. The physical address is obtained from the memory management unit but is intercepted by the PNC and packaged in the message. A remote PNC receiving a remote access request uses the supplied address to perform the operation on the local memory. The whole process of performing a remote memory access takes an order of magnitude longer to complete than a local reference. The processor does not experience any difficulties because of this; it is merely held in suspense until the action is completed. In addition to the remote memory access support, the PNC implements distributed-locking functions that are essential for multi-

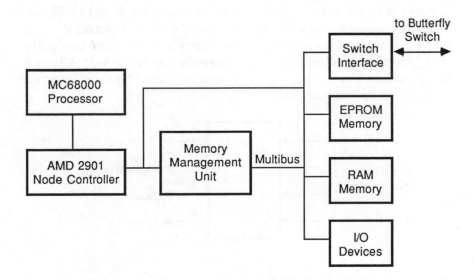

Figure 8-3. **Butterfly Processor Node**

processing. This is possible because of the suspension of the processor during a remote access, thereby allowing the PNC to perform atomic operations. The PNC also supports a block transfer mode for transferring large amounts of data over the switch.

The Butterfly switch forms the backbone of the processor. It is implemented as a collection of switching nodes, each node a 4×4 butterfly switch as that shown in Figure 8–4. Data, along with its address, arrives on any of the input paths and, depending on the address, exits on the appropriate path. A node is indexed by its address only; the route through the network is implicit in the address, as the bits are used at each switch node to pick the correct output path. Thus there is a path from every processor to every other one through the network, and these paths are all of exactly the same length. Each path through the switch can support a 32 Mbytes/sec transfer rate. When several processors are attempting to transmit data through the switch at once, a collision may occur in which two messages attempt to use the same switch output port for some switching node. In this case, one of the messages is allowed through and the other is retransmitted after a random delay time. For systems with more than 16 processors, redundant switching paths are used to reduce the contention problem just described and also to provide a measure of fault tolerance. When collisions occur as described above, the redundant path is used for the retransmission. A 16-node Butterfly processor is shown in Figure 8–5, showing several messages in transit and a collision. Note that a collision occurs only when an output is required by more than one message. Thus the 4×4 switch nodes may carry up to four messages at one time, provided they all take separate output paths (see Figure 8–5). Also note that the routing is automatic, with the destination address "used up" along the way to direct the switching nodes.

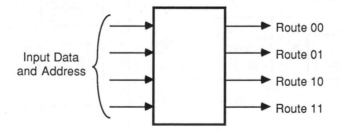

Figure 8–4.   **Butterfly Switch Node**

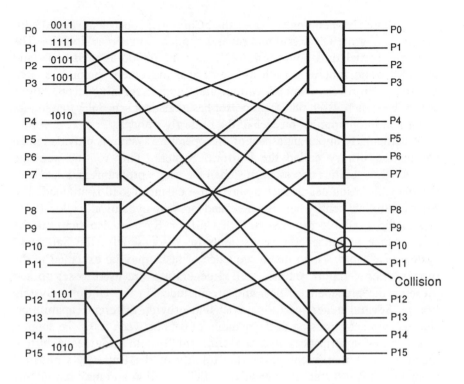

Figure 8–5. **A 16-node Butterfly**

I/O on the butterfly is performed by the attached Multibus peripherals on any of the processor nodes. The transfer rate of the processor node's I/O bus is approximately 2 Mbytes/sec. For applications that require a greater I/O bandwidth, a special I/O node can be attached directly to the switch, enabling I/O transfers to occur at speeds up to the maximum transfer rate of the switch paths.

Software on the Butterfly system has been mainly implemented using the C language, although FORTRAN and Lisp are also available for applications that require their specific features. The development of programs for the Butterfly is done using conventional software development tools for the 68000 processor, and is typically performed on an attached host processor (either a DEC VAX Computer or Sun Microsystems work station). A command interpreter called the bshell (Butterfly shell) runs on the Butterfly, and allows the loading and control of programs from the host processor.

The Butterfly operating system, called Chrysalis, consists of several entities, including the OS kernel and several application support libraries. The Chrysalis kernel runs both on the PNC and the 68000 at each node, and provides basic functions such as memory management support, switch control, interprocess communication, and support for atomic operations across the switch. Each 68000 processor has a resident scheduler that implements multiprogramming on each of the Butterfly's nodes.

A particularly important aspect of this operating system is provided in an application library called the Uniform System. This routine package provides the facilities necessary to spread the user's programs and data over the available resources in such a way that a balanced load is attained. The basic controllable entity here is a task, and tasks are dynamically allocated to any of the available processors. The Uniform System also supports the maintenance of predecessor constraints (as discussed for the Safeguard system of Chapter 7), so that a sequence of tasks may be executed in the proper order. Support routines, called generators, are used to set up and preserve the precedence rules, and are included in the Uniform System library. Several generator forms exist that provide different capabilities, such as parameter passing or the queuing of data between tasks. To support this form of multiprocessing, the Uniform System provides a virtual memory space that encompasses the totality of the Butterfly's physical memory. Thus tasks are not sensitive to their location and may run on any node in the system.

The implementation of the virtual address space supports the use of the object model described earlier for the 432 processor. Tasks, as discussed earlier, are organized as process objects, and they form the schedulable unit of work under the Chrysalis OS. Each node contains, as part of the OS, a deadline scheduler to allocate the processes over time on that node's 68000 processor. The OS contains facilities for creating communication queues between processes that can be used in the task precedence arrangement discussed earlier. Also, a built-in exception mechanism, called catch/throw, enables exceptions to be propagated upward through the execution trace.

Another support library contains the necessary functions to support an environment that is a suitable host for the CSP methodology discussed in Chapter 4. Note, however, that an actual CSP-like language is not supported here, only mechanisms that can be used to emulate the CSP concept.

The Butterfly represents a unique position in the domain of parallel processing, because it combines the advantages of the efficient, high-bandwidth switch with support for multiprocessing. Also, the deadline-scheduling algorithm and high-bandwidth, low-latency communication switch make the

Butterfly attractive for use on large, real-time problems. Further reading on the Butterfly can be found in [Goodhue85], [Thomas86], and the *IEEE Computer Architecture Technical Committee Newsletter,* Sept./Dec. 1985.

The Geometric Arithmetic Parallel Processor

The Geometric Arithmetic Parallel Processor, or GAPP, takes an approach that is based upon the systolic architecture concepts presented in Chapter 5. Developed by Martin Marietta and NCR, and manufactured by NCR, the GAPP incorporates 72 single-bit processors, integrated on a single VLSI chip. Each bit processor in the GAPP contains a one-bit ALU, a set of four registers, and a 128-bit RAM. Figure 8–6 shows the configuration of one processor on the GAPP chip and its connections to its neighbors. The ALU is simple, and it can perform addition, subtraction, and the normal complement of logical operations. The memory at each processor holds and receives operands to and from the ALU, and provides an externally addressable store for getting data on and off the chip. The processor array is arranged as a 16×12 rectangle with 6 PEs in the east/west direction and 12 in the north/south. Each processor is connected to its north, south, east, and west neighbors. A number of GAPP chips may be hooked together to form larger arrays without altering the interconnection pattern between chips. PE edge connections for each GAPP chip are dependent upon the application, and are wired external to the GAPP chip itself.

Each processor on the GAPP chip contains four single-bit registers that contain data from the north/south connection, the east/west connection, the carry bit of a processor's ALU, and an additional communication bit. Inputs to the registers are routed through a set of multiplexors that are controlled by the instruction that is currently executing. The communication line runs from south to north through all processing elements in a column, and can be used to communicate data into and out of the RAM. The north/south (NS) line connects to the south (S) input of the north neighbor and to the north (N) input of the south neighbor. The east/west connections are similar. The global outputs of all processing elements are ORed together into a single external output.

Programming the GAPP processor is accomplished using either GAPP assembly language or a subset of the C language, with special support constructs. In each GAPP instruction cycle, each of the five multiplexors can be independently controlled to move data bits in a number of ways. The instruc-

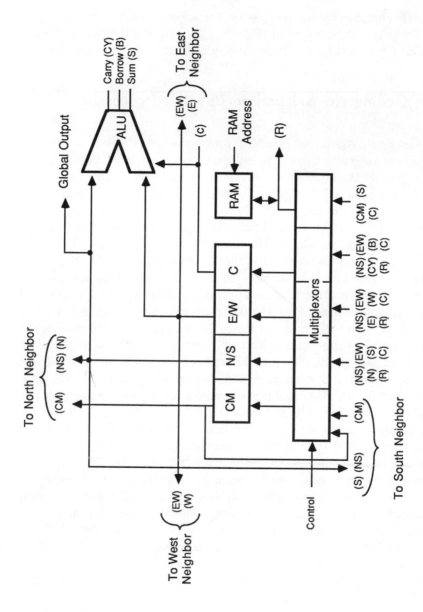

Figure 8–6. **GAPP Processing Element and Connections**

tions and RAM addresses for the GAPP are provided externally to the chip by a separate controller. The controller can be microprocessor-based or may consist of a state machine; either must provide instructions, addresses, and timing information to the GAPP chip. Thus the GAPP itself has no control or instruction fetch and decode circuitry; this must be provided by an external controller. The GAPP assembler and C subset compiler generate address and control sequences that can be loaded onto a controller for GAPP execution. More information on the GAPP can be found in [Davis84] and the NCR manufacturer's literature for the GAPP (NCR part NCR45CG72).

The Massively Parallel Processor (MPP)

In the late 1970's, NASA determined that a new source of computing power would be required to process large amounts of image data to be obtained from new, earth-orbiting satellites. With the initial concept developed at NASA, Goodyear Aerospace received a contract to construct the Massively Parallel Processor. The MPP is a large array processor, with a 128×128 square array of 16K simple processors. The processor interconnections are typical for an array processor, along with the associated edge connection possibilities discussed in Chapter 5. In order to provide some degree of reliability with such a large number of processing elements, an extra 512 processors, arranged in a 128×4 rectangle, are incorporated as spares that can be configured to replace failed components. Once a failed component in a processor column is found, that entire column is switched out and one of the extra columns takes its place. The basic configuration of the MPP is shown in Figure 8–7. Each of the components is discussed below.

As stated earlier, the array unit of the MPP is composed of 128×128 processing elements. Each PE is a single-bit processor that contains a number of single-bit registers, memory, and a simple ALU. Figure 8–8 shows a PE's structure. The transfer of data to and from a PE in the array is done through the S register, which has connections to the PE's east and west neighbors. As seen from the MPP block diagram, data flows through the array from west to east, through the S registers. To load or unload all of the S registers of the array (also called the S plane), 128 shifts from or to the staging memory are required. Once the S plane has been loaded, its contents can be transferred, via the data bus, to the PE memory. The reverse, from memory to S plane, is also possible. The P register can either load the data bus directly, or it may perform a logical operation on the old P register contents and the data bus value and store the result back in P. Connections to neighboring PEs are also

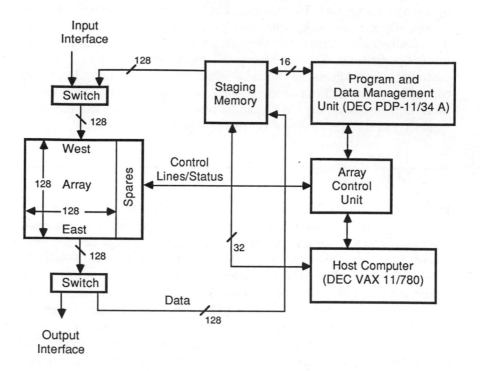

Figure 8–7. **MPP Block Diagram**

made via the P register so that it is the source and sink for array communications. Note that the task of getting data into and out of the array is done
not by the P register but by the S plane. The P and G registers may be compared on each PE to control certain operations (e.g., the result of the
compare can be loaded back into G). The G register, then, is a mask register
whose contents determine whether or not the PE is active on that cycle. The P
and A bit registers, along with the carry bit, are input to the adder for arithmetic operations. Results are deposited in the B register, and then out to the
data bus or through the shifter. The shifter can hold up to 30 bits and can
operate on shifter subsets of 2, 6, 10, 14, 18, 22, 26, or 30 bits, with the last
bit output to the A register. For example, in a 26-bit shift, the output of the
twenty-sixth bit is routed to the A register and bits 27 through 30 are not
used. The combination of the adder, the P, A, B, and C registers, and the

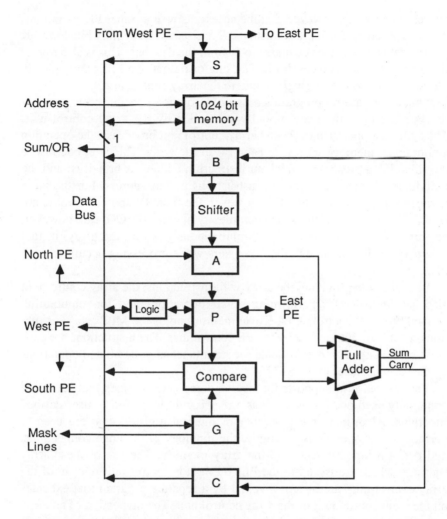

Figure 8–8.   **MPP Processing Element**

shifter, allow arithmetic operations on up to 30-bit operands by operating on one bit at a time, circulating the carry, and storing intermediate results in the shifter. In this way, the MPP can perform addition, subtraction, multiplication, and division.

Memory on each PE consists of a 1K-location, bit-addressable RAM. The same address in each PE memory is accessed simultaneously, using the global address lines. Note, however, that the access, as well as other PE operations, can be masked by the G bit. As with the S registers, the memory bits form 1K planes that can be loaded en masse to or from the data bus. This is also true of the other bit registers on each PE. The sum/or output of all PEs are logically ORed together to form a single output to the array control unit.

Since there are no program stores or instruction decode mechanisms at the PEs, all operations are globally controlled by the array control unit. Thus, on each operation cycle, the array control unit broadcasts the operation and optional memory address to each PE in the array. This is in contrast to the Illiac IV approach, in which an instruction address is broadcast and the individual PE memories contain instructions at that address. For the large number of processors in the MPP, however, the Illiac IV approach would not be feasible, because of the added complexity at each PE. One can, however, perform two different operations simultaneously within the array, in that data may be shifted through the S registers while processing occurs on each PE.

In addition to providing the array with instructions, the array control unit also has facilities for performing scalar operations and for maintaining general program control. A 64-Kbyte memory holds the MPP array instructions, which are interpreted by the PE control unit. The instructions are each eight bytes long and contain fields for simultaneous or combined operations on the various planes of the MPP.

The control unit supports the use of composite routines that represent commonly used operations, such as a matrix multiplication or user-defined functions. Also, there are a number of internal registers that are used to perform scalar operations, configure the topology of the edge connections, and perform indexed access to the array memory. The use of these array routines, which are issued to the PEs by the PE control unit portion of the array control unit, are in turn invoked by a separate program that executes on the main control unit of the array control unit. The invocation of an array operation by the main control unit is performed by placing the request in a queue for the PE control unit. The structure that supports this operation within the array control unit is shown in Figure 8–9. Note that this structure allows the simultaneous execution of scalar and array programs, as well as I/O, with the master control residing in the master control unit.

The staging memory on the MPP is used to assemble and disassemble data from the host computer data format (16 or 32 bits) into the 128-bit word width of the array, and vice versa. The memory is physically organized as a flexible number of banks (4, 8, 16, or 32), with up to 1M word (of 64-bit words) per bank. Accesses to the memory banks are interleaved so that con-

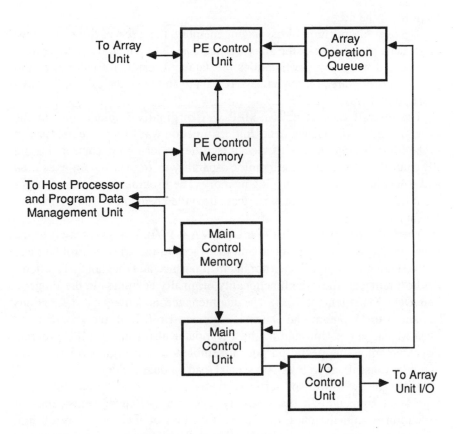

Figure 8–9.   **MPP Array Control Unit Structure**

secutive word addresses lie in different banks. This facilitates the rearrangement of data on a large scale (by 64-bit words) for processing by the array.

In addition to the word organization of the staging memory banks, bitwise permutations on the individual words are also possible. To accomplish this, the staging memory contains two (one on the input and one on the output) three-dimensional memory arrays that can be accessed in 128-bit quantities along various axes in the arrays. Each of these memories has eight planes, each plane with 128×128 bits of memory. An access can occur in column or row format on any of the planes, or may occur at specified intersections of column, row, and plane locations. An access mode control word determines the form of the access.

The overall operation of the staging memory, then, serves three purposes: to get data into and out of the array's S plane in 128-bit quantities; to perform bitwise and wordwise permutations for data and results formatting; and to provide a buffer area for the passage of data to and from the external devices (host processors).

The overall control of the MPP was originally implemented in the Program and Data Management Unit. Its function was to provide user access to the MPP through the use of special facilities to load main control unit and PE control unit programs, a monitor capability to trace program execution and a data interface to the staging memory. The Program and Data Management Unit also contains functions that allow the checking of MPP hardware for fault conditions.

The host computer, typically a DEC VAX 11/780, duplicates all of the Program and Data Management Unit interfaces to the array control unit and to the staging memory. Except for the maintenance and diagnostic functions, the host replaces all of the functionality originally contained in the Program and Data Management Unit. The maintenance and diagnostic functions remain in the Program and Data Management Unit. Both the Program and Data Management Unit and the host computer also support MPP program development with special-purpose assemblers and a high-level language compiler (Pascal), as well as with special load module builders.

There are two levels of software available for the MPP: assembly and high level language. At the assembly level, two languages exist, one for execution within the main control unit portion of the array control unit, called the main control language (MCL); and one for use on the array, called the PE array language (PRL). The MCL language is somewhat like a conventional assembly language, in that it contains the usual compliment of load, store, arithmetic, flow control, and other operation codes. A major difference, however, is the recognition of special data types such as arrays or bit planes, and the interface to special-purpose libraries for array, I/O, and control operations. Thus single MCL statements may in fact result in the performance of thousands of individual operations in the array. References of this type are linked to array programs via the array operation queue.

Routines written to run on the array unit are coded in the PRL language and loaded into the PE control memory of the array control unit. The processing element control unit reads these instructions and performs the appropriate array control actions to execute the instruction. The PRL language itself is a combination of array control and program control operations that can be mixed in a single instruction. The PRL array instruction control signals, along with the appropriate address, are broadcast to the PE array for execution. In a single array operation, each element of the individual PE can be controlled to achieve the desired effect. Control operations such as looping are performed on the PE control unit using internal scalar registers.

High-level language programming for the MPP is performed in Pascal. The extended language, called Parallel Pascal, retains the features of conventional Pascal with the addition of data reduction, permutation, and array conditional operations, as well as provision for the declaration of MPP-specific data types. The additional data-type definitions consist mainly of parallel arrays that are to be manipulated on the PE array. Along with this type of array definition, special array assignment operators are provided that allow the movement of entire arrays, rows, or column subsets of the arrays, and indexed access of array subsets.

A number of common array reduction functions are built into the language, such as summing an array's contents or finding its maximum. These functions operate on entire arrays or along subsets of the array that are of constant size (i.e., along a particular row). These functions operate within the PE array to produce either array or scalar results, depending upon the number of array dimensions that are reduced. For example, we may sum the columns of a two-dimensional array to produce a one-dimensional array result, or we may sum the entire array to produce a scalar result.

Permutations on array data in Parallel Pascal serve to rearrange the array data according to a specific rule. The MPP Parallel Pascal language supports permutations such as rotation, array transpose, and shift along an array dimension. Shifting and rotating are flexible in that the different dimensions of the array may be shifted or rotated by different amounts, thereby allowing nonuniform array operations.

Conditional operations on arrays allow the simultaneous condition testing of all or a subset of an array and the manipulation of only those elements that satisfy the test. This is accomplished with an extended Pascal statement, the where-do-otherwise, which is similar in operation to an if-then-else, except that the condition arguments and statement operands may be arrays. All of the standard Boolean operations are supported and translate into comparisons on the individual array elements. Note that the condition and statement operands (arrays) must be conformal (of the same dimensions and type).

A final feature of the MPP's Parallel Pascal language is the ability to perform bit-level access of array quantities. Expressions using this feature have the effect that a bit plane (as discussed earlier) is operated on by the PE array.

The combination of the above extensions and the standard Pascal capabilities provide a vehicle for application development for the MPP. The advantages of its usage over the assembly languages stem mainly from the automatic generation of the appropriate programs for both the PE control unit and the main control unit, and from the provision of useful, built-in array manipulation functions.

Additional information on the MPP architecture can be found in [Batcher82] and [Batcher80], and information on the actual implementation and programming of the MPP in [Potter85].

The Transputer

The Transputer architecture, developed by INMOS, consists of a family of processing elements designed to be interconnected to form arbitrary parallel processor configurations. Each Transputer processor is built around a standard building-block architecture that contains a processing engine, inter-PE link connections, external device interfaces, and control logic. Figure 8–10 shows the Transputer architecture for the 32-bit machine (a 16-bit version is also available). The Transputer is significant because it contains, on a single chip, the facilities necessary to construct many parallel architectures. Since each Transputer contains its own program counter and executes from its own local memory, parallel systems built using this component are inherently MIMD machines. We will discuss the significance of the different components of a Transputer and the various support devices that are available. Also, software on a Transputer system will be discussed.

The processor portion of a Transputer is a traditional microprocessor. Figure 8–10 shows the 32-bit version of the Transputer, and this discussion will focus on that version. The processor normally obtains its instructions and data from the internal 2-Kbyte RAM and an external memory that may consist of RAM and/or ROM. Data and instructions may also be obtained from the links, which will be discussed later. The external memory interface allows a single Transputer node to contain up to 4 Gbytes of addressable memory. For dynamic RAM implementations, refresh signals are automatically generated for the external memory, and they are programmable to allow different memory configurations. Also, a built-in DMA controller handles data transfers between the memory and the Transputer links. The internal 2-Kbyte RAM, which forms part of the total address space, has a 50-nsec cycle time and is useful for holding data that requires quick access.

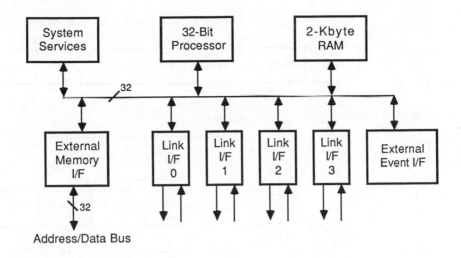

Figure 8–10.   **Transputer Processor Architecture**

The processor contains a short, internal stack for expression evaluation, registers for holding pointers to the memory work space and current instruction, as well as an operand register, whose usage will be discussed. All data fetches from memory are 32-bit accesses. The instruction size of the Transputer, however, is only 8 bits for most instructions (some require 16 bits). Four instructions, therefore, are typically loaded in each memory access. Each 8-bit instruction contains a 4-bit operation code field and a 4-bit operand field. This encoding was adopted based upon the rationale that most instruction and operand references are to locations near the current instruction, so that relative addressing is frequently used. Also, many immediate operands are small and can fit in the 4-bit operand space. Each normal instruction execution loads its data portion into the 4 least significant bits of the 32-bit operand register and then uses the entire 32 bits of the register as the operand. The OP code specifies the action to be taken. The upper 28 bits of the operand register can be loaded, 4 bits at a time, by a special instruction called prefix. Each prefix instruction shifts the operand register by 4 bits and loads the data field as described earlier. In this way, operand lengths can be built up in 4-bit quantities, up to a maximum size of 32 bits. After execution of an instruction using the operand register as the data source, its contents are cleared. Figure 8–11 shows the instruction fetch process with OP3 as the currently executing instruction.

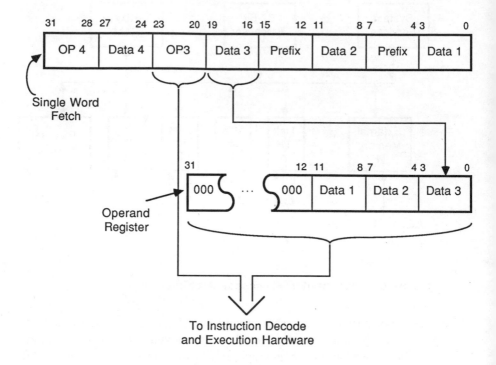

Figure 8–11.   **Transputer Instruction Mechanisms**

For those instructions that require 16 bits, the additional OP code bits are
loaded into the operand register using a prefix instruction, as described
earlier. The operand register is then used as the source for the OP code of the
new instruction. The use of the operand register in this way is forced by the
decoding and execution of a special 8-bit instruction, called operate, which
follows the prefix sequence.

Each Transputer link provides two unidirectional, 10 Mbit/sec serial
transmission paths that can be hooked up to any other Transputer link.
Transfers across the links occur a byte at a time, and each byte transfer is
acknowledged. Thus all byte exchanges are handshaked, and there may be
simultaneous communication in both directions on a single link and also on
all four Transputer links simultaneously. Figure 8–12 shows two-way
communication on a single link and the message formats for data and
acknowledge messages.

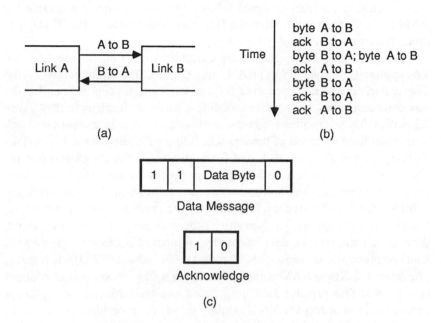

Figure 8–12. **Transputer (a) Link, (b) Example Communication Session, and (c) Message Formats**

The Transputer links are normally used for interprocess communication among a set of cooperating processes on different devices. The link can also be used, however, to load a program for execution on the embedded Transputer processor. In this case, the first message received after a reset on any of the Transputer links contains the length of the following program load. The bytes of the program message are loaded into prespecified memory locations. After the indicated number of program bytes have been transferred and loaded into RAM, execution begins at the first instruction. Whether the Transputer waits for a load message or simply boots from processor ROM is controlled by an input signal. Thus the function of each Transputer in a system may be changed upon reset by loading different startup programs over the links.

The initialization process just described is controlled by the embedded system services function. Also included in system services is an analyze signal input that freezes the state of the Transputer and regains control of the processor. This allows a link-loaded program to be run that can analyze the

Transputer's saved state or communicate the state over one of the links. Thus the sequence of an analyze signal followed by a reset does not disable the RAM refresh operation, so that the last operational state of the Transputer processor remains in memory for analysis.

Four programming languages are currently supported for use with the Transputer: C, Pascal, FORTRAN, and Occam. The architecture of the Transputer, however, is optimized for use with Occam programs, in that the link communication and process-scheduling hardware implement the Occam semantics for interprocess communication and process execution. Each Transputer has two levels of process scheduling built into the hardware. Two memory queues are provided, one for high-priority processes and one for low-priority ones. When no high-priority processes are present, the low-priority ones are time-multiplexed on the processor by the built-in scheduler. If high-priority processes are present, they are serviced one at a time from the high-priority queue. High-priority processes are not time-multiplexed, they run to completion unless interrupted or blocked because of an I/O wait. Blocked processes are requeued in a round robin fashion (FIFO) when ready. The internal 2-Kbyte RAM is typically used to hold process context information so that fast process switching times can be achieved. Interprocess communication occurs via block memory moves for coresident processes, or over the link interfaces for distributed processes. At the program level, interprocess communication is the same for coresident or distributed processes, so that Transputers can be added for increased performance without appreciably altering the existing process code.

The combination of Occam and the Transputer architecture allow for the construction of special purpose parallel systems. Also, more general purpose parallel architectures (e.g., vector, array, or pipeline processors) based on these components are possible. More information on the Transputer architecture and programming can be found in the manufacturer's literature, including [Inmos85].

The iPSC

The basic concept for the Intel iPSC computer was proposed by [Sullivan77] and developed at the California Institute of Technology [Seitz85], under a project called the Cosmic Cube. The project was sponsored by the United States Department of Energy and the United States Department of Defense's Advanced Research Projects Agency (DARPA). Under a license from Caltech, Intel developed its own hypercube-based architecture, utilizing existing Intel microcomputer and communication components. This section discusses the iPSC computer architecture and its software environment.

The Intel iPSC computer consists of a hypercube-architected machine along with an associated host processor called the Cube Manager. As explained in Chapter 5, an n dimensional hypercube has 2^n processing nodes, and each node is connected to n of its neighbors. In the iPSC architecture, as many as 128 nodes can be configured in a seven-dimensional hypercube system. Systems of five and six dimensions are also available. Each node in the iPSC consists of an Intel 80286 microprocessor and 80287 math coprocessor, 512 Kbytes of dual ported dynamic RAM, and 64 Kbytes of PROM. All nodes also contain eight channel connections, seven for internode communication, and one for global communication (see Figure 8–13). For each neighbor connection, a point-to-point serial link is used to transfer information. The global communication channel is connected to a baseband Ethernet local area network. The Ethernet network is a shared broadcast bus that uses the carrier sense, multiple access with collision detection protocol (CSMA/CD) to arbitrate access to the network. Both the internode and the global connections operate at a serial rate of 10 Mbits/sec.

Processor nodes are grouped into a set of 32 nodes called a computational unit (Figure 8–14). The RS-422 channels are used for low-level control of the processor nodes by the Cube Manager. They are also used for diagnostic and system maintenance. The unit services module implements the control over the multidrop RS-422 lines within the computational unit. The different iPSC configurations are built from these computational units in powers of two. Thus the five-dimensional system contains one computational unit, the six- and seven-dimensional ones contain two and four respectively.

In operation, each iPSC node executes using independent instruction and data streams. Each node runs an operating system kernel, called the Node Kernel, which supports the time-multiplexing of processes on the node, as well as message-based neighbor communications. The node's PROM contains a basic monitor function that supports rudimentary communication with the cube manager. When an application is developed, it is linked with the Node Kernel and loaded into the on-board RAM. The neighbor communications are implemented as interprocess channels that pass message blocks to and from the dual-ported RAM. Interprocess communication is not synchronized; a process may send without blocking. On the receiving side, a process may block if the expected message has not yet arrived, or may simply pick up a waiting message. Messages between processes may contain up to 16 Kbytes of information. When transferred, however, messages are broken into 1-Kbyte packets and reassembled at the destination node. This process is

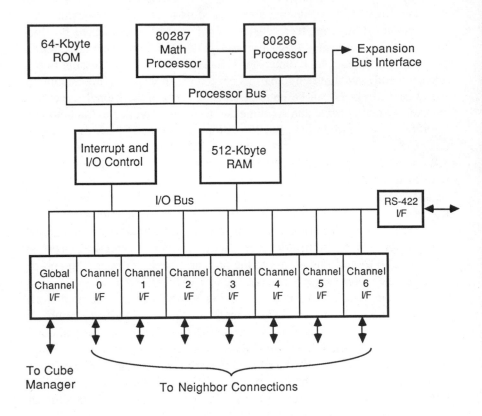

Figure 8–13. **iPSC Node Configuration**

handled automatically by the communication controllers, which reside at each channel interface. The dual-ported memory allows memory access from the processor bus and the I/O bus to occur simultaneously, provided that they are to different addresses. Thus processing and communication may proceed concurrently from the same memory.

Processes that execute within the cube are independently defined using standard program development utilities. Thus the program load for each node in the system is explicitly defined by the programmer or application system designer. Internode processing, then, is loosely coupled and the access to remote resources (such as another node's memory) is made entirely via the message-based communication system.

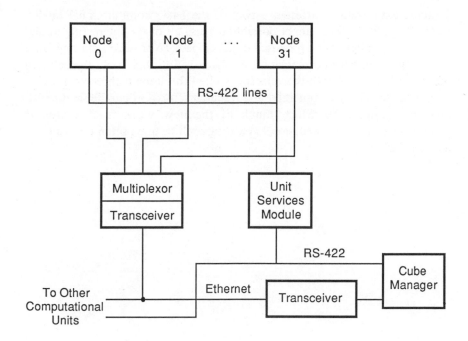

Figure 8–14. **iPSC Computational Unit**

The Cube Manager has several roles in the operation of the cube. First, it supports application program development and load module building through utilities for assembly language, FORTRAN, Lisp, and C. Second, it supplies the commands and load data for initializing applications on the iPSC. Finally, the Cube Manager can monitor the system's health, as well as collect and receive application results during an application's execution.

Using the basic cube architecture, different application structures can be emulated by the appropriate partitioning of the problem onto the cube nodes. [Rattner85] and [Organick85] discuss applications on cube machines. More information on the iPSC architecture in general can be found in [Asbury85] and in the manufacturer's literature.

In this section, architectural examples for many of the parallel and multiprocessor classes discussed in Chapter 5 have been given. Many more examples exist, however, and are discussed in both the manufacturer's literature and in the open literature. In several cases, machines of a given class are very similar in architecture and operation, even offering compatible instruction sets. In other areas, design philosophies are radically different, with each example exploiting a different aspect of the basic computational model. Regretfully, the author cannot possibly discuss all of the interesting implementations that have been proposed or developed. To provide a starting point for further research into machines not discussed in this book, the selected bibliography, along with the references cited throughout the text, provide references for many commercial and research efforts on parallel and multiprocessor computers. Since much of the new work in this area is evolutionary, a solid foundation in existing architectures often proves to be indispensable.

REFERENCES

Allen78. Allen A.D., *Probability, Statistics and Queueing Theory with Computer Science Applications*, Academic Press Inc., Orlando, Fla., 1978.

Allen85. Allen J.R. and Kennedy K., "A Parallel Programming Environment," *IEEE Software*, July 1985.

Asbury85. Asbury R., Frison S.G. and Roth T., "Concurrent Computers Ideal for Inherently Parallel Problems," *Computer Design*, September 1, 1985.

Backus82. Backus J., "Function-Level Programming," *IEEE Spectrum*, August 1982.

Baer80. Baer J., *Computer Systems Architecture*, Computer Science Press Inc., 1980.

Barr81. Barr A.A. and Feigenbaum E.A., *The Handbook of Artificial Intelligence Volume I*, William Kaufmann Inc., 1981.

Barr82. Barr A.A. and Feigenbaum E.A., *The Handbook of Artificial Intelligence Volume II*, William Kaufmann Inc., 1982.

Batcher74. Batcher K.E., "STARAN Parallel Processor System Hardware," *Proceedings of the 1974 National Computer Conference*, 1974.

Batcher82. Batcher K.E., "Bit-Serial Parallel Processing Systems," *IEEE Transactions on Computers*, May 1982.

Bouknight72. Bouknight W.J. et al, "The ILLIAC IV System," *Proceedings of the IEEE*, April 1972.

Boyse75. Boyse J.W. and Warn D.R., "A Straightforward Model for Computer Performance Prediction," *ACM Computing Surveys*, June 1975.

Brooks74. Brooks F.P., *The Mythical Man-Month: Essays on Software Engineering*, Addison-Wesley Publishing Co., 1974.

Burks62. Burks A.W., Goldstein H.H., von Neuman J., "Preliminary Discussion of the Logical Design of An Electronic Computing Instrument, Part II," *Datamation*, October 1962.

Clare73. Clare C. R., *Designing Logic Systems Using State Machines*, McGraw-Hill Inc., 1973.

Cohen82. Cohen P.R. and Feigenbaum E.A., *The Handbook of Artificial Intelligence VolumeIII*, William Kaufmann Inc., 1982.

Curnow76. Curnow H.J. and Wichman B.A., "A Synthetic Benchmark," *The Computer Journal*, February 1976.

Date81. Date C.J., *An Introduction to Database Systems*, Addison-Wesley, 1981.

Date83. Date C.J., *An Introduction to Database Systems Volume II*, Addison-Wesley, 1983.

Davis84. Davis R. and Thomas D., "Systolic Array Chip Matches the Pace of High-Speed Processing," *Electronic Design*, October 31, 1984.

Deitel83. Deitel H.M., *An Introduction to Operating Systems*, Addison-Wesley, 1983.

Denning78. Denning P.J. and Buzen J.P., "The Operational Analysis of Queueing Network Models," *ACM Computing Surveys*, September 1978.

Dennis79. Dennis J.B., "The Varieties of Data Flow Computers," Proceedings of the *First International Conference on Distributed Computing Systems*, October 1979.

Dennis80. Dennis J.B., "Data Flow Supercomputers," *IEEE Computer*, November 1980.

Desrochers84. Desrochers G.R. and Egan L.K., "Investigation of the Ada Language in a Fully Distributed Environment," Naval Underwater Systems Center Technical Memorandum No. 84-2032, NUSC, Newport, R.I., April 1984.

Enslow77. Enslow P.H., "Multiprocessor Organization - A Survey," *ACM Computing Surveys*, March 1977.

Enslow81. Enslow P.H., Saponas, T.G., "Distributed and Decentralized Control in Fully Distributed Processing Systems - A Survey of Applicable Models," Georgia Institute of Technology, Report No. GIT-ILS-81/02, February 1981.

Falk76. Falk H., "Reaching for a Gigaflop," *IEEE Spectrum*, October 1976.

Feng74. Feng T., "Data Manipulation Functions in Parallel Processors and their Implementations," *IEEE Transactions on Computers*, March 1974.

Fisher82. Fisher J.A., "The Enormous Longwood Instruction (ELI) Machine Progress and Research Plans," Yale University Research Report No. 241, July 1982.

Fisher84. Fisher J.A., "The VLIW Machine: A Multiprocessor for Compiling Scientific Code," *IEEE Computer*, July 1984.

Flynn66. Flynn M.J., "Very High Speed Computing Systems," *Proceedings of the IEEE*, December 1966.

Fortier85. Fortier P.J., *Design and Analysis of Distributed Real-Time Systems*, Intertext Inc./McGraw-Hill Inc., 1985.

Gajski85. Gajski D.D. and Peir J., "Essential Issues in Multiprocessor Systems," *IEEE Computer*, June 1985.

Gilbreath81. Gilbreath J., "A High Level Language Benchmark," BYTE, September 1981.

Gilbreath83. Gilbreath J. and Gilbreath G., "Eratosthenes Revisited - Once More through the Sieve," *BYTE*, January 1983.

Goodhue85. Goodhue J. and Starr E., "Development of a Butterfly Multiprocessor Test Bed: Description of Butterfly Components," Bolt Beranek and Newman Inc., Report No. 5872, March 1985.

Goodyear84. Goodyear Aerospace, "Functional Description of ASPRO the High Speed Associative Processor," Goodyear Aerospace Corp. Report GER 16868 Rev A, 16 July 1984.

Gregory63. Gregory J. and McReynolds R., "The Solomon Computer," *IEEE Transactions on Electronic Computers*, December 1963.

Harbaugh85. Harbaugh S. and Forakis J., "Timing Studies using a Synthetic Whetstone Benchmark," *ACM Ada Letters*, Vol. 4, No. 2, 1984.

Hayes78. Hayes J.P., *Computer Architecture and Organization*, McGraw-Hill Inc., 1978.

Hoare78. Hoare C.A.R., "Communicating Sequential Processes," *Communications of the ACM*, August 1978.

Hoare85. Hoare C.A.R., *Communicating Sequential Processes*, Prentice Hall International, 1985.

Huffman52. Huffman D.A., "A Method for the Construction of Minimum Redundancy Codes," *Proceedings of the IRG*, September 1952.

Inmos85. Inmos Limited, *Transputer Architecture Reference Manual*, Inmos Limited, 1985.

Intel80. Intel Corporation, *iAPX432 Object Primer*, Intel Corporation, 1980.

Intel81. Intel Corporation, *iAPX432 General Data Processor Architecture Reference Manual*, Intel Corporation, 1981.

Jackson57. Jackson J.R., "Networks of Waiting Lines," *Operations Research*, August 1957.

Jones77. Jones et al, "Software Management of CM* - A Distributed Multiprocessor," *Proceedings of the 1977 National Computer Conference*, 1977.

Kahn81. Kahn K. et al, "iMAX - A Multiprocessor Operating System for an Object-Based Computer," *Proceedings of the 8th Symposium on Operating Systems Principles*, December 1981.

Kleinrock75. Kleinrock L., *Queueing Systems: Volume I; Theory*, Wiley and Sons, New York, 1975.

Kleinrock76. Kleinrock L., *Queueing Systems: Volume II; Computer Applications*, Wiley and Sons, New York, 1976.

Kuck74. Kuck D.J., "A Survey of Parallel Machine Organization and Programming," *ACM Computing Surveys*, March 1977.

Kung82. Kung H.T., "Why Systolic Architectures?," *IEEE Computer*, January 1982.

Lavenberg83. Lavenberg S.S. ed., *Computer Performance Modeling Handbook*, Academic Press Inc., New York, 1983.

Lazowska84. Lazowska E.D., Zahorjan J., Graham G.S. and Sevcik K.C., *Quantitative System Performance: Computer System Analysis using Queueing Network Models*, Prentice Hall, Englewood Cliffs, N.J., 1984.

Lee84. Lee J.K.F. and Smith A.J., "Branch Prediction Strategies and Branch Target Buffer Design," *IEEE Computer*, January 1984.

Lerner84. Lerner E.J.,"Data-Flow Architecture," *IEEE Spectrum*, April 1984.

Linden76. Linden T.A., "Operating System Structures to Support Security and Reliable Software," *ACM Computing Surveys*, December 1976.

Madnick74. Madnick S.E. and Donovan J.J., *Operating Systems*, McGraw-Hill Inc., 1974.

McGraw82. McGraw J.R., "The VAL Language: Description and Analysis," *ACM Transactions on Programming Languages and Systems*, January 1982.

Millman72. Millman J. and Halkias C., *Integrated Electronics: Analog and Digital Circuits and Systems*, McGraw-Hill Book Company, 1972.

Organick85. Organick E.I., "Algorithms, Concurrent Processors and Computer Science Education," *ACMSIGSE Bulletin*, March 1985.

Papoulis84. Papoulis A., *Probability, Random Variables and Stochastic Processes*, McGraw-Hill Book Company, New York, 1984.

Potter85. Potter J.L. ed., *The Massively Parallel Processor*, The MIT Press, 1985.

Pountain86. Pountain D., *A Tutorial Introduction to Occam Programming*, INMOS Limited, 1986.

Pratt85. Pratt T., "Pisces: An Environment for Parallel Scientific Computation," *IEEE Software*, July 1985.

Preparata81. Preparata F.P. and Vaillemin J., "The Cube-Connected Cycles: A Versatile Network for Parallel Computation," *Communications of the ACM*, May 1981.

Pritsker79. Pritsker A.A.B. and Pedgen C.D., *Introduction to Simulation and SLAM*, John Wiley and Sons Inc., New York, 1979.

Purdum86. Purdum J., "Benchmark Philosophy and Methodology," *Computer Language*, February 1985.

Quinn84. Quinn M.J. and Narsingh D., "Parallel Graph Algorithms," *ACM Computing Surveys*, September 1984.

Ramamoorthy77. Ramamoorthy C.V. and Li H.F., "Pipeline Architecture," *ACM Computing Surveys*, March 1977.

Rattner85. Rattner J., "Concurrent Processing: A New Direction in Scientific Computing," *Proceedings of the 1985 AFIPS National Computer Conference*, 1985.

Sahni81. Sahni S. and Nassimi D., "Optimal BPC Permutations on a Cube Connected SIMD Computer," University of Minnesota Report, August 1981.

Seitz85. Seitz C.L., "The Cosmic Cube," *Communications of the ACM*, January 1985.

Siewiorek77. Siewiorek D.P. et al, "CM* - A Modular, Multi-Microprocessor," *Proceedings of the 1977 National Computer Conference*, 1977.

Snyder84. Snyder L., "Parallel Programming and the Poker Programming Environment," University of Washington Technical Report TR-84-04-02, April 1984.

Soh87. Soh J. and Paesano S., *Distributed Operating Systems*, Unpublished Manuscript, 1987.

Stone71. Stone H.S., "Parallel Processing with the Perfect Shuffle," *IEEE Transactions on Computers*, February 1971.

Stone80. Stone H.S. et al., *Introduction to Computer Architecture*, Science Research Associates Inc., 1980.

Stone82. Stone H.S., *Microcomputer Interfacing*, Addison-Wesley Publishing Company Inc., 1982.

Sullivan77. Sullivan H. and Brashkow T.R., "A Large-Scale Homogeneous Machine I & II," *IEEE Proceedings of the Fourth Annual Symposium on Computer Architecture*, New York, 1977.

Swan77. Swan R.J. et al, "The Implementation of the CM* Multi-Microprocessor," *Proceedings of the 1977 National Computer Conference*, 1977.

Thomas86. Thomas B. et al, "Butterfly Parallel Processor Overview," Bolt Beranek and Newmann Inc., Report No. 6148, March 6, 1986.

Thurber75. Thurber K.J. and Wald L.D., "Associative and Parallel Processors," *ACM Computing Surveys*, December 1975.

Trivedi82. Trivedi K., *Probability and Statistics with Reliability, Queueing and Computer Science Applications*, Prentice Hall, Englewood N.J., 1982.

Ullman82. Ullman J.D., *Database Systems*, Computer Science Press, 1982.

Walpole78. Walpole R.E. and Myers R.H., *Probability and Statistics for Engineers and Scientists*, Macmillan Publishing Company, New York, 1978.

Webster53. *Webster's New Collegiate Dictionary*, G.& C. Merriam Co., 1953.

Weicker84. Weicker R.P., "Dhrystone: A Synthetic Systems Programming Benchmark," *Communications of the ACM*, October 1984.

Wu83. Wu A.Y., "Embedding of Networks of Processors into Hypercubes," University of Maryland Report, December 1983.

Wulf80. Wulf W.A., "Trends in the Design and Implementation of Programming Language," *IEEE Computer*, January 1980.

Yau77. Yau S.S. and Fung H.S., "Associative Processor Architecture: A Survey," *ACM Computing Surveys*, March 1977.

BIBLIOGRAPHY

Ackerman W.B., "Data Flow Languages," *IEEE Computer*, February 1982.

Adams L.M. and Crockett C.T., "Modeling Algorithm Execution Time on Processor Arrays," *IEEE Computer*, July 1984.

Adams G.B and Siegal H.J, "The Extra Stage Cube: A Fault-Tolerant Interconnection Network for Supersystems," *IEEE Transactions on Computers*, May 1982.

Agrawal D.P., "High Speed Arithmetic Arrays," *IEEE Transactions on Computers*, March 1979.

Agrawal D.P., "Graph Theoretical Analysis and Design of Multistage Interconnection Networks," *IEEE Transactions on Computers*, July 1982.

Agrawal D.P. and Leu J.S., "Dynamic Accessibility Testing and Path Length Optimization of Multistage Interconnection Networks," *Proceedings of the 1984 International Conference on Distributed Computing Systems*, pp. 266-277, 1984.

Agrawal D.P., Janakiram V.K. and Pathak G.C., "Evaluating the Performance of Multicomputer Configurations," *IEEE Computer*, May 1986.

Agrawal D.P and Jain R., "A Pipelined Pseudoparallel System Architecture for Real-Time Dynamic Scene Analysis," *IEEE Transactions on Computers*, October 1982.

Ahmed H.M., Delsome J. and Morf M., "Highly Concurrent Computing Structures for Matrix Arithmetic and Signal Processing," *IEEE Computer*, January 1982.

Ahuja S., Carriero N. and Gelernter D., "Linda and Friends," *IEEE Computer*, August 1986.

Ajmone M. et al, "Modeling Bus Contention and Memory Interference in a Multiprocessing System," *IEEE Transactions on Computers*, Vol C-32, pp. 60-70, 1983.

Allen J.R. and Kennedy K., "PFC: A Program to Convert FORTRAN to Parallel Form," in *Supercomputers: Design and Applications*, K. Hwang ed., IEEE Computer Society Press, 1984.

Amdahl, G.M., Blaauw G.A. and Boorks F.J. Jr, "Architecture of the IBM System/360," *IBM Journal of Research and Development*, Vol. 8, No. 2, 1964.

Anderson J.P., Hoffman S.A., Shifman J. and Williams R.J., "D825-A Multiple Computer System for Command and Control," *Proceedings of the Fall Joint Computer Conference*, 1962.

Andrews G.J. and McGraw J.R., "Language Features for Parallel Processing and Resource Control," *Proceedings of the Conference on Design and Implementation of Programming Languages*, Ithica N.Y., October 1976.

Arden B.W. and Ginosar R., "MP/C: A Multimicroprocessor/Computer Architecture," *IEEE Transactions on Computers*, Vol. C-31, pp. 455-473, 1982.

Arden B.W. and Lee H., "Analysis of Chordal Ring Network," *IEEE Transactions on Computers*, April 1981.

Arnold C.N., "Performance Evaluation of Three Automatic Vectorizer Packages" *Proceedings of the International Conference on Parallel Processing*, pp. 235-242, 1982.

Arnold J.S., Casey D.P. and McKinstry R.H., "Design of Tightly-Coupled Multiprocessing Programs," *IBM Systems Journal*, No.1, 1974.

Arnold R.G., Berg R.O. and Thomas J.W., "A Modular Approach to Real-Time Supersystems," *IEEE Transactions on Computers*, Vol. C-31, pp. 385-398, 1982.

Arvind and Ianucci R.A., "A Critique of Multiprocessing von Neumann Style," Proceedings of the 10th Annual Symposium on Computer Architecture, pp. 426-436, 1983.

Arvind and Gostelow K.P., "The U-Interpreter," *IEEE Computer*, February 1982.

Arvind, Kathail V. and Pingali K., "A Data Flow Architecture with Tagged Tokens," *MIT Laboratory for Computer Science Technical Memorandum No. 174*, September 1980.

Baba T., et al, "Hierarchical Micro-Architectures of a Two-Level Microprogrammed Multiprocessor Computer," *Proceedings of the International Conference on Parallel Processing*, pp. 478-485, 1983.

Babb R.G., "Parallel Processing with Large Grain Data Flow Techniques," *IEEE Computer*, July 1984.

Backus J., "Can Programming be Liberated from the von Neumann Style? A Functional Style and its Algebra of Programs," *Communications of the ACM*, August 1978.

Baer J.L and Ellis C., "Model, Design and Evaluation of a Compiler for a Parallel Processing Environment," *IEEE Transactions on Software Engineering*, November 1977.

Bahandarkar D.P., "Analysis of Memory Interference in Multiprocessors," *IEEE Transactions on Computers*, September 1975.

Bain W.L. Jr. and Ahuja S.R., "Performance Analysis of High-Speed Digital Busses for Multiprocessing Systems," *Proceedings of the 8th Annual Symposium on Computer Architecture*, pp. 107-131, May 1981.

Barlow R.H., Evans D.J. and Shanehchi J., "Comparative Study of the Exploitation of Different Levels of Parallelism on Different Parallel Architectures," *Proceedings of the International Conference on Parallel Processing*, pp. 34-40, 1982.

Barnes G.H. and Lundstrom S.F., "Design and Validation of a Connection Network for Many-Processor Multiprocessor Systems," *IEEE Computer*, December 1981.

Batcher K.E., "The FLIP Network in Staran," *Proceedings of the 1976 International Conference on Parallel Processing*, Waldenwoods Mich., 1976.

Batcher K.E., "The Multidimensional Access Memory in Staran," *IEEE Transactions on Computers*, February 1977.

Baudet G.M., "Asynchronous Iterative Methods for Multiprocessors," *Journal of the ACM*, April 1978.

Bensoussan A., Clingen C.T. and Daley R., "The MULTICS Virtual Memory: Concepts and Design," *Communications of the ACM*, May 1972.

Bernstein A.J., "Analysis of Programs for Parallel Processing," IEEE Transactions on Electronic Computers, October 1966.

Bhandarkar D.P., *Analytical Models for Memory Interference in Multiprocessor Computer Systems*, Ph.D. Thesis, Carnegie Mellon University, September 1973.

Bhandarkar D.P., "Analysis of Memory Interference in Multiprocessors," *IEEE Transactions on Computers*, September 1975.

Bhandarkar D.P., "Some Performance Issues in Multiprocessor System Design," *IEEE Transactions on Computers*, May 1977.

Bhuyan L.N., "On the Performance of Loosely Coupled Multiprocessors," *Proceedings of the 11th Annual International Symposium on Computer Architecture*, pp. 256-262, June 1984.

Bhuyan L.N. and Agrawal D.P., "Design and Performance of Generalized Interconnection Networks," *IEEE Transactions on Computers*, December 1983.

Bhuyan L.N. and Agrawal D.P., "Generalized Hypercube and Hyperbus Structures for a Computer Network," *IEEE Transactions on Computers*, April 1984.

Bhuyan L.N. and Lee C.W., "An Interference Analysis of Interconnection Networks," *Proceedings of the International Conference on Parallel Processing*, pp. 2-9, 1983.

Bic L., "Execution of Logic Programs on a Dataflow Architecture," *Proceedings of the International Workshop on Computer Architecture*, pp. 1.20-1.25, May 1984.

Bisiani R., "A Class of Data-Flow Architectures for Speech Recognition," *Proceedings of the IEEE ICASSP 83*, 1983.

Bisiane R., Mauersberg H. and Reddy R., "Task Oriented Architecture," *Proceedings of the IEEE*, Vol. 71, No.7, 1983.

Booth M. and Misegades K., "Microtasking: A New Way to Harness Multi-processors," *Cray Channels*, Summer 1986.

Brent R., "The Parallel Evaluation of General Arithmetic Expressions," *Journal of the ACM*, April 1984.

Briggs F.A. and Davidson E.S., "Organization of Semiconductor Memories for Parallel-Pipelined Processors," *IEEE Transactions on Computers*, February 1977.

Briggs F.A, Dubois M. and Hwang K., "Throughput Analysis and Configuration Design of a Shared-Resource Multiprocessor System: PUMPS," *Proceeding of the 8th Annual Symposium on Computer Architecture*, May 1981.

Briggs F.A. and Dubois M., "Effectiveness of Private Caches in Multiprocessor Systems with Parallel-Pipelined Memories," *IEEE Transactions on Computers*, January 1983.

Briggs F.A., Fu K.S., Hwang K. and Wah B.W., "PUMPS Architecture for Pattern Analysis and Image Database Management," *IEEE Transactions on Computers*, October 1982.

Brooks E.D., "Performance of the Butterfly Processor - Memory Interconnection in a Vector Environment," *Proceedings of the 1985 International Conference on Parallel Processing*, pp. 21-24, 1985.

Hansen P.B., "The Programming Language Concurrent Pascal," *IEEE Transactions on Software Engineering*, June 1975.

Brock J.D. and Montz L.B., "Translation and Optimization of Data Flow Programs," *Proceedings of the 1979 International Conference on Parallel Processing*, pp. 46-54, August 1979.

Brode B., "Precompilation of FORTRAN Programs to Facilitate Array Processing," *IEEE Computer*, Vol. 14, No. 9, 1981.

Budnik P.P and Kuck D.J., "The Organization and Use of Parallel Memories," *IEEE Transactions on Computers*, December 1971.

Buehrer R.E. et al, "The ETH-Multiprocessor EMPRESS: A Dynamically Configurable MIMD System," *IEEE Transactions on Computers*, Vol. C-31, pp. 1035-1044, 1982.

Burkowski F.J., "A Vector and Array Multiprocessor Extension of the Sylvan Architecture," *Proceedings of the 11th Annual International Symposium on Computer Architecture*, pp. 4-11, June 1984.

Burnett G.J. and Coffman E.G., "A Study of Interleaved Memory Systems," *Proceedings of the AFIPS Spring Joint Computer Conference*, Vol. 36, pp. 467-474, 1970.

Bucher I.Y., "The Computational Speed of Supercomputers," *Proceedings of the ACM Sigmetrics Conference on Measurement and Modeling of Computer Systems*, pp. 151-165, 1983.

Butler J.M. and Oruc A.Y., "A Facility for Simulating Multiprocessors," *IEEE Micro*, October 1986.

Carlson W.W., "Algorithmic Performance of Dataflow Multiprocessors," *IEEE Computer*, December 1985.

Case R.P. and Padegs A., "Architecture of the IBM System 370," *Communications of the ACM*, January 1978.

Castan M. and Organick E.L., "u3L: An HLL-RISC Processor for Parallel Execution of FL-Language Programs," *Proceedings of the 9th Annual Symposium on Computer Architecture*, pp. 238-247, 1982.

Chamberlin D.D., Fuller S.H. and Liu L.Y., "An Analysis of Page Allocation Strategies for Multiprogramming Systems with Virtual Memory," *IBM Journal of Research and Development*, p. 17, 1973.

Chandy K.M., "Models for the Recognition and Scheduling of Parallel Tasks on Multiprocessor Systems," *Bulletin of the Operations Research Society of America*, Vol. 23, Supplement 1, Spring 1975.

Chang D., Kuck D.J. and Lawrie D.H., "On the Effective Bandwidth of Parallel Memories," *IEEE Transactions on Computers*, May 1977.

Charlesworth A.E., "An Approach to Scientific Array Processing: The Architectural Design of the AP-120/FPS-164 Family," *IEEE Computer*, December 1981.

Chen N.F. and Liu C.L., "On a Class of Scheduling for Multiprocessor Computing Systems," *Proceedings of the Conference on Parallel Processing*, August 1974.

Chen P. et al, "Interconnection Networks Using Shuffles," *IEEE Computer*, December 1981.

Chaing Y.P. and Fu K.S., "Matching Parallel Algorithm and Architecture," *Proceedings of the International Conference on Parallel Processing*, pp. 374-380, 1983.

Chin C.Y. and Hwang K., "Multipath Packet Switching Networks for Multiprocessors and Dataflow Computers," *IEEE Transactions on Computers*, October 1984.

Chin F.Y., Lam J. and Chen I.N., "Efficient Parallel Algorithms for Some Graph Problems," *Communications of the ACM*, Vol. 25, pp. 659-665, 1982.

Chow Y.C. and Kohler W.H., "Models for Dynamic Load Balancing in a Heterogeneous Multiple Processor System," *IEEE Transactions on Computers*, May 1979.

Chu Y. and Abrams M., "Programming Languages and Direct-Execution Computer Architecture," *IEEE Computer*, July 1981.

Chu Y. and Abrams M., "An Ada Concurrency Instruction Set," *Proceedings of the International Workshop on High-Level Computer Architecture*, Los Angeles, CA., pp 7.1-7.9, May 1984.

Clapp J.A and Hazle M., "Building Blocks for CCC Systems," *Mitre Corporation Report No. ESD-TR-77-360*, March 1983.

Cohen T., "Structured Flowcharts for Multiprocessing," *Computer Language*, Vol. 13, No.4, 1978.

Cohler E.U. and Storer J.E., "Functionally Parallel Architecture for Array Processors," *IEEE Computer*, Vol. 14, No. 9, 1981.

Conrad V. and Wallach H., "Iterative Solution of Linear Equations on a Parallel Processor System," *IEEE Transactions on Computers*, September 1977.

Cooper R.G., "The Distributed Pipeline," *IEEE Transactions on Computers*, November 1977.

Crane B.A., Gilmartin M.J., Huttenhoff J., Rus P.T. and Shively R.R., "PEPE Computer Architecture," *IEEE Compcon*, pp. 57-60, 1972.

Crowther W. et al, "Performance Measurements on a 128-Node Butterfly Parallel Processor," *Proceedings of the 1985 International Conference on Parallel Processing*, pp. 531-535, 1985.

Cuny J.E. and Snyder L., "A Model for Analyzing Generalized Interprocessor Communication Systems," *Purdue University Report No. CSD-TR-406*, October 1986.

Davidson E.S., "The Design and Control of Pipelined Function Generators," *Proceedings of the 1971 International Conference on Systems, Networks and Computers*, pp. 19-21, January 1971.

Davis A.L. and Keller R.M., "Data Flow Program Graphs," *IEEE Computer*, February 1982.

Davis C.G. and Couch R.L., "Ballistic Missile Defense: A Supercomputer Challenge," *IEEE Computer*, November 1980.

Dekel E., Nassimi D. and Sahni S.H., "Parallel Matrix and Graph Algorithms," *SIAM Journal of Computers*, Vol. 10, pp. 657-675, 1981.

Deminet J., "Experience with Multiprocessor Algorithms," *IEEE Transactions on Computers*, April 1982.

Denning P.J., "Operating System Principles for Data Flow Networks," *IEEE Computer*, July 1978.

Dennis J.B., "Data Flow Supercomputers," *IEEE Computer*, November 1980.

Dennis J.B., "The Varieties of Data Flow Computers," *Proceedings of the 1st International Conference on Distributed Computing Systems*, pp. 430-439, 1979.

Dennis J.B., Boughton G.A. and Leung C.K., "Building Blocks for Data Flow Prototypes," *Symposium on Computer Architecture*, pp. 193-200, May 1980.

Dennis J. and Gao R., "Maximum Pipelining of Array Operations on Static Dataflow Machine," *Proceedings of the 1983 International Conference on Parallel Processing*, pp. 23-26, August 1983.

Dennis J.B., Gao G.R. and Todd K.W., "Modeling the Weather with a Data Flow Supercomputer," *IEEE Transactions on Computers*, July 1984.

Department of Defense, *Reference Manual for the Ada Programming Language*, U.S. Department of Defense, July 1982.

Despain A.M. and Patterson D.A., "X-tree - A Tree Structured Multiprocessor Computer Architecture," *Proceedings of the 5th Symposium on Computer Architecture*, pp. 144-151, 1978.

Dias D.M. and Jump J.R, "Packet Switching Interconnection Networks for Modular Systems," *IEEE Computer*, December 1981.

Dijkstra E.W., "Solution of a Problem in Concurrent Programming," *Communications of the ACM*, September 1965.

Dimopoulos N., "The Homogeneous Multiprocessor Architecture-Structure and Performance Analysis," *Proceedings of the International Conference on Parallel Processing*, pp. 520-523, 1983.

Doran R.W., "The Amdahl 470 V/8 and the IBM 3033: A Comparison of Processor Designs," *IEEE Computer*, Vol. 15, No. 4, 1982.

Dongarra J.J. et al., *Linpack User's Guide*, Society of Industrial and Applied Mathematics, Philadelphia, 1979.

Dongarra J.J., "Performance of Various Computers Using Standard Linear Equations Software in a FORTRAN Environment," *Argonne National Laboratory Technical Memorandum No. 23*, January 22, 1987.

Dubois M. and Briggs F.A., "Effects of Cache Coherency in Multiprocessors," *IEEE Transactions on Computers*, November 1982.

Dubois M. and Briggs F.A., "Performance of Synchronized Iterative Processes in Multiprocessor Systems," *IEEE Transactions on Software Engineering*, July 1982.

Duckworth J.R., *Parallel Computation on a Multi-Stream Data Flow Machine*, Ph.D. Thesis, University of Mottingham, October 1984.

Emer J.S. and Davidson E.S, "Control Store Organizations for Multiple Stream Pipelined Processors," *Proceedings of the 1978 International Conference on Parallel Processing*, pp. 43-48, 1978.

Emrath P., "XYLEM: An Operating System for the Cedar Multiprocessor," *IEEE Software*, July 1985.

Enslow P.H., "Multiprocessor Organization," *ACM Computing Surveys*, March 1977.

Enslow P.H. ed., *Multiprocessors and Parallel Processing*, Wiley-Interscience, New York, N.Y., 1974.

Ericsson T and Danielsson P.E., "LIPP - A SIMD Multiprocessor Architecture for Image Processing," *Proceedings of the 10th Annual Symposium on Computer Architecture*, pp. 395-401, 1983.

Erikson O. and Staunstrup H., "Concurrent Algorithms for Root Searching," *Acta Informatica*, Vol. 18, pp. 361-376, 1983.

Evensen A.J. and Troy J.L, "Introduction to the Architecture of a 288-Element PEPE," *Proceedings of the Sagamore Conference on Parallel Processing*, pp. 162-169, 1973.

Fabry R.S., "Capability Based Addressing," *Communications of the ACM*, July 1974.

Faggin F., "How VLSI Impacts Computer Architecture," *IEEE Spectrum*, July 1978.

Fairbairn D.G., "VLSI: A New Frontier for System Designers," *IEEE Computer*, January 1982.

Farouki R.T. et al, "Computational Astrophysics on the Array Processor," *IEEE Computer*, Vol. 16, No. 6, 1983.

Fathi E.T. and Krieger M., "Multiple Processor Systems: What, Why and When," *IEEE Computer*, March 1983.

Feng T. Y., "Data Manipulation Functions in Parallel Processors and Their Implementations," *IEEE Transactions on Computers*, March 1974.

Feng T., "A Survey of Interconnection Networks," *IEEE Computer*, December 1981.

Fennell K.D. and Lesser V.R., "Parallelism in Artificial Intelligence Problem Solving: A Case Study of Hearsay II," *IEEE Transactions on Computers*, March 1977.

Fernbach S., "Applications of Supercomputers in the USA-Today and Tomorrow," in *Supercomputers: Design and Applications*, K. Hwang ed., IEEE Computer Society Press, 1984.

Fisher A.L. and Kung H.T., "Synchronizing Large Systolic Arrays," *Carnegie Mellon Report No. CMU-CS-82-133*, April 1982.

Fisher A.L. and Kung H.T., "Synchronizing Large VLSI Processor Arrays," *Proceedings of the 10th Annual Symposium on Computer Architecture*, pp. 54-58, 1983.

Fisher J.A., "Very Long Instruction Word Architectures and the ELI-512," *Proceedings of the 10th Annual Symposium on Computer Architecture*, pp. 140-149, 1983.

Flanders P.M., "A Unified Approach to a Class of Data Movements on an Array Processor," *IEEE Transactions on Computers*, Vol. C-31, pp. 809-819, 1982.

Floyd R.W. and Ullman J.D., "The Compilation of Regular Expressions into Integrated Circuits," *Journal of the ACM*, Vol. 29, pp. 603-622, 1982.

Flynn M.J., "Some Computer Organizations and Their Effectiveness," *IEEE Transactions on Computers*, September 1972.

Fontao R.O, "A Concurrent Algorithm for Avoiding Deadlocks in Multiprocess Multiple Resonance Systems," *Proceedings of the 3rd Symposium on Operating Systems Principles*, October 1971.

Forsstrom K.S., "Array Processors in Real-Time Flight Simulation," *IEEE Computer*, vol. 16, No. 6, 1983.

Fortes J.A.B. and Moldovan D.I., "Data Broadcasting in Linearly Scheduled Array Processors," *Proceedings of the 11th Annual International Symposium on Computer Architecture*, pp. 224-231, June 1984.

Foster C.C., *Content-Addressable Parallel Processors*, Van Nostrand Reinhold Co., New York, N.Y., 1976.

Franklin M.A. and Wann D. F., "Pin Limitation and VLSI Interconnection Networks:, *Proceedings of the International Conference on Parallel Processing*, pp. 253-258, 1981.

Franklin M. S. and Soong N. L., "One-Dimensional Optimization on Multiprocessor Systems," *IEEE Transactions on Computers*, Vol. C-30, pp. 61-66, 1981.

Fritsch G., Kleinoeder W., Linster C.U. and Volkert J., "EMSY 85-The Erlangen Multiprocessor System for a Broad Spectrum of Applications," *Proceedings of the 1983 International Conference on Parallel Processing*, pp. 325-330, 1983.

Fromm H. et al, "Experiences with Performance Measurement and Modeling of a Processor Array," *IEEE Transactions on Computers*, Vol. C-32, pp. 15-31, 1983.

Fuller S.H. and Harbison S.P., *The C.mmp Multiprocessor*, CMU Computer Science Department Technical Report, CMU, Pittsburgh. PA, 1978.

Fung L.W., "A Massively Parallel Processing Computer," in *High Speed Computer and Algorithm Organization*, D.J. Kuck et al eds, Acedemic Press, New York, 1977.

Gajski D.D. et al, "A Second Opinion on Data Flow Machines and Languages," *IEEE Computer*, February 1982.

Gaillat G., "The Design of a Parallel Processor for Image Processing On-Board Satellites: An Application Oriented Approach," *Proceedings of the 10th Annual Conference on Computer Architecture*, pp. 379-386.

Gajski D., "An Algorithm for Solving Linear Recurrence Systems on Parallel and Pipelined Machines," *IEEE Transactions on Computers*, March 1981.

Gajski D., Kuck D., Lawrie D. and Sameh A., "Cedar - A Large Scale Multiprocessor," *Proceedings of the 1983 International Conference on Parallel Processing*, pp. 524-529, 1983.

Gajski D. and Peir J.K., "Essential Issues in Multiprocessor Systems," *IEEE Computer*, June 1985.

Gallopoulos E.J. and McEwan S.D., "Numerical Experiments with the Massively Parallel Processor," *Proceedings of the 1983 International Conference on Parallel Processing*, pp. 29-35, 1983.

Gao Q.S. and Zhang X., "Another Approach to Making Supercomputers by Microprocessors -- Cellular Vector Computer of Vertical and Horizontal Processing with Virtual Common Memory," *Proceedings of the 1980 International Conference on Parallel Processing*, pp. 163-164, 1980.

Gao G. R., "Pipelined Mapping of Homogeneous Dataflow Programs," *Proceedings of the 1984 International Conference on Parallel Processing*, 1984.

Gaudet G. and Stevenson D., "Optimal Sorting Algorithms for Parallel Computers," *IEEE Transactions on Computers*, January 1978.

Gaudiot J.L., "The TX16: A Highly Programmable Multi-Microprocessor Architecture," *IEEE Micro*, October 1986.

Gaudiot J.L and Ercegovac M. D., "A Scheme for Handling Arrays in Dataflow Systems," *Proceedings of the 3rd International Conference on Distributed Computing Systems*, 1982.

Gehringer E.F., Jones A.K. and Segall Z.Z., "The Cm* Testbed," *IEEE Computer*, October 1982.

Georgiadis P.I., Papazoglou M.P. and Maritasas D.G., "Towards a Parallel SIMULA Machine," *Proceedings of the 8th Annual Symposium on Computer Architecture*, pp. 263-178, 1981.

Goke R. and Lipovski G.J., "Banyan Networks for Partitioning on Multiprocessor Systems," *Proceedings of the 1st Annual Symposium on Computer Architecture*, pp. 21-30, 1973.

Goldschlager L.M., "A Universal Interconnection Pattern for Parallel Computers," *Journal of the ACM*, Vol. 29, pp. 1073-1086, 1982.

Gonzales M. J., "Deterministic Processor Scheduling:, *ACM Computing Surveys*, September 1977.

Gonzales T. and Sahni S., "Preemptive Scheduling of Uniform Processor Systems," *Journal of the ACM*, January 1978.

Goodman J.R. and Sequin C.H., "Hypertree: A Multiprocessor Interconnection Topology," *IEEE Transactions on Computers*, Vol. C-30, pp. 923-933, 1981.

Goodyear Aerospace Co., "Massively Parallel Processor (MPP)," *Technical Report No. 16684*, July 1984.

Gosden J.A., "Explicit Parallel Processing Description and Control in Programs for Multi and Uni-Processor Computers," *AFIPS Fall Joint Computer Conference*, pp. 651-660, 1966.

Gostelow K.P. and Thomas R.E., "Performance of a Simulated Dataflow Computer," *IEEE Transactions on Computers*, October 1980.

Gottlieb A., Grishman R., Kruskal C.P., McAaliffe K.P., Randolph L. and Snir M., "The NYU Ultracomputer - Designing an MIMD Shared Memory Parallel Computer," *IEEE Transactions on Computers*, February 1983.

Gottlieb A. and Schwartz J.T., "Networks and Algorithms for Very Large-Scale Parallel Computation," *IEEE Computer*, January 1982.

Grinberg J., Nudd G.R. and Etchells R.D., "A Cellular VLSI Architecture," *IEEE Computer*, Vol.17, No. 1, 1984.

Grit D.H. and McGraw J.R., "Programming Divide and Conquer on a Multiprocessor," *Lawrence Livermore National Lab Report No. UCRL-88710*, 1983.

Grohoski G.R., and Patel J.H., "A Performance Model for Instruction Prefetch in Pipelined Instruction Units," *Proceedings of the 1982 International Conference on Parallel Processing*, pp. 248-252, 1982.

Gurd J. and Watson I., "Data Driven System for High Speed Parallel Computing Part I," *Computer Design*, June 1980.

Gurd J. and Watson I., "Data Driven System for High Speed Parallel Computing Part II," Computer Design, July 1980.

Habra N.R., *The Design and Analysis of a Parallel Processing Language*, Ph.D. Thesis, Columbia University, 1979.

Hack J.J., "Peak v.s. Sustained Performance in Highly Concurrent Vector Machines," *IEEE Computer*, September 1986.

Hagiwara H. et al., "A Dynamically Microprogrammable Computer with Low Level Parallelism," *IEEE Transactions on Computers*, Vol. C-29, 1980.

Halstead R.H., "Parallel Symbolic Computing," *IEEE Computer*, August 1986.

Handler W., "The Impact of Classification Schemes on Computer Architecture," *Proceedings of the 1977 International Conference on Parallel Processing*, pp. 7-15, 1977.

Handler W., Schreiber H. and Sigmund V., "Computational Structures Reflected in General Purpose and Special Purpose Multiprocessor Systems," *Proceedings of the 1979 International Conference on Parallel Processing*, pp. 95-102, 1979.

Hanscn P.B., *The Architecture of Concurrent Programs*, Prentice-Hall, Engwood Cliffs, N.J., 1977.

Harris J.A. and Smith D.R., "Hierarchical Multiprocessor Organizations," *Proceedings of the 4th Symposium on Computer Architecture*, 1977.

Hayes J.P. et al, "A Microprocessor-based Hypercube Supercomputer," *IEEE Micro*, October 1986.

Haynes L.S. et al, "A Survey of Highly Parallel Computing," *IEEE Computer*, January 1982.

Hedlund K.S., *Wafer Scale Integration of Parallel Processors*, Ph.D. Thesis, Computer Science Department, Purdue University, Lafayette I.N., 1082.

Heidelberger P. and Lavenberg S.S., "Computer Performance Evaluation Methodology," *IEEE Transactions on Computers*, December 1984.

Hewitt C. and Lieberman H., "Design Issues in Parallel Architectures for Artificial Intelligence," *MIT Artificial Intelligence Laboratory Report No. AIM 750*, November 1983.

Higbie L.C., "Applications of Vector Processing," *Computer Design*, April 1978.

Hillis W.D., *The Connection Machine*, MIT Press, 1985.

Hirale T., Shimada T. and Nishida K., "A Hardware Design of the SIGMA-1, a Data Flow Computer for Scientific Computations," *Proceedings of the 1984 International Conference on Parallel Processing*, pp. 524-531, 1984.

Hoare C.A.R., "Monitors: An Operating System Structuring Concept," *Communications of the ACM*, October 1974.

Hockney R.W., "MIMD Computing in the USA-1984," *Parallel Computing*, Vol. 2, pp. 119-136, 1985.

Hockney R.W., "Characterizing Computers and Optimizing the FACR (L) Poisson-Solver on Parallel Unicomputers," *IEEE Transactions on Computers*, Vol. C-22, pp. 933-941, 1983.

Hockney R.W. and Jesshope C.R., *Parallel Computers: Architecture, Programming and Algorithms*, Adam Hilger Ltd, Bristol England, 1981.

Hogenauer E.B., Newbold R.F. and Inn Y.J., "DDSP - A Data Flow Computer for Signal Processing," *Proceedings of the 1982 International Conference on Parallel Processing*, pp. 126-133, 1982.

Holgate R.W. and Ibbett R.N., "An Analysis of Instruction-Fetching Strategies in Pipelined Computers," *IEEE Transactions on Computers*, Vol. C-29, pp. 325-329, 1979.

Holley L.H. et al., "VM/370 Asymmetric Multiprocessing," *IBM Systems Journal*, Vol. 18, No. 1, 1979.

Holliday M.A. and Vernon M.K., "Exact Performance Estimates for Multiprocessor Memory and Bus Interference," *IEEE Transactions on Computers*, January 1987.

Holt R.C., "Some Deadlock Properties of Computer Systems," *ACM Computing Surveys*, September 1972.

Holt R.C., Graham G.S., Lazowska E.D., and Scott M.A., *Structured Concurrent Programming with Operating System Applications*, Addison-Wesley, 1978.

Hoogendoorn C.H., "A General Model for Memory Interference in Multiprocessors," *IEEE Transactions on Computers*, October 1977.

Hopkins A.L., Smith B. and Lala J.H., "FTMP - A Highly Reliable Fault-Tolerant Multiprocessor for Aircraft," *Proceedings of the IEEE*, October 1978.

Hopper A. and Wheeler D., "Binary Routing Networks," *IEEE Transactions on Computers*, Vol. C-28, No. 10, 1979.

Horowotz E. and Zorat A., "The Binary Tree as an Interconnection Network: Applications to Multiprocessor Systems and VLSI," *IEEE Transactions on Computers*, April 1981.

Hoshino T. et al., "Highly Parallel Processor Array 'PAX' for Wide Scientific Applications," *Proceedings of the 1983 International Conference on Parallel Processing*, pp. 95-105, 1983.

Hovesty K. and Jenny C.J., "Partitioning and Allocating Computational Objects in Distributed Computing Systems," *Proceedings of IFIP 80*, pp. 593-598, 1980.

Hsiao D.K. ed., *Advanced Database Machine Architecture*, Prentice Hall Inc., Englewood Cliffs, N.J., 1983.

Huang K.H. and Abraham J.A., "Efficient Parallel Algorithms for Processor Arrays," *Proceedings of the 1982 International Conference on Parallel Processing*, pp. 271-279, 1982.

Hufnagel S., "Comparison of Selected Array Processor Architectures," *Computer Design*, March 1979.

Hwang K. ed., *Tutorial - Supercomputers: Design and Applications*, IEEE Computer Society Press, 1984.

Hwang K. and Yao. S.B., "Optimal Batched Searching of Tree-Structured Files in Multiprocess Computer System," *Journal of the ACM*, July 1977.

Hwang K. and Ni L.M., "Resource Optimization of a Parallel Computer for Multiple Vector Processing," *IEEE Transactions on Computers*, September 1980.

Hwang K., Su S.P. and Ni L.M., "Vector Computer Architecture and Processing Techniques," in *Advances in Computers*, Vol. 20, M.C. Yovits ed., Academic Press, New York, N.Y., 1981.

Hwang K. and Cheng Y.H., "Partitioned Matrix Algorithms for VLSI Arithmetic Systems," *IEEE Transactions on Computers*, December 1982.

Hwang K. and Briggs F.A., *Computer Architecture and Parallel Processing*, McGraw Hill, New York, N.Y., 1984.

Ignizio J.P., Palmer D.F. and Murphy C.M., "A Multicriteria Approach to Supersystem Architecture Definition," *IEEE Transactions on Computers*, Vol. C-31, pp. 410-418, 1982.

Intel Corp., *iAPX 432 Object Primer*, Intel Corporation, 1981.

Intel Corp., *Introduction to the iAPX 432 Architecture*, Intel Corporation, 1981.

Irani K.B. and Chen K.W., "Minimization of Interprocessor Communication for Parallel Computation," *IEEE Transactions on Computers*, Vol. C-31, pp. 1067-1075, 1982.

Ishikawa Y. and Tokoro M., "The Design of an Object Oriented Architecture," *Proceedings of the 11th Annual International Symposium on Computer Architecture*, pp. 178-187, 1984.

Isloor S.S. and Marsland T.A., "The Deadlock Problem: An Overview," *IEEE Computer*, September 1980.

Ja'Ja' J. and Simon J., "Parallel Algorithms in Graph Theory: Planarity Testing," *SIAM Journal on Computers*, Col. 11, pp. 314-328, 1982.

Jagadish H.V. et al, "A Study of Pipelining in Computing Arrays," *IEEE Transactions on Computers*, May 1986.

Jenevein R.M. and Browne J.C., "A Control Processor for a Reconfigurable Array Computer," *Proceedings of the 9th Annual Symposium on Computer Architecture*, pp. 81-89, 1982.

Jess J.A.G. and Kees H.G.M., "A Data Structure for Parallel L/U Decomposition," *IEEE Transactions on Computers*, Vol. C-31, pp. 231-238, 1982.

Jesshope C.R., "The Implementation of Fast Radix-2 Transforms on Array Processors" *IEEE Transactions on Computers*, Col C-29, pp. 20-27, 1980.

Jin L., "A New General-Purpose Distributed Multiprocessor Structure," *Proceedings of the 1980 International Conference on Parallel Processing*, pp. 153-154, 1980.

Johnson P.M., "An Introduction to Vector Processing," *Computer Design*, February 1978.

Jones A.K. and Schwartz P., "Experience Using Multiprocessor Systems: A Status Report," *CMU Computer Science Department Report No. CME-CS-79-146*, October 1979.

Jones A.K. and Gehringer E.F. eds., *The Cm* Multiprocessor Project: A Research Review*, CMU Computer Science Department, July 1980.

Jordan H.F., "Experience with Pipelined Multiple Instruction Streams," *Proceedings of the IEEE*, Vol. 72, No. 1, 1984.

Jordan H.F., Scalabrin M. and Calvert W., "A Comparison of Three Types of Multiprocessor Algorithm," *Proceedings of the 1979 International Conference on Parallel Processing*, pp. 231-238, 1979.

Jordan K.E., "Performance Comparison of Large-Scale Scientific Computers: Scalar Mainframes, Mainframes with Integrated Vector Facilities, and Supercomputers," *IEEE Computer*, March 1987.

Jump J.R. and Ahuja S.R., "Effective Pipelining of Digital Systems," *IEEE Transactions on Computers*, September 1978.

Kapauan A.A. et al, "The Pringle Parallel Computer," *University of Washington Report No. TR-84-04-01*, April 1984.

Kapauan A.A. et al., "The Pringle Parallel Computer," *Proceedings of the 11th Annual International Symposium on Computer Architecture*, pp. 12-20, 1984.

Karp A.H., "Programming for Parallelism," *IEEE Computer*, May 1987.

Karplus W.J. and Cohen D., "Architectural and Software Issues in the Design and Application of Peripheral Array Processors," *IEEE Computer*, September 1981.

Kartashev S.I. and Kartasjev S.P., "Problems of Designing Supersystems with Dynamic Architectures," *IEEE Transactions on Computers*, December 1980.

Katsuki D. et al, "Pluribus - An Operational Fault-Tolerant Multiprocessor," *Proceedings of the IEEE*, October 1978.

Kaufman M.T., "An Almost Optimal Algorithm for the Assembly Line Scheduling Problem," *IEEE Transactions on Computers*, November 1976.

Kavi K.M., Buckles B.P. and Bhat V.N., "A Formal Definition of Data Flow Graph Models," *IEEE Transactions on Computers*, November 1986.

Keller R.M., Patil S.S. and Lindstrom G., "A Loosely Coupled Applicative Multiprocessing System," *Proceedings of the 1979 AFIPS National Computer Conference*, 1979.

Kennedy K, "Optimization of Vector Operations in an Extended FORTRAN Compiler," *IBM Research Report No. RC-7784*, 1979.

Keyes R.W., "Fundumental Limits in Digital Information Processing," *Proceedings of the IEEE*, Col. 69, No. 2, 1981.

Kinney L.L and Arnold R.G., "Analysis of a Multiprocessor System with a Shared Bus," *Proceedings of the 5th Annual Symposium on Computer Architecture*, pp. 89-95, 1978.

Kishi M, Yasuhara H. and Kawamura Y., "DDDP: A Distributed Data Driven Processor," *Proceedings of the 10th Annual Symposium on Computer Architecture*, pp. 236-242, 1983.

Klappholz D., "The Symbolic High-Level Language Programming of an MIMD Machine," *Proceedings of the 1981 International Conference on Parallel Processing*, pp. 61-53, 1981.

Knight J.C. and Dunlop D.D., "Measurements of an Optimizing Compiler for a Vector Computer," *Proceedings of the 1981 International Conference on Parallel Processing*, pp. 58-59, 1981.

Kogge P.M., "Algorithm Development for Pipelined Processors," *Proceedings of the 1977 Conference on Parallel Processing*, 1977

Kogge P.M., *The Architecture of Pipelined Computers*, McGraw Hill, 1981.

Kogge P.M. and Stone H.S., "A Parallel Algorithm for the Efficient Solution of a General Class of Recurrence Equations," *IEEE Transactions on Computers*, Vol. C-22, pp. 786-793, 1973.

Koren I., "A Reconfigurable and Fault Tolerant VLSI Multiprocessor Array," *Proceedings of the 8th Annual Symposium on Computer Architecture*, pp. 425-442, 1981.

Kornfeld W.A. and Hewitt C., "The Scientific Community Metaphor," *MIT A.I. Memo No. 641*, January 1981.

Kozdrowicki E.W. and Theis D.J., "Second Generation of Vector Supercomputers," *IEEE Computer*, November 1980.

Kruskal C.P., "Results in Parallel Searching, Merging and Sorting," *Proceedings of the 1982 International Conference on Parallel Processing*, pp. 196-198, 1982.

Krygiel A.J., "Synchronous Nets for Single Instruction Stream Multiple Data Stream Computers," *Proceedings of the 1981 International Conference on Parallel Processing*, pp. 266-273, 1981.

Kuck D.J., "A Survey of Parallel Machine Organization and Programming," *ACM Computing Surveys*, March 1977.

Kuck D.J. et al eds., *High Speed Computer and Algorithm Organization*, Academic Press, New York, N.Y., 1977.

Kuck D.J., Kuhn R.H., Seasure B and Wolfe M., "The Structure of an Advanced Retargetable Vectorizer," in *Supercomputers: Design and Applications*, K. Hwang ed., IEEE Computer Society Press, 1984.

Kuck D.J. and Stokes R.A., "The Burroughs Scientific Processor (BSP)," *IEEE Transactions on Computers*, May 1982.

Kuhn R.H. and Padau D.A. eds., *Tutorial on Parallel Processing*, IEEE Computer Society Press, Los Angeles C.A., 1981.

Kumar M. and Hirschberg D.S., "An Efficient Implementation of Batcher's Odd-Even Merge Algorithm and its Application in Parallel Sorting," *IEEE Transactions on Computers*, Vol. C-32, pp. 254-264, 1983.

Kung H.T., "Why Systolic Architectures?," *IEEE Computer*, January 1982.

Kung H.T. and Lam M., "Wafer-Scale Integration and Two-Level Pipelined Implementations of Systolic Arrays," *Journal of Parallel and Distributed Computing*, August 1984.

Kung S.Y., "On Supercomputing with Systolic/Wavefront Array Processors," Proceedings of the IEEE, July 1984.

Kung S.Y., Arun K.S., Galezer R.J. and Rao D.V.B., "Wavefront Array Processor: Language, Architecture and Applications," *IEEE Transactions on Computers*, November 1982.

Kurtzberg J.M., "On the Memory Conflict Problem in Multiprocessor Systems," *IEEE Transactions on Computers*, March 1974.

Kushner T., Wu A.Y. and Rosenfeld A., "Image Processing on ZMOB," *IEEE Transactions on Computers*, Vol. C-31, pp. 943-951, 1982.

Kushner T. et al, "Image Processing on the MPP," *University of Maryland Report No. AFOSR TR-81-0367*, February 1981.

Lai T.H. and Sahni S., "Anomalies in Parallel Branch-and-Bound Algorithms," *Proceedings of the 1983 International Conference on Parallel Processing*, pp. 183-190, 1983.

Lamport L., "Proving the Correctness of Multiprocess Programs," *IEEE Transactions on Software Engineering*, March 1977.

Lang T. and Stone H.S., "A Shuffle-Exchange Network with Simplified Control," *IEEE Transactions on Computers*, January 1976.

Larson J.L., "Multitasking on the CRAY X-MP/2 Multiprocessor," *IEEE Computer*, July 1984.

Lawrie D.H., "Access and Alignment of Data in an Array Processor," *IEEE Transactions on Computers*, December 1975.

Lawrie D.H. and Vora C.R., "The Prime Memory System for Array Access," *IEEE Transactions on Computers*, October 1982.

Lee M. and Wu. C.L., "Performance Analysis of Circuit Switching Baseline Interconnection Networks," *Proceedings of the 11th Annual International Symposium on Computer Architecture*, pp. 82-90, 1984.

Lee R.B. and Wiemann A.L., "New Design Methodologies and Circuits Needed for Parallel VLSI Supercomputers," *Proceedings of the 1982 International Conference on Circuits and Computers*, pp. 224-231, 1982.

Lev G., Pippenger N. and Valiant L.G., "A Fast Parallel Algorithm for Routing in Permutation Networks," *IEEE Transactions on Computers*, Vol. C-30, pp. 93-100, 1981.

Levy H.M., *Capability-Based Computer Systems*, Digital Press, Bedford M.A., 1983.

Li G.J. and Wah B.W., "Computational Efficiency of Parallel Approximate Branch-and-Bound Algorithms," *Proceedings of the 1984 International Conference on Parallel Processing*, 1984.

Li H.F., "Scheduling Trees in Parallel Pipelined Processing Environments," *IEEE Transactions on Computers*, November 1977.

Lincoln N.R., "Technology and Design Trade Offs in the Creation of a Modern Supercomputer," *IEEE Transactions on Computers*, May 1982.

Lincoln N.R., "Supercomputers = Colossal Computations + Enormous Expectations + Renowned Risk," *IEEE Computer*, Vol. 16, No. 5, 1983.

Lint B. and Agerwala T., "Communication Issues in the Design and Analysis of Parallel Algorithms," *IEEE Transactions on Software Engineering*, March 1981.

Lipovski G.J. and Tripathi A., "A Reconfigurable Varistructured Array Processor," *Proceedings of the 1977 International Conference on Parallel Processing*, pp. 165-174, 1977.

Liu J.W.S. and Liu C.L., "Performance Analysis of Multiprocessor Systems Containing Functionally Dedicated Processors," *Acta Informatica*, Vol. 10, No. 1, 1978.

Louie J., "Array Processors: A Selected Bibliography," *IEEE Computer*, Vol. 14, No. 9, 1981.

Lubeck O. et al, "A Benchmark Comparison of Three Supercomputers: Fujitsu VP-200, Hitachi S810/20, and CRAY X-MP/2," *IEEE Computer*, December 1985.

Lundstrom S.F. and Barnes G.H., "A Controllable MIMD Architecture," *Proceedings of the 1980 International Conference on Parallel Processing*, pp. 19-27, 1980.

Ma P.Y.R, Lee E.Y.S. and Tsuchiya M., "A Task Allocation Model for Distributed Computing Systems," *IEEE Transactions on Computers*, January 1982.

MacDougall M.H., "Instruction Level Program and Processor Modelling," *IEEE Computer*, July 1984.

Maekawa M., "Optimal Processor Interconnection Topologies," *Proceedings of the 8th Annual Symposium on Computer Architecture*, pp. 171-186, 1981.

Maenner R., Shoemaker R.L. and Bartels P.H., "The Heidelberg Polyp System," *IEEE Micro*, February 1987.

Maples C., "Analyzing Software Performance in a Multiprocessor Environment," *IEEE Software*, July 1985.

Marathe M. and Fuller S.H., "A Study of Multiprocessor Contention for Shared Data in C.mmp," *ACM SIGMETRICS Conference*, December 1977.

Maron N. and Brengle T.S., "Integrating an Array Processor into a Scientific Computing System," *IEEE Computer*, Vol. 14, No. 9, 1981.

Martin J.L. ed, "International Parallel Processing Projects: A Software Perspective," *IEEE Software*, July 1985.

Mashburn H.H., "The C.mmp/Hydra Project: An Architectural Overview," in *Computer Structures: Principles and Examples*, D.P. Siewiorek, C.G. Bell and A. Newell eds, McGraw Hill Book Company, 1982.

Matelan N., "The FLEX/32 Multicomputer," *Proceedings of the 1985 International Symposium on Computer Architecture*, pp. 209-213.

McDowell C.E., "A Simple Architecture for Low Level Parallelism," *Proceedings of the 1983 International Conference on Parallel Processing*, pp. 174-477, 1983.

McGraw J.R., "Data Flow Computing-Software Development," *IEEE Transactions on Computers*, December 1980.

McGraw J.R. and Skedzielewski S.K., "Streams and Iteration in Val: Additions to a Data Flow Language," *Proceedings of the 3rd International Conference on Distributed Computing Systems*, pp. 730-739, 1982.

McMillen R.J. and Siegel H.J., "MIMD Machine Communication Using the Augmented Data Manipulator Network," *Proceedings of the Seventh Symposium on Computer Architecture*, June 1980.

Mead C. and Conway L., *Introduction to VLSI Systems*, Addison-Wesley, Reading M.A., 1980.

Mehra S.K. and Majithia J.C., "Reconfigurable Computer Architectures," *IEE Proceedings*, July 1982.

Mehra S.K., Wong J.W. and Majithia J.C., "A Comparative Study of Some Two Processor Organizations," *IEEE Transactions on Computers*, Vol. C-29, pp. 44-49, 1980.

Miranker G.S., "Implementation of Procedures on a Class of Data Flow Processors," *Proceedings of the 1977 International Conference on Parallel Processing*, pp. 77-86, 1977.

Miura K. and Uchida K., "FACOM Vector Processor System VP-100/VP-200," in *Supercomputers: Design and Applications*, K. Hwang ed, IEEE Computer Society Press, 1984.

Moldovian D.I., "On the Design of Algorithms for VLSI Systolic Arrays," *Proceedings of the IEEE*, January 1983.

Montoye R.K. and Lawrie D.H., "A Practical Algorithm for the Solution of Triangular Systems on a Parallel Processing System," *IEEE Transactions on Computers*, Vol. C-31, pp. 1076-1082, 1982.

Moto-oka T., "Overview of the Fifth Generation Computer System Project," *Proceedings of the 10th Annual Symposium on Computer Architecture*, pp. 417-422, 1983.

Mudge T.N., Hayes J.P., Buzzard G.D. and Winsor D.C., "Analysis of Multiple Bus Interconnection Networks," *Proceedings of the 1984 International Conference on Parallel Processing*, pp. 228-232, 1984.

Mukai H., "Parallel Algorithms for Solving Systems of Nonlinear Equations," *Computers and Mathematics with Applications*, Vol. 7, pp. 235-250, 1981.

Muntz R.R. and Coffman E.G., "Optimal Preemptive Scheduling on Two Processor Systems," *IEEE Transactions on Computers*, November 1969.

Murata T. and Chern M.Y., "Efficient Matrix Multiplications on a Concurrent Data Loading Array Processor," *Proceedings of the 1983 International Conference on Parallel Processing*, pp. 90-94, 1983.

Nassimi D. and Sahni S., "Optimal BCP Permutations on a Cube Connected SIMD Computer," *IEEE Transactions on Computers*, Vol. C-31, pp. 338-341, 1982.

Newton G., "Deadlock Prevention, Detection and resolution: An Annotated Bibliography," *ACM Operating Systems Review*, April 1979.

Ni L.M. and Hwang K., "Optimal Load Balancing Strategies for a Multiple Processor System," *Proceedings of the 1981 International Conference on Parallel Processing*, pp. 352-357, 1981.

Ni L.M. and Hwang K., "Performance Modeling of Shared Resource Array Processors," *IEEE Transactions on Software Engineering*, July 1981.

Norrie C., "Supercomputers for Super-problems: An Architectural Introduction," *IEEE Computer*, March 1984.

Nutt C., "A Parallel Processor Operating System," *IEEE Transactions on Software Engineering*, November 1977.

Oleinick P.N., *The Implementation and Evaluation of Parallel Algorithm on C.mmp*, Ph.D. Dissertation, Carnegie Mellon University, Pittsburg P.A., 1978.

Olson R., "Parallel Processing in a Message-based Operating System," *IEEE Software*, July 1985.

Owicki S. and Gries D., "Verifying Properties of Parallel Programs," *Communications of the ACM*, May 1976.

Oxley D.W., "Motivation for a Combined Data Flow - Control Flow Processor," *SPIE Vol. 298 Real Time Signal Processing IV*, 1981.

Padua D. A., Kuck D.J. and Lawrie D.H., "High Speed Multiprocessors and Compiling Techniques," *IEEE Transactions on Computers*, September 1980.

Parker D.S. and Raghavendra C.S, "The Gamma Network: A Multiprocessor Interconnection Network with Redundant Paths," *Proceedings of the 9th Annual Symposium on Computer Architecture*, pp. 73-80, 1982.

Parkinson D. and Liddel H.M., "The Measurement of Performance on a Highly Parallel System," *IEEE Transactions on Computers*, Volume C-32, 1983.

Patel J.II., "Performance of Processor-Memory Interconnections for Multi-processors," *IEEE Transactions on Computers*, October 1981.

Paul G., "VECTRAN and the Proposed Vector/Array Extensions to ANSI FORTRAN for Scientific and Engineering Computation," in *Supercomputers: Design and Application*, K. Hwang ed., IEEE Computer Society Press, 1984.

Paul G. and Wilson M.W., "The VECTRAN Language: An Experimental Language for Vector/Matrix Array Processing," *IBM Palo Alto Scientific Center Report No. 6320-3334*, 1975.

Paul G. ed, "Special Issue on Supercomputers - Their Impact on Science and Technology," *Proceedings of the IEEE*, January 1984.

Pearce R.C. and Majitjia J.C., "Analysis of a Shared Resource MIMD Computer Organization," *IEEE Transactions on Computers*, January 1978.

Pease M.C., "The Indirect Binary n-cube Microprocessor Array," *IEEE Transactions on Computers*, May 1977.

Perron R. and Mundie C., "The Architecture of the Alliant FX/8 Computer," *Digest of Papers COMPCON Spring*, 1986.

Perrott R.H., "A Language for Array and Vector Processors," *ACM Transactions on Programming Languages and Systems*, October 1979.

Perrott R.H. et al., "Implementation of an Array and Vector Processing Language," *Proceedings of the 1983 International Conference on Parallel Processing*, pp. 232-239, 1983.

Peterson J.L., "Petri Nets," *ACM Computing Surveys*, September 1977.

Peterson W.P., "Vector FORTRAN for Numerical Problems on the Cray-1," *Communications of the ACM*, Vol. 26, pp. 1008-1021, 1983.

Pfister G.F. et al., "The IBM Research Parallel Processor Prototype (RP3)," *Proceedings of the 1985 International Conference on Parallel Processing*, 1985.

Philipson L., "VLSI Based Design Principles for MIMD Multiprocessor Computers with Distributed Memory Management," *Proceedings of the 11th Annual Symposium on Computer Architecture*, pp. 319-3327, 1984.

Pleszkun A.R. and Davidson E.S., "Structured Memory Access Architecture," *Proceedings of the 1983 International Conference on Parallel Processing*, pp. 461-471, 1983.

Potter J.L., "Image Processing on the Massively Parallel Processor," *IEEE Computer*, Vol. 16, No. 1, 1983.

Pradhan D.K. and Kodandapani K.L., "A Uniform Representation of Single and Multistage Interconnection Networks Used in SIMD Machines," *IEEE Transactions on Computers*, September 1980.

Preparata F.P. and Vuillemin J.E., "The Cube-Connected Cycles: A Versatile Network for Parallel Computation," *Proceedings of the 20th Symposium on the Foundations of Computer Science*, pp. 140-147, 1979.

Priester R.W. et al., "Signal Processing with Systolic Arrays," *Proceedings of the 1981 International Conference on Parallel Processing*, pp. 207-215, 1981.

Purcell C.J., "The Control Data STAR-100 - Performance Measurements," *Proceedings of the AFIPS National Computer Conference*, pp. 385-387, 1974.

Radoy C.H. and Lipovski G.J., "Switched Multiple Instruction Multiple Data Stream Processing," *Proceedings of the 2nd Annual Symposium on Computer Architecture*, pp. 183-187, 1974.

Ramamoorthy C.V., Chandy K.M. and Gonzalez M.J., "Optimal Scheduling Strategies in a Multiprocessor System," *IEEE Transactions on Computers*, February 1972.

Ramamoorthy C.V. and Li H.F., "Pipelined Architecture," *ACM Computing Surveys*, March 1977.

Ramamoorthy C.V. and Wah B.W., "An Optimal Algorithm for Scheduling Requests on Interleaved Memories for a Pipelined Processors," *IEEE Transactions on Computers*, Vol C-31, 1981.

Rattner J., "Concurrent Processing: A New Direction in Scientific Computing," *AFIPS Conference Proceedings*, No. 51., pp. 159-166, 1985.

Ravishanakar C.V. and Goodman J.R., "VLSI Considerations that Influence Data Flow Architectures," *Proceedings of the 24th IEEE Computer Society International Conference*, February 1982.

Raw B.R., "Program Behavior and the Performance of Interleaved Memories," *IEEE Transactions on Computers*, March 1979.

Reed D.A., "A Simulation Study of Multimicrocomputer Networks," *Proceedings of the 1983 International Conference on Parallel Processing*, pp. 161-163, 1983.

Reeves A.P., "A Systematically Designed Binary Array Processor," *IEEE Transactions on Computers*, Vol C-29, pp. 278-287, 1980.

Requa J.E., "The Piecewise Data Flow Architecture Control Flow and Register Management," *Proceedings of the 10th Annual Symposium on Computer Architecture*, pp. 84-89, 1983.

Requa J.E. and McGraw J.R., "The Piecewise Data Flow Architecture: Architectural Concepts," *IEEE Transactions on Computers*, May 1983.

Rettberg R. and Thomas R., "Contention Is No Obstacle to Shared-Memory Multiprocessing," *Communications of the ACM*, Vol. 29, pp. 1202-1212, 1986.

Robinson J.T., "Analysis of Asynchronous Multiprocessor Algorithms with Applications to Sorting," *Proceedings of the 1977 International Conference on Parallel Processing*, pp. 128-135, 1977.

Rodrigue G., Giroux E.D. and Pratt M., "Perspective on Large-Scale Scientific Computations," *IEEE Computer*, October 1980.

Rodrigue G. ed., *Parallel Computations*, Academic Press, 1982.

Rosene A.F., "Memory Allocation for Multiprocessors," *IEEE Transactions on Electronic Computers*, October 1967.

Rosenfeld A., "Parallel Image Processing Using Cellular Arrays," *IEEE Computer*, Vol. 16, No. 1, 1983.

Rumbaugh J., "A Data Flow Multiprocessor," *IEEE Transactions on Computers*, February 1977.

Russel R.M., "The CRAY-1 Computer System," *Communications of the ACM*, January 1978.

Sasidhar J. and Shin K.G., "Design of a General-Purpose Multiprocessor with Hierarchical Structure," *Proceedings of the 1981 International Conference on Parallel Processing*, pp. 141-150, 1981.

Sastry K.V. and Kain R.Y., "On the Performance of Certain Multiprocessor Computer Organizations," *IEEE Transactions on Computers*, November 1975.

Satyanarayanan M., "Commercial Multiprocessing Systems," *IEEE Computer*, Vol. 13, No. 5, 1980.

Satyanarayanan M., "Multiprocessing: An Annotated Bibliography," *IEEE Computer*, Vol. 13, No. 5, 1980

Schaefer D.H., "Spatially Parallel Architectures: An Overview," *Computer Design*, August 1982.

Schwartz J.T., "Ultracomputers," *ACM Transactions on Programming Languages and Systems*, October 1980.

Seitz C.L., "Concurrent VLSI Architectures," *IEEE Transactions on Computers*, December 1984.

Seitz C.L., "The Cosmic Cube," *Communications of the ACM*, Vol. 28, pp. 22-33, 1985.

Sequin C.H., "Doubly Twisted Torus Networks for VLSI Processing Arrays," *Proceedings of the 8th Annual Symposium on Computer Architecture*, pp. 471-480, 1981.

Sethi A.S. and Deo N, "Interference in Multiprocessor Systems with Localized Memory Access Probabilities," *IEEE Transactions on Computers*, February 1979.

Shar L.E. and Davidson E.S., "A Multiminiprocessor System Implemented Through Pipelining," *IEEE Computer*, February 1975.

Shaw D.E., "SIMD and MSIMD Variants of the NON-VON Supercomputer," *Proceedings of COMPCON Spring 84*, pp. 360-363, 1984.

Shin K.G., Lee Y.H. and Sasidhar J., "Design of HM2P - A Hierarchical Multimicroprocessor for General Purpose Applications," *IEEE Transactions on Computers*, Vol. C-31, pp. 1045-1053, 1982.

Siegel H.J., "A Model of SIMD Machines and a Comparison of Various Interconnection Networks," *IEEE Transactions on Computers*, December 1979.

Siegel H.J., "The Theory Underlying the Partitioning of Permutation Networks," *IEEE Transactions on Computers*, September 1980.

Siegel H.J., *Interconnection Networks for Large-Scale Parallel Processing: Theory and Case Studies*, D.C. Heath & Company, Lexington M.A., 1984.

Siegel H.J., Siegel L.J., Kemmerer F.C., Mueller P.T., Smalley H.E. and Smith S.D., "PASM: A Reconfigurable SIMD/MIMD System for Image Processing and Pattern Recognition," *IEEE Transactions on Computers*, December 1981.

Siegel H.J. and McMillen R.J., "The Multistage Cube: A Versatile Interconnection Network," *IEEE Computer*, December 1981.

Siewiorek D.P. et al., "A Case Study of C.mmp, Cm' and C.vmp Part I: Experience with Fault Tolerance in Multiprocessor Systems," *Proceedings of the IEEE*, October 1978.

Sintz R.H., "Optimal Use of a Vector Processor," *Proceedings of COMPCON 1980*, pp. 277-281, 1980.

Sips H.J., "Bit Sequential Arithmetic for Parallel Processors," *IEEE Transactions on Computers*, January 1984.

Sites R.L., "An Analysis of the Cray-1 Computer," *Proceedings of the 5th Annual Symposium on Computer Architecture*, pp. 101-106, 1978.

Slotnick D.L., Borck W.C. and McReynold R.C., "The SOLOMON Computer," *Proceedings of the AFIPS Fall Joint Computer Conference*, pp. 97-107, 1962.

Smith A.J., "Multiprocessor Memory Organization and Memory Interference," *Communications of the ACM*, October 1977.

Smith A.J., "Cache Memories," ACM Computing Surveys, September 1982.

Smith B.J., "A Pipelined Shared Resources MIMD Computer," *Proceedings of the 1978 International Conference on Parallel Processing*, pp. 6-8, 1978.

Smith B.J., "Architecture and Application of the HEP Multiprocessor Computer System," *Real Time Signal Processing IV*, August 1982.

Snyder L., "Introduction to the Configurable, Highly Parallel Computer," *IEEE Computer*, January 1982.

Snyder L., "Overview of the CHiP Computer," *Purdue University Report No. CSD-TR-377*, August 1981.

Snyder L., "Programming Processor Interconnection Structures," *Purdue University Report No. CSD-TR-381*, October 1981.

Sovis F., "Uniform Theory of the Shuffle-Exchange Type Permutation Network," *Proceedings of the 10th Annual Symposium on Computer Architecture*, pp. 185-193, 1983.

Sowa M. and Murata T., "A Data Flow Computer Architecture with Program and Token Memories," *IEEE Transactions on Computers*, Vol. C-31, pp. 820-824, 1982.

Sternberg S.R., "Biomedical Image Processing," *IEEE Computer*, Vol. 16, No. 1, 1983.

Stevens K., "CFD: A FORTRAN-Like Language for the Illiac IV," *SIGPLAN Notices*, March 1975.

Stevenson D.K., "Numerical Algorithm for Parallel Computers," *Proceedings of AFIPS National Computer Conference*, pp. 357-361, 1980.

Stolfo S.J. and Miranker D.P., "DADO: A Parallel Processor for Expert Systems," *Proceedings of the 1984 International Conference on Parallel Processing*, pp. 74-82, 1984.

Stone H.S., "Parallel Processing with the Perfect Shuffle," *IEEE Transactions on Computers*, February 1971.

Stone H.S., "Multiprocessor Scheduling with the Aid of Network Flow Algorithms," *IEEE Transactions on Software Engineering*, January 1977.

Stone H.S., "Computer Rescarch in Japan," *IEEE Computer*, March 1984.

Su S.P. and Hwang K., "Multiple Pipeline Scheduling in Vector Supercomputers," *Proceedings of the 1982 International Conference on Parallel Processing*, pp. 226-234, 1982.

Sugarman R., "Superpower Computers," *IEEE Spectrum*, April 1980.

Swan R.J., Bechtholsheim A., Lai K.W. and Ousterhout J.K., "The Implementation of the Cm* Multimicroprocessor," *Proceedings of AFIPS 1977 National Computer Conference*, pp. 645-655, 1977.

Swartzlander E.E. jr. and Gilbert B.K., "Supersystems: Technology and Architecture, *IEEE Transactions on Computers*, Vol. C-31, pp. 399-409, 1982.

Syre J.C., Comte D. and Hifdi N., "Pipelining, Parallelism and Asynchronism in the LAU System," *Proceedings of the 1977 International Conference on Parallel Processing*, pp. 87-92, 1977.

Takahashi N. and Amamiya M., "A Dataflow Processor Array System: Design and Analysis," *Proceedings of the 10th Annual Symposium on Computer Architecture*, pp. 243-251, 1983.

Tanaka H., "A Parallel Inference Machine," *IEEE Computer*, May 1986.

Tannenbaum A,, "Implication of Structured Programming for Computer Architecture," *Communications of the ACM*, March 1978.

Tanimoto S.L., "A Pyramidal Approach to Parallel Processing," *Proceedings of the 10th Annual Symposium on Computer Architecture*, pp. 372-378, 1983.

Tesler L.G. and Enea H., "A Language for Concurrent Processes," *Proceedings of the AFIPS Spring Joint Computer Conference*, 1968.

Theis D.J., "Special Tutorial: Vector Supercomputers," *IEEE Computer*, April 1974.

Theis D.J., "Guest Editor's Introduction: Applications for Array Processors," *IEEE Computer*, June 1983.

Thompson C.D., "Generalized Connection Networks for Parallel Processor Intercommunication," *IEEE Transactions on Computers*, December 1978.

Thompson C.D. and Kung H.T., "Sorting on a Mesh-Connected Parallel Computer," *Communications of the ACM*, April 1977.

Thornton J.E., "Parallel Operation in the Control Data 6600," Proceedings of AFIPS Fall Joint Computer Conference, 1964.

Thurber K.J., *Large Scale Computer Architecture - Parallel and Associative Processors*, Hayden Book Co., N.J., 1976.

Thurber K.J., "Parallel Processor Architectures - Part I: General Purpose Systems," *Computer Design*, January 1979.

Thurber K.J., "Parallel Processor Architectures - Part II: Special Purpose Systems," *Computer Design*, February 1979.

Tohru M.O., "Overview of the Fifth Generation Computer System Project," *Proceedings of the 10th Annual Symposium on Computer Architecture*, pp. 417-422, 1983.

Treleaven P.C., "Exploiting Program Concurrency in Computing Systems," *IEEE Computer*, January 1979.

Treleaven P.C., Brownbridge D.R. and Hopkins R.P., "Data Driven and Demand Driven Computer Architecture," *ACM Computing Surveys*, March 1982.

Treleaven P.C. and Lima I.G., "Future Computers: Logic, Dataflow,..., Control Flow?," *IEEE Computer*, March 1984.

Trigg R., "Software on ZMOB: An Object Oriented Approach," *Proceedings of IEE Workshop on CAPAIDM*, November 1981.

Tyner P, *iAPX 432 General Data Processor Architecture Reference Manual*, Intel Corporation, 1981.

Ungar D., Blau R., Foley P., Samples D. and Patterson D., "Architecture of SOAR: Smalltalk on a RISC," *Proceedings of the 11th Annual Symposium on Computer Architecture*, pp. 188-197, 1984.

VanAken J. and Zick G., "The Expression Processor: A Pipelined Multiprocessor Architecture," *IEEE Transactions on Computers*, Vol. C-30, pp. 525-536, 1981.

van Tilborg A., "Distributed Operating System Implementation," *Calspan Advanced Technology Center Report No. 6927-S-4*, June 1983.

Vegdahl S.R., "A Survey of Proposed Architectures for the Execution of Functional Languages," *IEEE Transactions on Computers*, December 1984.

Vick C.R., Kartashev S.P. and Kartachev S.I., "Adaptable Architectures for Supersystems," *IEEE Computer*, Vol. 13, No. 11, 1980.

Vuillemin J., "A Combinational Limit to the Computing Power of VLSI Circuits," *IEEE Transactions on Computers*, Vol. C-32, pp.294-300, 1983.

Wagner R.A., "The Boolean Vector Machine," *Proceedings of the 10th Annual Symposium on Computer Architecture*, pp. 59-66, 1983.

Wallqvist A., Berne B.J. and Pangali C., "Exploiting Physical Parallelism Using Supercomputers: Two Examples from Chemical Physics," *IEEE Computer*, May 1987.

Wann D.F., and Franklin M.A., "Asynchronous and Clocked Control Structures for VLSI Based Interconnection Networks," *IEEE Transactions on Computers*, Vol. C-32, pp. 284-293, 1983.

Wang R.Q., Zhang X. and Gao Q.S., "SP2I Interconnection Network and Extension of the Iteration Method of Automatic Vector-Routing," *Proceedings of the 1982 International Conference on Parallel Processing*, pp. 16-25, 1982.

Watson I. and Gurd J., "A Practical Data Flow Computer," *IEEE Computer*, February 1982.

Watson W.J., "The TI ASC: A Highly Modular and Flexible Super Computer Architecture," *Proceedings of AFIPS Fall Joint Computer Conference*, 1972.

Watson W.J. and Carr H.M., "Operational Experiences with the TI Advanced Scientific Computer," *Proceedings of AFIPS National Computer Conference*, pp. 389-397, 1974

Weide B.W., "Modeling Unusual Behavior of Parallel Algorithms," *IEEE Transactions on Computers*, Vol. C-31, pp. 1126-1130, 1982.

Weiss S. and Smith J.E., "Instruction Issue Logic for Pipelined Supercomputers," *Proceedings of the 11th Annual Symposium on Computer Architecture*, pp. 110-118, 1984.

Whitby-Strevens C., "The Transputer," *Proceedings of the 12th International Symposium on Computer Architecture*, pp. 292-300, 1985.

Widdoes L.C. Jr., "The S-1 Project: Developing High Performance Digital Computers," *Digest of Papers IEEE COMPCON*, pp. 282-291, 1980.

Wilson A., Siewiorek D. and Segall Z., "Evaluation of Multiprocessor Interconnect Structures with the CM* Testbed," *Proceedings of the 1983 International Conference on Parallel Processing*, pp. 164-171, 1983.

Wing O. and Huang J.W., "A Computational Model of Parallel Solution of Linear Equations," *IEEE Transactions on Computers*, Vol. C-29, pp. 632-638, 1980.

Wittmayer W.R., "Array Processor Provides High Throughput Rates," *Computer Design*, March 1978.

Wu C.L. and Feng T.Y., "On a Class of Multistage Interconnection Networks," *IEEE Transactions on Computers*, August 1980.

Wu C.L. and Feng T.Y., "Universality of the Shuffle Exchange Network," *IEEE Transactions on Computers*, May 1981.

Wu S.B. and Liu M.T., "A Cluster Structure as an Interconnection Network for Large Multimicrocomputer Systems," *IEEE Transactions on Computers*, April 1981.

Wulf W.A. et al., "Overview of the HYDRA Operating System," *Proceedings of the 5th Symposium on Operating System Principles*, pp. 122-121, 1975.

Wulf W.A., Levin R. and Harbison S.P., *HYDRA/C.mmp: An Experimental Computer System*, McGraw-Hill, New York N.Y., 1981.

Yasumura M. Tanaka Y. and Kanada Y., "Compiling Algorithms and Techniques for the S-810 Vector Processor," *Proceedings of the 1984 International Conference on Parallel Processing*, pp. 1192-1201, 1984.

Yalamanchili S. and Aggarwal J.K., "Reconfiguration Strategies for Parallel Architectures," *IEEE Computer*, December 1985.

Yau S.S. and Fung H.S., "Associative Processor Architecture - A Survey," *ACM Computing Surveys*, March 1977.

GLOSSARY

2-1/2 D Memory Organization

A memory structure characterized by the storage of a two-dimensional array of words per memory block such that a block address and a word select are required to extract the appropriate word.

2 D Memory Organization

A memory structure characterized by the storage of a one-dimensional array of words per memory block such that a block address is sufficient to extract the appropriate word.

3 D Memory Organization

A memory characterized by the storage of a two-dimensional array of bits per memory block such that both a block address and a bit select are necessary to extract the appropriate bit from a block. The concatenated bits form the desired word.

Absolute Address

A reference descriptor that contains the actual bits to be directly decoded into activation signals for a peripheral device or memory. Also referred to as direct address.

Accumulator

A CPU register that is the primary source and sink for data to and from the ALU as well as for external data transfers.

Acknowledgment

A short message sent from the receiver to the sender to indicate whether a previous message was received without error.

Actor

In a data flow graph, a node that consists of an operation and a firing rule.

Address Mode

The definition of the method by which an address is used to retrieve or deposit a data item. A single computer may support several different addressing modes.

Adjacency Matrix (A)

A square matrix, indexed by node number for both row and columns, whose entries denote the existence of a directed or undirected edge between the nodes at the intersection of a row and column. Successive powers (denoted K) of the adjacency matrix yield directed paths of length K at the row and column intersections.

Adjacent From

In a graph, indicates the existence and direction of a directed edge (e.g., A adjacent from B denotes the existence of the edge e<B,A>).

Adjacent To

In a graph, indicates the existence and direction of a directed edge (e.g., A adjacent to B denotes the existence of the edge e<A,B>).

Algorithm

A sequence of steps that are followed to solve a specific problem.

Analytical Model

A mathematical description of a system that can be used to evaluate and predict various system quantities.

Anticipatory Paging

The practice, by an operating system, of reading in several memory pages when a memory page fault occurs, with the hope that the additional pages will be required by the application.

Arbitrate

To allocate the use of a resource (e.g., communication link, CPU) to waiting users according to some specified rule or rules.

Architecture

Applied to computers, the description of the organization and interrelationships between the constituent parts of a computer or operating system.

Arithmetic Logic Circuit

The core circuitry of an ALU that performs all of the arithmetic and logical operations on the data.

Arithmetic Logic Unit (ALU)

The combination of arithmetic logic circuitry, limited register storage, the necessary gating, interconnections and external interfaces. An ALU is controlled to perform arithmetic, logic, and permutation functions on registers or externally provided data.

Array

An orderly, regular organization of things. Applied to data and processing elements.

Array Processor

(1) A parallel architecture that contains a two dimensional array of interconnected processing elements and that is adept at performing applications that exhibit two dimensional parallelism.

(2) A parallel processor architecture characterized by a rectangular grid of processing elements, each connected to its north, south, east, and west neighbors. Array processors are typically SIMD machines.

Arrival

The event of a customer entering a queue for service.

Arrival Process

A distribution or function that produces arrivals for a queuing model.

ASCII

American Standard Code for Information Interchange. A code that assigns specific bit patterns to represent a set of characters.

Assembly Language

The "native" language of a given computer. Assembly language has a one-to-one correspondence with the basic operations that are performed by the CPU.

Associative Memory

Data storage that is addressed by content rather than by location. An associative memory has comparison logic that is coupled with the storage locations so that memory data can be located by association with a set of search conditions.

Asynchronous

A mode of operation where events are not time-ordered by a regular spacing scheme but instead occur in relation to each other.

Asynchronous Transmission

The transferral of data where the arrival time of the next data block cannot be predicted, but whose data block words are regularly spaced at known intervals.

Atomic Operation

An operation that is indivisible; that is, it's parts cannot be interleaved with those of another operation.

Autonomy

A system property whereby a portion of a system may work independently on a problem while the other portions of the system work on other problems.

Backplane Bus

A parallel electrical interface onto which processors, memory, and peripherals attach for the purpose of communication and control.

Backus-Naur Form (BNF)

A metalanguage that is used to specify programming language syntax.

Bandwidth

The raw data carrying capacity of a connection or system, measured in units per second. Also defined as the difference in frequency between the lowest and highest signalling rate of a connection or system.

Base

The quantity in a number system whose successive powers define the sequence in the system. Also called radix.

Baud

A unit of signalling speed that corresponds to one unit per second. In serial transmission, baud refers to the number of encoded bits per second.

Benchmark Program

A standard program (usually written in a high-level language) that is used to measure and compare speed and efficiency of computers, language, compilers, or other system elements.

Binary Tree

A graph where each node has at most two children and exactly one parent.

Birth-and-Death Process

A process that has the Markovian property and satisfies the flow balance premise.

Bit-Associative

Refers to an associative processor where there is a single bit logic unit associated with each word in the associative memory.

Bit-time

The time interval within which a bit of data can be uniquely determined.

Block Transfer

Referring to the movement of a number of data words at once with a minimal amount of control (i.e., only at initiation and termination).

Boolean Logic

Algebraic operations on two-valued variables. Boolean operators accept and produce True/False quantities.

Bottleneck

A point in a system that limits the maximum throughput attainable. The slowest or most restrictive step in a multistep process.

Branch

A decision point in a program where one of several possible execution paths must be taken.

Branch Prediction

The problem of anticipating where a program branch will lead so that the appropriate target address can be fetched.

Branch Target

The address that is the destination of a branch instruction, if it is taken. Typically, a branch instruction has two possible execution paths, the next sequential instruction and the instruction at the branch target.

Branch Target Buffer

A memory that holds the addresses of possible branch targets. When a branch instruction is encountered, the target address is placed in the buffer for use with future branches.

Breadth First Search

A method of searching a graph where the root node is examined first, then the nodes adjacent to the root, then the nodes adjacent to those, and so on until the desired node is found or the graph is exhausted.

Burst Mode Transfer

A form of direct memory transfer where a burst of data is sent over the processor bus. During the transfer, the processor is prevented from using the bus.

Bus

A set of conductors that connect the components of a computer system. Buses can be parallel, with several bits of data transferred simultaneously, or serial, with with single bit transfers. Bus access is controlled by a protocol that specifies when a transfer may occur.

Butterfly Switch

A type of communication switch.

Cache Memory

A limited amount of storage that holds quantities that are frequently accessed by the CPU, but that acts as part of main memory. Cache memory typically operates at speeds close to that of the CPU.

Capability

A reference descriptor that contains both the address of the desired object and a set of access rights and privileges to the object.

Capability-Based Addressing

An addressing scheme where every reference is made via a capability such that access rights are always checked.

Cell

In a data flow architecture, a packaged unit containing an operator, control information, operands and result destination information.

Central Processing Unit (CPU)

The computational unit that typically consists of an ALU, control unit, register set, and interface circuitry.

Chaining

A method of organizing data using a linked list.

Channel Capacity

The capability of a connection, usually measured in data units per unit of time. The measurement of a channel's ability to transfer data from one point to another.

Circular Dependency

Refers to the condition where two or more nodes are all data dependent upon each other.

Clock

A periodic signal that is used to time and synchronize circuitry and operations.

Communicating Sequential Processes (CSP)

A set of statements and their associated syntax used for expressing concurrent, interacting processes.

Communication Bus

Typically, a serial bus that is shared by the attached devices and allocated according to an access protocol.

Compile

The process of translating a higher-level program to a set of lower-level instructions to produce an executable image.

Complete Graph

Refers to a directed graph where for every pair of nodes A and B, there exists at least one directed path from A to B or from B to A.

Compute Bound

The condition of not having enough computational power to solve a given application in the required time.

Computer Aided Design/Computer Assisted Manufacture (CAD/CAM)

The automation of the design and manufacturing process using computer design tools and control programs.

Computer-Based Control Unit

A type of CPU control unit that derives its controlling signals from a counter whose outputs are decoded through combinational logic circuits for each counter state.

Concurrent Execution

Pertaining to the simultaneous processing of two or more instruction streams (versus the sequential execution of two or more instruction streams or the simultaneous execution of parts of the same instruction stream).

Confluence

The process of executing an instruction in phases.

Connection

A data path between two communicating entities.

Content-Addressable Memory

See Associative Memory.

Context

For an executing program or procedure, the physical and logical environment that defines the process state, physical or logical memory configuration, and references to associated execution history and scope information.

Continuous Simulation

A simulation method where the dependent variables behave in a continuous manner with respect to the independent variable (usually time).

Control Unit

A unit that manages the operation of other components in a computer system. See also Controller.

Controller

In a CPU architecture, the portion that manages the timing and operation of the internal CPU components by providing a series of timed gating signals.

Core Memory

A nonvolatile binary storage medium that incorporates magnetic "doughnuts" and the associated write, sense, and addressing logic.

Crossbar Switch

A rectangular grid that contains a switch at each of the grid intersections and connections to communicating components along the grid edges.

Crosstalk

A condition that results when a signal in one conductor induces a corresponding unwanted signal in another conductor, which is usually parallel to the first.

Cube

A parallel processor architecture characterized by the logical placement of processing elements at the corners of a cube and the processing element interconnections along the cube edges. Also called a Boolean n-cube.

Cube Connected Cycles

A cube-like architecture where each corner of the cube actually contains a ring of processing elements.

Cycle

A loop consisting of a complete iteration of a set of elemental operations. In a CPU, the combined sequence of actions that transfer data from internal register storage to the ALU input(s), perform the desired ALU and post-ALU operations, and return the data to internal register storage. Assembly-level machine instruction performance is usually specified in numbers of cycles necessary to complete a given instruction. Also called machine cycle. For a memory, a complete read or write operation, including addressing and data transfer.

Cycle Time

In a CPU, the time required to complete a machine cycle. In a memory, the minimum time allowable between successive accesses to memory.

Data

Information, represented in some consistent form, to which a meaning may be assigned.

Data Consistency

The condition where two or more items have the exact same values at the same time, plus or minus a tolerance value.

Data Driven

Refers to a mode of execution where operations are performed as the data and execution vehicle become available, rather than in some predetermined order.

Data Flow

A mode of operation where execution is controlled by the availability of data, operands and execution vehicles rather than by the passage of control from one instruction to the next.

Data Flow Computer

A parallel architecture characterized by a data driven operation.

Data Output Dependency

The time ordering of statements where the output of a previous statement is required for a later statement to execute, thus making the later dependent upon the completion of the former.

Daughter Board

A small circuit board, usually containing just a few components, that plugs into a connector on a larger circuit board.

Deadline Scheduling

A dynamic scheduling algorithm that places entries with the nearest completion deadline at the front of the queue.

Departure

In a queuing model, a customer that is leaving the model after service.

Depth First Search

A method of searching a graph where the root node is examined first, then one node that is adjacent to the root, then one node that is adjacent to that node, and so on until the end of the graph is reached. Then another node that is adjacent to the root is examined and the process repeats until the desired node is found or the graph is exhausted.

Dhrystone

A single-program benchmark that is representative of system software.

Digital Device

An electronic circuit that has two stable states which can be uniquely identified and assigned binary values.

Direct Access Memory

A storage device that is characterized by the fact that an access may reference any storage location in constant time.

Direct Memory Access (DMA)

The mechanisms by which blocks of data may be transferred to and from a processor's main memory without the direct involvement of the processor. Possessing the capability to address and control memory as the processor does.

Directed Edge

In a graph, an edge that implies a "to" or "from" relationship between the connected nodes.

Directed Graph

A graph that consists of nodes and directed edges.

Directed Path

A path consisting of directed edges.

Directory

In a file system, a list of the contents of the system, usually ordered and/or structured according to some criteria.

Dirty Bit

An indicator associated with every page in main memory that indicates whether the page contents should be saved on secondary storage before a new page is brought in.

Dynamic RAM

A random access semiconductor memory that must be periodically refreshed in order to retain the stored data.

Dynamic Scheduling Algorithm

Any method of ordering the contents of a queue, which depends upon the passage of time. Thus a queue with the same contents at time t as at time t+m may have different orderings for times t and t+m.

Edge

In a graph, a representation of the relationship between the elements of the problem set. Also called link, connection, branch and arc.

Effective Address

The address that is presented to the memory or memory management system from the CPU. The effective address may be an absolute address or a virtual address that still requires translation.

Explicit Parallelism

Parallelism that is purposefully constructed from sections of a program.

Fetch

The process of retrieving a word from memory by the CPU. Usually associated with instruction fetch.

File Network

An interconnection network constructed from a series of switches that allows various permutations of the input data to occur.

Firing Rule

A set of conditions that must be met before a specified operation can proceed.

First In First Out (FIFO) Scheduling

A static scheduling discipline where jobs are served in the order in which they arrive. Also called first come first served (FCFS).

Floppy Disk

A removable magnetic mass storage device that is organized in tracks and sectors along which data is stored.

Flow Balance Premise

An assumption in a state transition diagram that the flow of events into a state (e.g., arrivals) equals the flow of events out of that state (e.g., departures) at steady state.

Flow Chart

A specialized graph that has functional sections for nodes and flow of control for edges.

Fourier Transform

A signal analysis technique where the signal of interest is broken down into a sum of a series of elementary, basic signals.

Front End

Refers to a computer that is used as an interface to a more capable machine.

Fully Connected

Refers to a graph with at least one edge between every pair of nodes.

Fully-Parallel Distributed Logic

Refers to an associative processor where there is logic associated with groups of bits in the associative memory.

Fully-Parallel Word Organized

Refers to an associative processor where there is logic associated with every bit in the associative memory.

Functional Programming

A form of programming where all expressions are functions and no assignment statements are allowed.

Granularity

In the organizational space, the qualitative measure of a processing element's power.

Graph

A representation of a set of elements and their relationships that reflect the structure of a given problem. A graph consists of nodes that represent the elements of the set, and edges that represent the element relationships.

Graph Cycle

A path that originates and terminates at the same node and that passes through at least one other node.

Handler

A section of code that is dedicated to servicing a specific type of activity, such as a message reception or error occurrence.

Handshake

An exchange of signals or data words that indicate that a particular transfer has been completed successfully.

Hard Disk

A fixed magnetic mass storage device organized as sectored tracks along which data is stored.

High-Level Language

A computer language that is independent of the structure of the computer upon which it is run. Also called higher-order language.

Huffman Encoding

A variable length encoding technique for representing data sets (e.g., instructions, alphabet) where the items that appear more frequently are assigned a correspondingly shorter code and vice versa.

Hypercube

An architecture comprised of multiple cubes that are interconnected at the corners. A cube architecture with dimension greater than three.

I/O Bound

The condition where there is not sufficient I/O bandwidth to perform a given application in the required time.

Idempotent Matrix

A matrix that has the characteristic that, after attaining a given power K, will result in the same identical matrix for all powers of the matrix greater than or equal to K.

Immediate Operand

An operand whose value is contained directly in the instruction word.

Implicit Parallelism

Parallelism that is embedded in the normal structure of a program.

Indegree

A measure of the number of directed edges that are adjacent from any other nodes on the node in question.

Indexed Addressing

An addressing method where the effective address is formed from the combination of the base address plus and offset (the index value).

Indirect Addressing

A mode of addressing where a reference to a specific location does not contain the desired data but rather another address where the data is located. Indirect addresses can usually be nested so that a sequence of indirect accesses may be necessary to finally arrive at the desired data location.

Instruction Encoding

The unique pattern of bits that are assigned to each instruction in an instruction set.

Instruction Set

The collection of basic operations that make up a computer's assembly language.

Integrated Computerized Manufacturing Definition Methods (IDEF)

A design methodology that uses functional, behavioral, and informational perspectives to model the system under design.

Interleaved Memory

A memory that is structured into banks so that consecutive accesses are directed to different banks, thereby reducing the effective cycle time of the total memory.

Intermediate-Level Language

A computer language that has both the structure and semantics of a high-level language and the capability to perform machine-dependent operations.

Interpreter

A program execution environment that accepts high-level language statements and performs the desired operations "on the fly," without compilation.

Interrupt-Driven I/O

A type of input/output where the processor execution is forced from the normal instruction stream to a special I/O service routine, whenever a hardware interrupt line is activated.

Kendall Notation

A notation that is used to represent the various parameters of a queuing model.

Layered Dependency

Found within nested program loops, a form of data dependency that is not present when the statements in question are considered in the context of an inner loop, but is present when the statements are considered in the context of an outer loop.

Least Frequently Used Strategy

A paging strategy whereby the main memory page with the lowest recorded frequency of access is replaced when a page swap is performed.

Least Recently Used (LRU) Strategy

A page replacement strategy used in memory management where the page that has the oldest recorded access is replaced with a new page from secondary storage.

Linear Code

A program or section of code that does not contain any branch or jump type instructions.

Link

A connection over which communication may occur.

Linpack

A single-program benchmark that is often used to test vector processors and supercomputers.

Local Area Network (LAN)

A shared communication bus with a limited range (usually within a building or complex).

Lock

Any mechanism that is used to grant exclusive access of a resource by one of several users.

Lockstep

A mode of operation where all of the operations in a multiple operation sequence are performed simultaneously and where

all of the operations of a single step must complete before the
operations of the subsequent step may begin.

Loose Coupling

A degree of interconnection characterized by the lack of
direct sharing of processor address spaces. A level of communication that is necessarily message-based.

Main Memory

The storage that is directly addressable within a processor's
address space. Also called primary memory.

Markovian Property

A process characteristic which states that future events are
not dependent upon previous events. Also called the memoryless property.

Mask

A series of bits that are ANDed together with a data word in
order to allow only certain data bits to pass.

Master/Slave Relationship

A form of control where one participant exercises direct
control over the actions of another.

Memory-Mapped I/O

An input/output organization where memory and I/O device
addresses are within the same address space, and where the
I/O device addresses are accessed using memory control
signals.

Memoryless Property

See Markovian Property.

Microinstruction

A machine-specific collection of bit fields that directly control a CPU's components during a CPU cycle.

Microprogram

At the lowest level in the programming language hierarchy, a microprogram consists of a series of microinstructions, with each microinstruction containing bit fields that directly control CPU components.

Microprogrammed Control Unit

A type of CPU control unit that derives its controlling signals from the execution of a microprogramn.

Modular Structure

Having the property that the principal entities are organized as components from which the total entity is constructed.

Modulo

An operation that results in the remainder of the division of the operands. Thus, a modulo b results in the remainder of a/b. Also called mod.

Multi-Function Pipeline

A set of operation stages that are connected by multiple paths and thus are capable of performing different sequences of operations on the data stream.

Multidimensional Access Memory (MDA)

An associative memory that can also be access by conventional means and that can be configured to have different word lengths.

Multiple Instruction Stream Multiple Data (MIMD)

A class of computer organization where several different instructions operate simultaneously on several different data within a single computer.

Multiple Instruction Stream Single Data (MISD)

A class of computer organization where a several instructions operate simultaneously on a single datum within a single computer.

Multiple-Program Benchmarks

A set of related programs that together test several aspects of a computing system through the use of certain sequences of high-level language statements, subprogram calls, and inter-process communication.

Multiported Memory

A memory structure that can support simultaneous access to it's contents, as long as no two simultaneous accesses are to the same location.

Multiprocessor

A form of parallel architecture characterized by coarse grained processing elements and a shared memory space.

Multistage Network

A network composed of several cascaded switching elements.

N-Dimensional Parallelism

A class of parallelism where the elements of a set are operated on simultaneously and where element interactions can occur at any time.

Network

A collection of communication lines that is used to interconnect processing elements.

Node

In a graph, a representation of the elements of the problem set. Also called vertex, point and object.

Non-Linear Code

A program or section of code that contain a branch or jump type instructions.

Not Recently Used Strategy

A paging strategy whereby any main memory page with a latest recorded usage that is older than some threshold is replaced when a page swap is performed. Similar to the least

recently used strategy without having to find the oldest referenced page, just an old one.

Object

A logical structure that contains information in an organized
manner, has a set of operations defined to manipulate the
data, can be referenced with a single identifier, and has a type
associated with it.

Onion Diagram

A representation of a system where the outer layers are built
upon the capabilities of the inner layers, with the core representing the unembellished base of the system being
represented.

Operand

A datum that is used in the performance of an operation. The
part of an instruction that is operated on.

Operating System

The collection of executive routines, utility programs, and
system operational policies that enable a computer system to
operate. The operating system provides the environment
within which application programs execute.

Operating System Kernel

The basic part of an operating system upon which all other
operating system capability is based. This may include such
functions as processor management, basic device interfaces
and program load and execution utilities.

Operation Code (OP Code)

An encoded string of bits that specify an operation to be performed.

Outdegree

A measure of the number of directed edges that are adjacent
to a node.

Packet

> A collection of data words that are routed together from source to destination.

Packet Switching

> A mode of communication where entire data packets are individually switched through a network and where the individual packets of a single message may not follow the same path.

Page Swapping

> The practice, in memory management, of writing (if necessary) main memory pages to secondary storage and then reading secondary storage pages into the locations vacated by the written pages.

Paged Memory

> A memory management strategy that breaks up the processor's address space into equal sized contiguous blocks that can be individually filled from or written to secondary storage.

Parallel I/O

> Input/Output that occurs word-by-word by transmitting a number of bits simultaneously over the same number of conductors.

Path

> In a graph, the set of edges to be traversed in going from one node to another.

Pipeline Parallelism

> A class of parallelism where the elements in a data set are operated on in stages so that several elements are at various degrees of completion at the same time.

Pipelined Processor

> A parallel processing architecture that performs operations in a pipelined fashion.

Plus Minus 2^i (PM2I)

The interconnection strategy used in the inverse augmented data manipulator network.

Polled I/O

A type of input/output where the processor periodically checks the I/O devices to determine if any need servicing

Principle of Locality of Reference

The premise that the next program reference will be to a location near (usually sequential from) the currently referenced location.

Process

An independent sequence of events that occur to accomplish a given job.

Processing Element

One of a set of identical components of a parallel processor, each of which performs the majority of operations on the total data set.

Pure If Block

A sequence of statements that consists solely of If statements.

Q Matrix

The product of R and R Transpose whose elements indicate mutual reachability between the nodes at the row and column intersections.

Quantum Time

In an time shared operating system, the amount of CPU time each process is allowed before it is requeued for execution. Also called quantum.

Queue

A waiting line in which customers wait for service.

Queuing Model

A representation of an operational system that consists of an arrival process, a queue, a server, and a queuing discipline.

Queuing Network

A series of connected queuing, models and the associated routing functions.

Random Access Memory (RAM)

A type of semiconductor memory that has direct access characteristics.

Reachability Matrix (R)

Formed by summing the powers of the adjacency matrix and the identity matrix, the reachability matrix elements indicate the existence of a directed path between the nodes at the row and column intersections.

Read-Modify-Write Operation

See test and set operation.

Reduced Instruction Set Computer (RISC)

A computer with a minimal number of instructions which each execute in a small number of CPU cycles.

Redundancy

In a computer system, the replication of critical components for the purpose of fault tolerance.

Reflexive Node

In a graph, a node with a directed edge to itself.

Refresh

The process of periodically reading and then re-writing stored data in order to retain the data.

Reservation Table

A data structure that shows when data will encounter a given pipeline stage and therefore can be used to schedule the entrance of the next item into the pipe.

Response Time

The measurement of the duration between a request for service and the completion of the service.

Root Node

The starting or uppermost node in a hierarchical graph.

Routing Function

A discipline for determining what path a customer will follow after leaving a queue or a server.

Scalar

A single data unit that is composed of only one part.

Scalar Unit

A processor that operates on scalar quantities only.

Scan Scheduling

A disk access scheduling algorithm that works by continually scanning the disk head from the outer track to the inner track and back again, servicing requests as the appropriate tracks pass under the head.

Secondary Memory

Memory that is used not as the processor's main memory, but rather as the source and sink for many sets of main memory data.

Segmented Memory

A method of breaking up the memory address space into a number of pieces, all of which may not be the same size.

Self Referential Cyclic Dependency

The condition that occurs when a single statement contains the same variable on both the left hand and right hand side of an expression.

Semantic Level

A qualitative measure of the closeness of correspondence between the symbols or constructs of a language and the underlying hardware upon which it executes.

Sequential Memory

A storage device in which data can only be deposited by stepping serially through the data until the desired position is found.

Serial I/O

Input/Output that occurs bit-by-bit along a single conductor. Serial I/O data is disassembled at the sender into bits for transmission, and reassigned at the receiver into the appropriate data format.

Server

An entity that provides service to a customer based upon a service time distribution.

Service Process

A distribution or function that produces service times for each customer at a server.

Shortest Seek Time First (SSTF) Scheduling

A disk access scheduling algorithm that attempts to optimize disk seek time. Disk accesses are ordered such that the request with the track closest to the one the disk head is currently at is the next one serviced.

Shortest Time First (STF) Scheduling

A static scheduling discipline where jobs are ordered according to the estimated execution time, from shortest to longest.

Shuffle Network

A network whose interconnections serve to shuffle the communicated data, much like cards in a deck are shuffled.

Simulation

The representation or modelling of a system by another system (in this context, a software system).

Single Assignment Programming

A form of programming where only value type variables are allowed.

Single Function Pipeline

A set of operation stages connected by a single path and thus are capable of performing only one sequence of operations on the data stream.

Single Instruction Stream Multiple Data Stream (SIMD)

A class of computer organization where each instruction that is executed causes the same operation to be performed simultaneously on several different data within a single computer.

Single Instruction Stream Single Data (SISD)

A class of computer organization in which a single instruction operates on a single datum during each instruction cycle within a single computer.

Single-Program Benchmark

A single program that tests several aspects of a computing system through the use of certain sequences of high-level language statements and subprogram calls.

Software Environment

The combined set of constraints, limits and conditions within which a program must execute.

Stage

A point in a pipeline where a designated operation on the data takes place.

State

The combined condition of the components in a system or subsystem. For a process, the state is the combined condition of the state variables and the processor state.

State Table Control Unit

A type of CPU control unit that derives its controlling signals from an embedded state table.

State Transition Table

A square data array that is indexed by state and transition events and contains the next state for each combination of current state and transition events.

State Variable

A quantity that represents the condition or part of the condition or the state.

Statement Substitution

A technique for achieving parallelism in a sequence of statements by substituting expressions for calculating variables in place of variable references in order to remove data dependencies along a sequential execution path.

State Transition Diagram

A graph whose nodes represent the state space and whose directed edges represent transition events.

Static RAM

A random access semiconductor memory in which the stored data remains intact, without refresh, provided that applied power is maintained.

Static Scheduling Algorithm

Any method of ordering the contents of a queue, which does not depend upon the passage of time. Thus, a queue with the same contents at time t as at time t+m will be ordered exactly the same at time t as at time t+m.

Steady-State Behavior

The response of a system to a nonvarying external stimulus.

Stochastic Process

A process whose outcome is determined probabilistically.

Storage Efficiency

The relative measure of the amount of memory required to store a data set given a certain data set encoding scheme.

Strong Typing

In a programming language, refers to the mandatory declaration of the name and type of every variable, data structure, and function used in the program.

Strongly Connected Graph

Refers to a directed graph where for every pair of nodes A and B, A is both adjacent from and adjacent to B (i.e., the edges e<A,B> and e<B,A> exist for every pair A and B).

Supernode

In a graph, a collection of nodes that are strongly connected so that all nodes in the supernode can be reached if any one can be reached.

Switch

In a network, a device than can route an incoming message over any one of the switch's output paths.

Switching Frequency

The maximum rate at which two different signal levels may be alternated on a conductor or within a device.

Synchronous Transmission

The transferral of data where the arrival time of the next data block is known and regulated by a controlling clock.

Systolic Processor

A parallel architecture characterized by the flow of both data and results within the processor, and by the interaction of data and partial results.

Test-And-Set Operation

A two part, atomic operation that either sets a value to a variable or does nothing depending upon the current value of the variable.

Throughput

A measure of the amount of work per unit time that a system is capable of performing.

Tight Coupling

A degree of interconnection characterized by the direct sharing of processor address spaces. A level of communication that is word-at-a-time.

Token

In a data flow computer, refers to operands and/or data that are waiting for matching and execution.

Topology

In the organizational space, the qualitative measure of the density and capability of the interconnections between the processing elements of an architecture.

Trace Scheduling

A technique, used for VLIW processors, where each path through series of sequential statements is compacted into a single, wide statement, and where the appropriate code is inserted to ensure that the sequence of wide statements produce the intended results when executed.

Transient Behavior

The response of a system to a varying external stimulus.

Transparent Multiprocesing

The situation that occurs when the number of available processors for an application may be changed without altering or recompiling the application code.

Undirected Edge

In a graph, an edge that does not imply a "to" or "from" relationship between the connected nodes.

Undirected Graph

A graph that consists of nodes and undirected edges only.

Undirected Path

A path consisting of undirected edges.

Update Synchronization

Refers to the problem of ensuring that multiple changes to a datum, possibly from different sources, occur in the proper order so that the resulting datum value is correct.

Utilization

The percentage amount of a system's total capacity that is being used.

Value Function Scheduling

A dynamic scheduling algorithm that orders the queue entries based upon a calculated benefit of that particular ordering. This type of scheduling attempts to maximize the "value" of the queue ordering according to some predefined calculation.

Value Matrix

An adjacency matrix whose elements carry some value such as edge length or cost to traverse an edge.

Variable-Length Encoding

A method of assigning different length, unique representations for each item in a set. Huffman encoding is an example of this.

Vector

A quantity, consisting of an ordered set of like elements, that possesses both quantity and direction.

Vector Parallelism

A class of parallelism where the elements of a set of data are operated on simultaneously with element interactions occurring only at set intervals.

Vector Processor

A form of parallel architecture that is optimized for performing vector operations.

Vectorizing Compiler

A compiler that accepts a regular, high-level language program, detects the program constructs that can result in vector computations, and provides executable code that is suitable for execution on a vector processor.

Very High-Level Language

A class of programming languages characterized by the emphasis of what is to be done rather than how it is to be accomplished.

Very Large-Scale Integration (VLSI)

Refers to the technology associated with fabricating a large amount of electronic devices on a single silicon chip, and to the relative dimensions of each device.

Very Long Instruction Word (VLIW) Processor

A parallel architecture where a sequence of operations are converted to a number of parallel operations which are then executed simultaneously on a single, very wide execution unit.

Virtual Device Interface

An interface program that gives a user program the illusion that it is controlling a physical device when it is actually communicating with another program.

Virtual Memory

A memory organization where the actual physical size of memory and the number of addresses that can be accessed are not equal. Usually, virtual memory is implemented such that it appears that the amount of available memory is much greater than the amount that is physically present. Requires an address translation scheme to map virtual addresses to absolute addresses.

Volatile

The description applied to a memory that loses the stored data when applied power is removed.

von Neumann Architecture

A classic computer architecture characterized by the storage of both programs and data in the same memory space.

von Neumann Bottleneck

Refers to the single address space for accessing both programs and data and to the performance limitation of the interface to that address space.

Whetstone

A single-program benchmark containing mainly floating point operations.

Word-Serial Associative

Refers to an associative processor where there is one logic unit associated with each associative memory.

Write Through

Applied to cache memory, refers to the mechanisms or practice of initiating a write to main memory data whenever the corresponding cache data is written to. This practice attempts to maintain data consistency between the cache and main memory.

Write-Once Memory

A mass storage device that cannot be reused.

THE LINPACK BENCHMARK

One benchmark that has been receiving much attention recently is the so-called linpack benchmark. This benchmark program is based upon the linpack FORTRAN subroutine package for solving linear equations. The benchmark actually solves a system of 100 linear equations using the LU decomposition technique. The benchmark uses the linpack routines to perform this decomposition, hence the name linpack benchmark. This benchmark program is popular because the solution is computationally intense and is representative of many scientific applications. The linpack benchmark listed here is the double precision version and was obtained from the Argonne National Laboratory. The linpack routines were developed by Dongarra, Bunch, Moeller, and Stewart [Dongarra79], and the routines used in the benchmark are from that package. The benchmark itself has been used to test a number of conventional computers, personal and small systems, and supercomputers. Those who use the benchmark are encouraged to report their results to J. Dongarra at the Argonne National Laboratory; a result collection and distribution service is graciously provided there. The address for reporting results is: J. Dongarra, Mathematics and Computer Science Division, Argonne National Laboratory, Argonne, Illinois 60439.

```
c
c Linpack Benchmark Program in Double Precision
c
      double precision aa(200,200),a(201,200),b(200),x(200)
      double precision time(8,6),cray,ops,total,norma,normx
      double precision resid,residn,eps,epslon
      integer ipvt(200)
      lda = 201
      ldaa = 200
c
c set up the data and perform the solution
c using the linpack routines
c
      n = 100
      cray = .056
      ops = (2.0d0*n**3)/3.0d0 + 2.0d0*n**2
c
          call matgen(a,lda,n,b,norma)
          t1 = second()
          call dgefa(a,lda,n,ipvt,info)
          time(1,1) = second() - t1
          t1 = second()
          call dgesl(a,lda,n,ipvt,b,0)
          time(1,2) = second() - t1
          total = time(1,1) + time(1,2)
c
c     compute a residual to verify results.
c
          do 10 i = 1,n
             x(i) = b(i)
   10     continue
          call matgen(a,lda,n,b,norma)
```

```
          do 20 i = 1,n
             b(i) = -b(i)
   20     continue
          call dmxpy(n,b,n,lda,x,a)
          resid = 0.0
          normx = 0.0
          do 30 i = 1,n
             resid = dmax1( resid, dabs(b(i)) )
             normx = dmax1( normx, dabs(x(i)) )
   30     continue
          eps = epslon(1.0d0)
          residn = resid/( n*norma*normx*eps )
          write(6,40)
   40     format
      $   ('      norm. resid        resid            machep',
      $           '           x(1)           x(n)')
          write(6,50) residn,resid,eps,x(1),x(n)
   50     format(1p5e16.8)
c
          write(6,60) n
   60     format(//
      $     '     times are reported for matrices of order ',i5)
          write(6,70)
   70     format(6x,'dgefa',6x,'dgesl',6x,'total',5x,
      $           'mflops',7x,'unit',6x,'ratio')
c
          time(1,3) = total
          time(1,4) = ops/(1.0d6*total)
          time(1,5) = 2.0d0/time(1,4)
          time(1,6) = total/cray
          write(6,80) lda
   80     format(' times for array with leading dimension of'
      $           ,i4)
          write(6,110)  (time(1,i),i=1,6)
c
          call matgen(a,lda,n,b,norma)
          t1 = second()
          call dgefa(a,lda,n,ipvt,info)
          time(2,1) = second() - t1
```

```
        t1 = second()
        call dgesl(a,lda,n,ipvt,b,0)
        time(2,2) = second() - t1
        total = time(2,1) + time(2,2)
        time(2,3) = total
        time(2,4) = ops/(1.0d6*total)
        time(2,5) = 2.0d0/time(2,4)
        time(2,6) = total/cray
c
        call matgen(a,lda,n,b,norma)
        t1 = second()
        call dgefa(a,lda,n,ipvt,info)
        time(3,1) = second() - t1
        t1 = second()
        call dgesl(a,lda,n,ipvt,b,0)
        time(3,2) = second() - t1
        total = time(3,1) + time(3,2)
        time(3,3) = total
        time(3,4) = ops/(1.0d6*total)
        time(3,5) = 2.0d0/time(3,4)
        time(3,6) = total/cray
c
        ntimes = 10
        tm2 = 0
        t1 = second()
        do 90 i = 1,ntimes
           tm = second()
           call matgen(a,lda,n,b,norma)
           tm2 = tm2 + second() - tm
           call dgefa(a,lda,n,ipvt,info)
  90    continue
        time(4,1) = (second() - t1 - tm2)/ntimes
        t1 = second()
        do 100 i = 1,ntimes
           call dgesl(a,lda,n,ipvt,b,0)
 100    continue
        time(4,2) = (second() - t1)/ntimes
        total = time(4,1) + time(4,2)
```

```
          time(4,3) = total
          time(4,4) = ops/(1.0d6*total)
          time(4,5) = 2.0d0/time(4,4)
          time(4,6) = total/cray
c
          write(6,110) (time(2,i),i=1,6)
          write(6,110) (time(3,i),i=1,6)
          write(6,110) (time(4,i),i=1,6)
   110    format(6(1pe11.3))
c
          call matgen(aa,ldaa,n,b,norma)
          t1 = second()
          call dgefa(aa,ldaa,n,ipvt,info)
          time(5,1) = second() - t1
          t1 = second()
          call dgesl(aa,ldaa,n,ipvt,b,0)
          time(5,2) = second() - t1
          total = time(5,1) + time(5,2)
          time(5,3) = total
          time(5,4) = ops/(1.0d6*total)
          time(5,5) = 2.0d0/time(5,4)
          time(5,6) = total/cray
```

```
c
      call matgen(aa,ldaa,n,b,norma)
      t1 = second()
      call dgefa(aa,ldaa,n,ipvt,info)
      time(6,1) = second() - t1
      t1 = second()
      call dgesl(aa,ldaa,n,ipvt,b,0)
      time(6,2) = second() - t1
      total = time(6,1) + time(6,2)
      time(6,3) = total
      time(6,4) = ops/(1.0d6*total)
      time(6,5) = 2.0d0/time(6,4)
      time(6,6) = total/cray
c
      call matgen(aa,ldaa,n,b,norma)
      t1 = second()
      call dgefa(aa,ldaa,n,ipvt,info)
      time(7,1) = second() - t1
      t1 = second()
      call dgesl(aa,ldaa,n,ipvt,b,0)
      time(7,2) = second() - t1
      total = time(7,1) + time(7,2)
      time(7,3) = total
      time(7,4) = ops/(1.0d6*total)
      time(7,5) = 2.0d0/time(7,4)
      time(7,6) = total/cray
c
      ntimes = 10
      tm2 = 0
      t1 = second()
      do 120 i = 1,ntimes
         tm = second()
         call matgen(aa,ldaa,n,b,norma)
         tm2 = tm2 + second() - tm
         call dgefa(aa,ldaa,n,ipvt,info)
  120 continue
      time(8,1) = (second() - t1 - tm2)/ntimes
      t1 = second()
```

```
          do 130 i = 1,ntimes
             call dgesl(aa,ldaa,n,ipvt,b,0)
  130     continue
          time(8,2) = (second() - t1)/ntimes
          total = time(8,1) + time(8,2)
          time(8,3) = total
          time(8,4) = ops/(1.0d6*total)
          time(8,5) = 2.0d0/time(8,4)
          time(8,6) = total/cray
c
          write(6,140) ldaa
  140     format(/' times for array with leading dimension of'
     $            ,i4)
          write(6,110) (time(5,i),i=1,6)
          write(6,110) (time(6,i),i=1,6)
          write(6,110) (time(7,i),i=1,6)
          write(6,110) (time(8,i),i=1,6)
      stop
      end
c
c This subroutine is a stub for the second function.
c It should be removed and the system dependent time
c function or subroutine should be used.
c
      function second()
      second = 5
      return
      end
c
c This section contains the linpack subroutines
c
      subroutine matgen(a,lda,n,b,norma)
      double precision a(lda,1),b(1),norma
c
      init = 1325
      norma = 0.0
      do 30 j = 1,n
         do 20 i = 1,n
             init = mod(3125*init,65536)
```

```
            a(i,j) = (init - 32768.0)/16384.0
            norma = dmax1(a(i,j), norma)
   20    continue
   30 continue
      do 35 i = 1,n
         b(i) = 0.0
   35 continue
      do 50 j = 1,n
         do 40 i = 1,n
            b(i) = b(i) + a(i,j)
   40    continue
   50 continue
      return
      end
c
c
c

      subroutine dgefa(a,lda,n,ipvt,info)
      integer lda,n,ipvt(1),info
      double precision a(lda,1)
c
c     dgefa factors a double precision matrix
c     by gaussian elimination.
c
c     dgefa is usually called by dgeco, but it can be called
c     directly with a saving in time if rcond is not needed.
c     (time for dgeco) = (1 + 9/n)*(time for dgefa) .
c
c     on entry
c
c        a       double precision(lda, n)
c                the matrix to be factored.
c
c        lda     integer
c                the leading dimension of the array  a .
c
c        n       integer
c                the order of the matrix  a .
```

```
c
c      on return
c
c         a     an upper triangular matrix and the multipliers
c               which were used to obtain it.
c               the factorization can be written a = l*u where
c               l is a product of permutation and unit lower
c               triangular matrices and u is upper triangular.
c
c         ipvt  integer(n)
c               an integer vector of pivot indices.
c
c         info  integer
c               = 0   normal value.
c               = k   if  u(k,k) .eq. 0.0 this is not an error
c            condition for this subroutine, but it does
c            indicate that dgesl or dgedi will divide by zero
c            if called. use rcond in dgeco for a reliable
c            indication of singularity.
c
c      linpack. this version dated 08/14/78 .
c      cleve moler, univ. of new mexico, argonne national lab.
c
c      subroutines and functions
c
c      blas daxpy,dscal,idamax
c
c      internal variables
c
       double precision t
       integer idamax,j,k,kp1,l,nm1
c
c
c      gaussian elimination with partial pivoting
c
       info = 0
       nm1 = n - 1
       if (nm1 .lt. 1) go to 70
```

```
      do 60 k = 1, nm1
         kp1 = k + 1
c
c         find l = pivot index
c
         l = idamax(n-k+1,a(k,k),1) + k - 1
         ipvt(k) = l
c
c      zero pivot implies this column already triangularized
c
         if (a(l,k) .eq. 0.0d0) go to 40
c
c            interchange if necessary
c
            if (l .eq. k) go to 10
               t = a(l,k)
               a(l,k) = a(k,k)
               a(k,k) = t
   10       continue
c
c            compute multipliers
c
            t = -1.0d0/a(k,k)
            call dscal(n-k,t,a(k+1,k),1)
c
c            row elimination with column indexing
c
            do 30 j = kp1, n
               t = a(l,j)
               if (l .eq. k) go to 20
                  a(l,j) = a(k,j)
                  a(k,j) = t
   20          continue
               call daxpy(n-k,t,a(k+1,k),1,a(k+1,j),1)
   30       continue
         go to 50
   40    continue
            info = k
```

```
50      continue
60 continue
70 continue
   ipvt(n) = n
   if (a(n,n) .eq. 0.0d0) info = n
   return
   end
```

```
c
c
c
      subroutine dgesl(a,lda,n,ipvt,b,job)
      integer lda,n,ipvt(1),job
      double precision a(lda,1),b(1)
c
c     dgesl solves the double precision system
c     a * x = b  or  trans(a) * x = b
c     using the factors computed by dgeco or dgefa.
c
c     on entry
c
c        a        double precision(lda, n)
c                 the output from dgeco or dgefa.
c
c        lda      integer
c                 the leading dimension of the array  a .
c
c        n        integer
c                 the order of the matrix  a .
c
c        ipvt     integer(n)
c                 the pivot vector from dgeco or dgefa.
c
c        b        double precision(n)
c                 the right hand side vector.
c
c        job      integer
c                 = 0         to solve  a*x = b ,
c                 = nonzero   to solve  trans(a)*x = b  where
c                             trans(a)  is the transpose.
```

```
c
c      on return
c
c         b          the solution vector  x .
c
c      error condition
c
c         a division by zero will occur if the input factor
c         contains a zero on the diagonal.  technically this
c         indicates singularity but it is often caused by
c         improper arguments or improper setting of lda .  it
c         will not occur if the subroutines are called
c         correctly and if dgeco has set rcond .gt. 0.0 or
c         dgefa has set info .eq. 0 .
c
c      to compute  inverse(a) * c  where  c  is a matrix
c      with  p  columns
c            call dgeco(a,lda,n,ipvt,rcond,z)
c            if (rcond is too small) go to ...
c            do 10 j = 1, p
c               call dgesl(a,lda,n,ipvt,c(1,j),0)
c         10 continue
c
c      linpack. this version dated 08/14/78 .
c      cleve moler, univ. of new mexico, argonne national lab.
c
c      subroutines and functions
c
c      blas daxpy,ddot
c
c      internal variables
c
       double precision ddot,t
       integer k,kb,l,nm1
c
       nm1 = n - 1
       if (job .ne. 0) go to 50
c
```

```
c          job = 0 , solve  a * x = b
c          first solve  l*y = b
c
           if (nm1 .lt. 1) go to 30
           do 20 k = 1, nm1
              l = ipvt(k)
              t = b(l)
              if (l .eq. k) go to 10
                 b(l) = b(k)
                 b(k) = t
   10         continue
              call daxpy(n-k,t,a(k+1,k),1,b(k+1),1)
   20      continue
   30      continue
c
c          now solve  u*x = y
c
           do 40 kb = 1, n
              k = n + 1 - kb
              b(k) = b(k)/a(k,k)
              t = -b(k)
              call daxpy(k-1,t,a(1,k),1,b(1),1)
   40      continue
         go to 100
   50 continue
c
c          job = nonzero, solve  trans(a) * x = b
c          first solve  trans(u)*y = b
c
           do 60 k = 1, n
              t = ddot(k-1,a(1,k),1,b(1),1)
              b(k) = (b(k) - t)/a(k,k)
   60      continue
c
c          now solve trans(l)*x = y
c
           if (nm1 .lt. 1) go to 90
           do 80 kb = 1, nm1
```

```
            k = n - kb
            b(k) = b(k) + ddot(n-k,a(k+1,k),1,b(k+1),1)
            l = ipvt(k)
            if (l .eq. k) go to 70
               t = b(l)
               b(l) = b(k)
               b(k) = t
   70       continue
   80    continue
   90    continue
  100 continue
      return
      end
c
c
c
      subroutine daxpy(n,da,dx,incx,dy,incy)
c
c     constant times a vector plus a vector.
c     jack dongarra, linpack, 3/11/78.
c
      double precision dx(1),dy(1),da
      integer i,incx,incy,ix,iy,m,mp1,n
c
      if(n.le.0)return
      if (da .eq. 0.0d0) return
      if(incx.eq.1.and.incy.eq.1)go to 20
c
c        code for unequal increments or equal increments
c          not equal to 1
c
      ix = 1
      iy = 1
      if(incx.lt.0)ix = (-n+1)*incx + 1
      if(incy.lt.0)iy = (-n+1)*incy + 1
      do 10 i = 1,n
        dy(iy) = dy(iy) + da*dx(ix)
        ix = ix + incx
```

```
         iy = iy + incy
   10 continue
      return
c
c        code for both increments equal to 1
c
   20 continue
      do 30 i = 1,n
         dy(i) = dy(i) + da*dx(i)
   30 continue
      return
      end
c
c
c


      double precision function ddot(n,dx,incx,dy,incy)
c
c     forms the dot product of two vectors.
c     jack dongarra, linpack, 3/11/78.
c
      double precision dx(1),dy(1),dtemp
      integer i,incx,incy,ix,iy,m,mp1,n
c
      ddot = 0.0d0
      dtemp = 0.0d0
      if(n.le.0)return
      if(incx.eq.1.and.incy.eq.1)go to 20
c
c        code for unequal increments or equal increments
c          not equal to 1
c
      ix = 1
      iy = 1
      if(incx.lt.0)ix = (-n+1)*incx + 1
      if(incy.lt.0)iy = (-n+1)*incy + 1
      do 10 i = 1,n
         dtemp = dtemp + dx(ix)*dy(iy)
         ix = ix + incx
```

```
          iy = iy + incy
   10 continue
      ddot = dtemp
      return
c
c        code for both increments equal to 1
c
   20 continue
      do 30 i = 1,n
         dtemp = dtemp + dx(i)*dy(i)
   30 continue
      ddot = dtemp
      return
      end
```

```
c
c
c
      subroutine   dscal(n,da,dx,incx)
c
c     scales a vector by a constant.
c     jack dongarra, linpack, 3/11/78.
c
      double precision da,dx(1)
      integer i,incx,m,mp1,n,nincx
c
      if(n.le.0)return
      if(incx.eq.1)go to 20
c
c        code for increment not equal to 1
c
      nincx = n*incx
      do 10 i = 1,nincx,incx
        dx(i) = da*dx(i)
   10 continue
      return
c
c        code for increment equal to 1
c
   20 continue
      do 30 i = 1,n
        dx(i) = da*dx(i)
   30 continue
      return
      end
c
c
      integer function idamax(n,dx,incx)
c
c     finds the index of element having max. dabsolute value.
c     jack dongarra, linpack, 3/11/78.
c
      double precision dx(1),dmax
```

```
      integer i,incx,ix,n
c
      idamax = 0
      if( n .lt. 1 ) return
      idamax = 1
      if(n.eq.1)return
      if(incx.eq.1)go to 20
c
c         code for increment not equal to 1
c
      ix = 1
      dmax = dabs(dx(1))
      ix = ix + incx
      do 10 i = 2,n
         if(dabs(dx(ix)).le.dmax) go to 5
         idamax = i
         dmax = dabs(dx(ix))
    5    ix = ix + incx
   10 continue
      return
c
c         code for increment equal to 1
c
   20 dmax = dabs(dx(1))
      do 30 i = 2,n
         if(dabs(dx(i)).le.dmax) go to 30
         idamax = i
         dmax = dabs(dx(i))
   30 continue
      return
      end
c
c
c
      double precision function epslon (x)
      double precision x
c
c     estimate unit roundoff in quantities of size x.
```

```
c
      double precision a,b,c,eps
c
c     this program should function properly on all systems
c     satisfying the following two assumptions,
c        1. the base used in representing dfloating point
c           numbers is not a power of three.
c        2. the quantity  a  in statement 10 is represented to
c           the accuracy used in dfloating point variables
c           that are stored in memory.
c     the statement number 10 and the go to 10 are intended to
c     force optimizing compilers to generate code satisfying
c     assumption 2.
c     under these assumptions, it should be true that,
c            a  is not exactly equal to four-thirds,
c            b  has a zero for its last bit or digit,
c            c  is not exactly equal to one,
c            eps  measures the separation of 1.0 from
c                 the next larger dfloating point number.
c     the developers of eispack would appreciate being
c     informed about any systems where these assumptions do
c     not hold.
c
c     ********************************************************
c     this routine is one of the auxiliary routines used by
c     eispack iii to avoid machine dependencies.
c     ********************************************************
c
c     this version dated 4/6/83.
c
      a = 4.0d0/3.0d0
   10 b = a - 1.0d0
      c = b + b + b
      eps = dabs(c-1.0d0)
      if (eps .eq. 0.0d0) go to 10
      epslon = eps*dabs(x)
      return
      end
```

```
c
c
c
      subroutine mm (a, lda, n1, n3, b, ldb, n2, c, ldc)
      double precision a(lda,*), b(ldb,*), c(ldc,*)
c
c   purpose:
c      multiply matrix b times matrix c and store
c      the result in matrix a.
c
c   parameters:
c
c      a double precision(lda,n3),
c      matrix of n1 rows and n3 columns
c
c      lda integer, leading dimension of array a
c
c      n1 integer, number of rows in matrices a and b
c
c      n3 integer, number of columns in matrices a and c
c
c      b double precision(ldb,n2),
c      matrix of n1 rows and n2 columns
c
c      ldb integer, leading dimension of array b
c
c      n2 integer,
c      number of columns in matrix b, and number of rows in
c      matrix c
c
c      c double precision(ldc,n3),
c      matrix of n2 rows and n3 columns
c
c      ldc integer, leading dimension of array c
c
c ------------------------------------------------------------
c
      do 20 j = 1, n3
         do 10 i = 1, n1
            a(i,j) = 0.0
```

```
      10     continue
             call dmxpy (n2,a(1,j),n1,ldb,c(1,j),b)
      20 continue
c
      return
      end
c
c
c

      subroutine dmxpy (n1, y, n2, ldm, x, m)
      double precision y(*), x(*), m(ldm,*)
c
c   purpose:
c      multiply matrix m times vector x and add the
c      result to vector y.
c
c   parameters:
c
c      n1 integer,
c      number of elements in vector y, and number of rows in
c      matrix m
c      y double precision(n1),
c      vector of length n1 to which is added
c      the product m*x
c
c      n2 integer,
c      number of elements in vector x, and number of columns
c      in matrix m
c
c      ldm integer, leading dimension of array m
c
c      x double precision(n2), vector of length n2
c
c      m double precision(ldm,n2),
c      matrix of n1 rows and n2 columns
c
c   cleanup odd vector
c
          j = mod(n2,2)
          if (j .ge. 1) then
```

```
          do 10 i = 1, n1
             y(i) = (y(i)) + x(j)*m(i,j)
  10      continue
        endif
c
c   cleanup odd group of two vectors
c
        j = mod(n2,4)
        if (j .ge. 2) then
          do 20 i = 1, n1
             y(i) = ( (y(i))
     $                  + x(j-1)*m(i,j-1)) + x(j)*m(i,j)
  20      continue
        endif
c
c   cleanup odd group of four vectors
c
        j = mod(n2,8)
        if (j .ge. 4) then
          do 30 i = 1, n1
             y(i) = ((( (y(i))
     $                  + x(j-3)*m(i,j-3)) + x(j-2)*m(i,j-2))
     $                  + x(j-1)*m(i,j-1)) + x(j)   *m(i,j)
  30      continue
        endif
c   cleanup odd group of eight vectors
        j = mod(n2,16)
         if (j .ge. 8) then
           do 40 i = 1, n1
              y(i) = ((((((( (y(i))
     $                 + x(j-7)*m(i,j-7)) + x(j-6)*m(i,j-6))
     $                 + x(j-5)*m(i,j-5)) + x(j-4)*m(i,j-4))
     $                 + x(j-3)*m(i,j-3)) + x(j-2)*m(i,j-2))
     $                 + x(j-1)*m(i,j-1)) + x(j)   *m(i,j)
  40      continue
        endif
c   main loop - groups of sixteen vectors
        jmin = j+16
```

```
do 60 j = jmin, n2, 16
   do 50 i = 1, n1
      y(i) = ((((((((((((((( (y(i))
$                + x(j-15)*m(i,j-15)) + x(j-14)*m(i,j-14))
$                + x(j-13)*m(i,j-13)) + x(j-12)*m(i,j-12))
$                + x(j-11)*m(i,j-11)) + x(j-10)*m(i,j-10))
$                + x(j- 9)*m(i,j- 9)) + x(j- 8)*m(i,j- 8))
$                + x(j- 7)*m(i,j- 7)) + x(j- 6)*m(i,j- 6))
$                + x(j- 5)*m(i,j- 5)) + x(j- 4)*m(i,j- 4))
```

```
     $                  + x(j- 3)*m(i,j- 3)) + x(j- 2)*m(i,j- 2))
     $                  + x(j- 1)*m(i,j- 1)) + x(j)    *m(i,j)
50      continue
60 continue
   return
   end
```

INDEX

DATE DUE

MAR 3 0 2005			
	261-2500		Printed in USA